There Was a Little Girl

The Real Story of My Mother and Me

BROOKE SHIELDS

A PLUME BOOK

PLUME
An imprint of Penguin Random House LLC
375 Hudson Street
New York, New York 10014

First published in the United States of America by Dutton, an imprint of
Penguin Random House LLC, 2014
First Plume printing 2015
Plume ISBN 978-0-14-751656-5

 REGISTERED TRADEMARK—MARCA REGISTRADA

THE LIBRARY OF CONGRESS HAS CATALOGED THE DUTTON HARDCOVER EDITION AS FOLLOWS:
Shields, Brooke, 1965–
There was a little girl : the real story of my mother and me / Brooke Shields.
pages cm
ISBN 978-0-525-95484-2
1. Shields, Brooke, 1965- 2. Shields, Teri, 1933-2012. 3. Mothers and daughters—United
States—Biography. 4. Actors—United States—Biography. 5. Models (Persons)—United
States—Biography. I. Title.
PN2287.S37195A3 2015
791.4302'8092—dc23
[B]
2014036032

Printed in the United States of America
10 9 8 7 6 5 4 3 2 1

Original hardcover book design by Alissa Rose Theodor

While the author has made every effort to provide accurate telephone numbers, Internet
addresses, and other contact information at the time of publication, neither the publisher nor
the author assumes any responsibility for errors or for changes that occur after publication.
Further, the publisher does not have any control over and does not assume any responsibility
for author or third-party websites or their content.

Penguin is committed to publishing works of quality and integrity.
In that spirit, we are proud to offer this book to our readers;
however, the story, the experiences, and the words
are the author's alone.

A PLUME BOOK

THERE WAS A LITTLE GIRL

BROOKE SHIELDS is an award-winning actress and a *New York Times* best-selling author. She starred in iconic films such as *Pretty Baby*, *The Blue Lagoon*, and *Endless Love*. She is a renowned model and starred in the long-running TV show *Suddenly Susan* and the critically acclaimed *Lipstick Jungle*. She has appeared on Broadway multiple times and wrote and performed her one-woman show, *In My Life*. She wrote the *New York Times* bestseller *Down Came the Rain* and also penned two children's books. She lives in New York City with her husband, writer and producer Chris Henchy, and their two daughters.

Praise for *There Was a Little Girl*

"A well-crafted and insightful read from beginning to end. . . . A thoughtful, poignant, and provoking story about a girl and her mom. . . . A remarkably clear-eyed examination."   —Associated Press

"This story of Brooke's career as a model and actress unfolds from the perspective of an adult child of an alcoholic. Her voice in this memoir is unguarded and raw and deals head-on with the damage alcohol causes in intimate relationships. For a celebrity of her stature to write so honestly and intelligently about emotional wounds is a refreshing change. The book will appeal not only to Shields's fans, but also to readers who seek out memoirs about surviving dysfunctional families. Brooke Shields is still our sister, just more real and imperfect."   —*BookPage*

"A raw, honest tale of a mother and daughter that will appeal not only to celebrity watchers but to mothers and daughters."   —*Library Journal*

"Shields writes with considerable reflection; she's done the hard work of making sense of the contradictions in her mother, and now we get the benefit of her sharing what she's learned."   —*Kirkus Reviews*

Contents

> **when she was good she was very, very good…and when she was bad she was**

—*Brooke Shields's baby photo album, 1965*

There was a little girl,

And she had a little curl

Right in the middle of her forehead.

When she was good

She was very, very good,

And when she was bad she was horrid.

—*Henry Wadsworth Longfellow*

There Was a
Little Girl

Introduction

'm told that even decorated soldiers' last words are often calling for "Mommy."

That is the first feeling that washed over me.

And on November 5, 2012, six days after I watched my mother die right in front of me, I opened up the *New York Times* obituaries and the feeling hit again . . . but it came with a wave of anger. I was so hurt my vision blurred. I couldn't believe what I'd just read, and I asked myself: How could I have been so stupid and so naïve? How could I have let my guard down? How could they have done this to my mommy?

Days earlier, I'd written my own simple and rather short obituary about my mom and had sent in the required $1,500. The following afternoon I got a call from the *Times* saying they wanted to print it on the front page of the obituary section. I said they could position it wherever they wanted.

They explained that they thought Mom deserved to have a more prominent placement. This made me feel like maybe after all these years, Mom would finally get some modicum of respect. And deep down we all want to know our moms deserve respect, don't we? The *Times* added that they didn't want me to pay the $1,500, but I explained that I was fine paying and thanked them for the offer. Suddenly the person on the other end of the phone stated that the obituary was, in fact, already being moved to a more prominent part of the paper, so a bit more copy would be needed. This was the first red flag.

"I am not giving an interview. Publish my written obit, please."

"Well, we may just need one or two additional facts that you could clarify."

"Listen, I submitted my personally written obituary about my mother and I sent in a check. Thank you."

"OK, we don't want to upset you. . . . How about we just take your obit and print that but add one or two additional facts about her up-bringing and the like?"

"Fine."

They indeed called and asked one question about her deceased brother and if she had lived in any other city in New Jersey before moving to New York City. It was a two-minute phone call and it seemed fine. I was satisfied.

A few days later, on the stoop of my apartment, I was shocked and horrified to read a piece I'd known nothing about. It was a scathing, judgmental critique of my mother's life. I gasped and stared, wide-eyed, at the nasty, venomous piece of so-called journalism.

The first line read, "Teri Shields, who began promoting her daughter, Brooke, as a child model and actress when she was an infant and allowed her to be cast as a child prostitute . . . died on Wednesday." What an opener!

The obituary's author highlighted—completely out of context—the most salacious facts and quotes. He painted her as a desperate single mom who sold her daughter into prostitution and nudity for her own profit. He even distorted Mom's most famous quote, mistaking her wry humor for deep abuse—"Fortunately, Brooke was at an age where she couldn't talk back." This quote referred to the fact that I'd been eleven months old when I shot my first ad, for Ivory soap, not to human trafficking of a minor into the sex trade.

Who the fuck did this guy think he was to write about a woman he never knew? How could he hurl such vicious allegations when an obit was supposed to be fact based? The piece was shocking and of the lowest common denominator, which was especially terrible coming from somebody who called himself a reputable journalist.

Reading the obit, I felt myself beginning to lose it. I started to take deep breaths, trying not to panic or pass out. I ran into the kitchen and began pacing around the table as I sobbed and rambled: Why are they so cruel? Why can't they let her be? Why can't they let her die without being nasty? Why can't they be kind to her just once? Why was it so easy and acceptable for him to degrade her? Where was the human decency? Someone's mother just died.

I walked in circles, crying and choking on my tears, and then left the kitchen and walked up the stairs to my bedroom. I bawled my eyes out and ranted for only a few minutes longer. Then I began to sense the rage. It was like a hot liquid traveling up my legs and all the way to my cheeks and actually radiating from my face.

The anger was terrible, but then I took a step back mentally and thought: Who is this guy? What is it about his own life and parental dynamic that caused him to write with such ignorance and venom? Why the drive to assassinate the character of a woman of whom he had no personal recollection, and whose path he had never crossed? What did she symbolize to him?

If this dead seventy-nine-year-old woman could elicit such a vehement response and vicious reaction so many years after her prominence in the public eye had faded—never mind that a man who had never been a mother or a daughter penned it—there was something there that needed to be explored. The relationships between mothers and their daughters are often fraught and fascinatingly complicated. I knew mine was. But what did she trigger in him? Why did he care?

Almost immediately, I knew what I wanted to do. It was time to tell our story—my mother's and my own. The story of my mother's trajectory through her life and through mine. The story of how I became who I am because of all she was.

This book is about everything that went into being Teri Shields. It is not a *Mommie Dearest* tale. But I'm not holding her up on a pedestal, either. There has been so much written about my mom, and most of it has been quite negative. This is by no means an attempt to idealize her or condemn her. It is simply my turn to tell the story as I saw and felt it. It's about the forty-eight years that I knew—yet never really knew—my mother.

My life—those forty-eight years of it—always existed somehow in relation to hers. She affected everything in my life. She was at the apex of it all. Nearly everything I did was for her, in response to her, because of her, or in spite of her. I was either emulating her or trying to define my independence from her. I was either trying to escape her or crash into her.

I thought about her all the time. She was part of my every day. Even though I worked hard and succeeded at creating a healthy private life and home with my grounded husband and beloved daughters, as long as she was alive, Mom's needs were never far away.

I remained preoccupied by her until she passed away. And afterward as well, obviously, because I am writing about her every day.

As a child, I literally couldn't imagine life without her. I used to think that if Mom died, I'd die, too.

Now I'm still here, with two daughters of my own, and this book is about understanding what came before, and what comes next.

Part One

My feelings about my mother and about our relationship are so confused that to write them down with clarity would mean I had them all figured out, which I do not.

—*Brooke Shields's diary*

Chapter One

Teri Terrific

Who was my mother? I believe that I knew her better than anybody else did. And I didn't know her at all. I could wax philosophical and venture to say that my mother never fully knew herself, and that the persona she created became her reality. She saw herself the way she wanted others to see her and built up the necessary barricades between her real character and what she presented. She made it impossible for even her daughter to chisel past the myth.

For years, I thought she was the strongest, most honest and forthright woman ever. Looking back, I see that she was the most truthful white liar I will ever know.

I understand a great deal about my mother and about her complex nature, but there were facts hidden, brushed over, and manipulated. There was information lost in translation and lost to booze. And there was much sadness and pain and deep insecurity. I have always felt that to really know another person, it requires a certain willingness to be vulnerable. Vulnerability equaled weakness in my mother's eyes.

I have asked myself these questions: How well did I know Mom? How deeply do any of us really know our mothers? And how well do they really know us?

Ultimately, how much of who I am is my mother? Do I have to know her better to know myself?

Of course, there is a lot I do know. There are stories, the ones she told me and the ones I heard from others. And pictures—so many pictures! They tell a story all their own.

I know that my mother, Theresa Anna Lillian Schmon, was born in Newark, New Jersey, on August 11, 1933. She had an older brother and a younger sister, who was the apple of my mom's eye. Mom was a perfect example of a middle child. She overcame her low self-esteem by rebelling and being a trailblazer. I smile thinking of her as a sweet but tough little kid whose attitude and humor made her a survivor. I am proud of my mom as a little girl. But for the most part, when I think about what I know of my mom's childhood, I just feel sad.

Evidently her mother, also named Theresa, was forced to stop going to school at nine years old to become the primary caregiver of her three siblings. My grandmother's mother had passed away, and she became an instant mother to three kids. Later on, she lost her younger brother to a freak drowning accident in Newark. I can only imagine the guilt and anger that comes from losing a sibling at such a young age and while on your watch. While researching my genealogy at the Newark History Society, I found a microfiche document that reported that in addition to these children, my grandmother's father had an entirely different family he was supporting on the other side of town. I am not sure if my grandmother ever found out about her father's double life, but I have a feeling that all these circumstances of her own life had to take a toll. This must be where her hardened personality began to develop. My grandmother was always a cold person in my eyes and would often throw out barbs about Mom. She resented her for something, and I saw it when we visited. Grandma never credited my mother for the things she had given her but instead gave acknowledgment to her other daughter. I guess she resented my mom for leaving her instead of staying and caring for her forever. If I did something annoying when we were visiting, her idea of a perfect insult would be to say, "Ugh, you're just like your mother!"

I took this as a compliment and thanked her. She'd then scoff at me, saying I was a sarcastic brat. One day Grandma offered to show me her dentures. I sat on her lap and grabbed her front teeth with my thumb and index finger, and she told me to pull. I did and her teeth came out in my hands. I burst into tears and thought I had ripped her head apart by the jaw. She laughed hysterically.

Eventually, when my grandmother grew up, there was a light at the end of the tunnel. She met and married John Schmon. They had three children: Johnny, Louise, and my mother, Teri. My mother's name was originally spelled the same way as her mother's, but she was forced to change the spelling because there were too many other Terrys and Theresas in her grammar school class.

As a child, Mom was left on her own a great deal and learned to be quite independent. She was a very cute little brunette with huge, dark-brown eyes. In pictures her eyes always stood out because of how dark and round her pupils were. She was a sweet, silly, and popular little girl who had an honest sense of humor. In first grade the teacher once asked the class why they thought that their area of Newark was nicknamed the Ironbound section. Mom raised her hand and exclaimed that it was because they were so tough!

Mom's father drove a bus. Her mom got a job at a doughnut shop and was the one who filled the doughnuts with the cream and the jelly.

She evidently ended up getting fired for filling the doughnuts with too much jelly. She had other jobs but was basically a stay-at-home mom. It was the Depression, and it wasn't uncommon for women to work various jobs in pastry shops and the like or to clean houses. Even my mother worked, cleaning houses in Newark starting at a very young age.

Mom told me that before Easter one year she really wanted a little chick she had seen in the window of a toy store. The chick cost only two cents, but her mom would not give her the money for something so frivolous. Mom told me she cleaned houses after school for two weeks straight to make the two cents. But by the time she got to the store to buy it for herself, it was closer to Easter and the price had been raised to three cents. She never got the chick.

But she was always smart and ingenious. At about age seven, she did make a dollar by sending in an idea to a soap factory. Her idea was to layer in decals in the center of the soap to encourage kids to bathe. They couldn't see the next fun decal until they washed the layers of soap away. She sent in a handwritten note to the company, and they sent her back a thank-you and a one-dollar bill. She claimed the company went on to make the soap and make a great deal of money from her invention. Mom gave her mother the dollar.

She was imaginative and adventurous, too, and her inventive way of thinking ended up giving me confidence to think outside the box and trust that my thoughts were unique. Of course, she was also OK with causing a little trouble, even then. When she was a very little girl, probably around four or five, she would run away from home and sneak into the movie theatre by getting on her tippy-toes and craning her neck to declare to the ticket lady, "My mommy's in there." The lady would wave her on inside and never notice if she did or did not come back out. Once inside the safety of the un-air-conditioned theatre, Mom would settle into a seat in the middle row and get lost in the stories told on the big screen. This was around 1938, and according to my mother, it was in a time when movies played all day long and periodicals played in between the screenings. World news would be sandwiched in between movies like *The Adventures of Robin Hood*, *Holiday*, or *Bringing Up Baby*.

Whenever her mother finally discovered—usually four or five hours later—that she had run away, they knew where to find her. The theatre lights would suddenly blast on and uniformed policemen would burst in with Mom's mother and come to retrieve the runaway. The minute her mother would grab hold of her tiny arm, Mom would just point up at the screen and say, "Movin' pictures, movin' pictures!" Inevitably, Mom would get a whupin'.

All her life Mom simply loved movies. She would escape into the darkness of the theatre, and that's where she found her home. She told me she usually went alone, and inevitably some guy would try to be inappropriate with her. She claimed it got to the point where she would just scream out, "*Put that away!*" She said it happened once and three separate men jumped up to leave. Nothing derailed her love of the movin' pictures. She was enamored of the glamour of movies and the fantasies they created. They were her original escape. It was fitting, I guess, for her to raise a child who would end up an actress.

Mom never seemed close to her mother, but she worshipped her father. They shared a special bond and a similar sense of humor. They both had a willingness to be silly. And neither cared about looking bad. Since birth he'd had a hole through the cartilage in his nose, and he would put a pencil through it and make a funny face to make Mom laugh. He'd imitate Charlie Chaplin in the movie *The Gold Rush* by sticking forks in two separate buns so they looked like little shoes and making the little bread feet dance on a tabletop. He'd chime in singing, "Now this is *abundance!*"

But even though Mom seemed to have revered her dad, I never got the impression that he was warm or overtly affectionate. Years later, upon my mom's graduation from grammar school, he could muster up the sensitivity to write "Phooey" in her yearbook. I found it later and saw that Mom had asked only her father and one of her teachers to sign her book.

He worked hard to support his family during very difficult times. Even though I got the impression that my grandmother never cared for my mother and in fact even grew to resent her, to me it seemed that Mom did genuinely feel loved by her father.

Sadly, though, Mom's dad died of lung cancer shortly after the "Phooey" incident. She was fourteen years old and this would be her first real loss of love. Mom's hero was gone and her mother was left yet again with three children to raise on her own.

Mom was able to stay in school and met the first love of her life in high school. He was a nice Italian boy named Salvatore Piccarillo and they became high school sweethearts. Mom would tell me stories about how she felt a part of his family and how his grandmother taught her to take one step at a time in life and not rush things or "sweat the small stuff." She also taught my mother the importance of perseverance and progress. This little old Italian grandmother would place her fingers on the kitchen table, touching her pinky to her thumb. She would separate her pinky from her thumb and then slide her thumb to meet it. The back of her hand would arch up every time her thumb met her pinky, and as she continued, over the length of the table, it looked very much like a huge caterpillar slowly making its way to a place in the shade. She'd made it all the way to the end of the table by taking little steps.

Mom and her beau, Sal, spent all their time together, and they became the standout couple at their high school. I loved the idea that he was a football player, and I imagined them as prom king and queen. These seemed to be some of the better years of Mom's life in Newark. She was said to light up every room she entered. She was special in every way.

After she graduated, Mom got a job working at Krueger Brewing Company, on an assembly line as a capper. She modeled a bit and was also often called out of work for photo opportunities to show her beautiful gams or greet various men in uniform. They would pluck her from the grind of the factory job and she'd have an interesting experience and hours off. Just like Marilyn Monroe in the famous photo from *Yank* magazine, it was always my mom who they wanted to show off the product or be the mascot of a factory. She looked like she was imitating the famous Betty Grable pinup photo in the bathing suit. She wore only fire engine–red lipstick and always showed off her long, sexy legs. She was stunningly beautiful, and her laugh was infectious. She excelled at everything she tried, and she read people astutely. She knew she was somehow different from her peers and wasn't the type to want to settle down.

Soon my mother started setting her sights past Newark and across the Hudson River to the bright lights and more cosmopolitan Manhattan. She wanted more. She wanted a big, fabulous life, and I guess she felt Newark couldn't provide it. She showed no regrets in leaving anyone behind. I often wonder what her life would have been like if she'd stayed. It seems impossible that she would have been content.

Mom started to take the bus into New York City every day for work and eventually got a job at the famous Gaslight Café. Her salary was minimal, and she made the majority of her money in tips. She was a coat-check girl who met the regular customers with just a smile and a nod, as she was always horrible with names. Once, while introducing a boyfriend to her mother, she forgot her own mom's name. She mumbled something and then just kept repeating her boyfriend's first name, feeling relieved that she could at least access *somebody's* name in this horrible moment.

Well, this inability to recall names plagued her forever, but particularly at the Gaslight, where remembering the clientele's names ensured a larger tip. To counterbalance her deficiency, Mom would take the coat, cock her head with a wink, and go to the coat-check closet to retrieve a number check in its place. In the back, Mom kept a small notepad log of characteristics of the customers or tidbits about their lives—things they had mentioned or she had overheard. For instance: This man had a kid going off to college, had a sick family member, or had spent a holiday in a certain place. She also made a note of tie color or hair color or physical characteristics. She'd write: "red hair with crooked nose: Bob" or "slick side part and black hair, smells of Old Spice: Jack." For the ones with no name, she would simply bring the claim ticket to the man and in a flirty tone, hands on hips, say, "Now you, how come you're not wearing my favorite yellow tie? Shame on you! Next time I want to see it. Enjoy your evening."

The men all felt special and, with stoked egos, reached farther into their pockets for a tip.

Mom crumpled her cash tips and shoved them in her pockets. At the end of the night she'd take the bus back to Newark, and her mom would be waiting with the ironing board up and the iron hot and ready. Mom would dump out the balled-up money and give them to her mom, who stayed up ironing the bills until they were all flat and in a stack. I'm not sure my mother ever got to keep any of this cash for herself. I suspect it all went to her mother for the care of the family. Mom never seemed to resent this and instead began to clock the prospects of a bigger world, one that didn't involve a daily bus commute.

She began to grow away from Sal. They always remained friends (until the day she died), but she decided to go off on her own and move to New York City. She set out to get an apartment and was able to secure one with decent rent on the east side in the Fifties. She then began working in the Garment District in various stockrooms and, sometimes, as a model. Mom continued to send her mother money when she could. I have found thank-you notes from my grandmother and my great-aunt Lil thanking Mom for the rent money.

My mother wanted a more upscale career but had no experience or education in sales or management. But she didn't see that as an obstacle. She often said to me growing up, "Brookie, where there's a will, there's a way. Don't take no for an answer and never let 'em see you sweat. Figure out what you want and find a way."

She applied and got a job at the makeup counter of the posh uptown department store Lord and Taylor. It would be here that she would meet her longtime friend and my eventual godmother, Lila Wisdom. Lila was from Tucson, Arizona, and was younger than Mom by a few years. They became the best of friends, but Mom always saw herself as the captain of the ship. I only knew my mom as the captain of the ship, so this made sense to me. Lila was from a small town and had graduated from college. Mom acted like her bossy big sister, and their dynamic worked.

Because Mom also had zero training in the world of makeup beyond applying her ever-present fire engine–red lipstick and matching nails, she had to be creative and seemingly confident. Her job was to make up the customers and subsequently sell them products. Mom was right-handed and unable to use her left steadily or contort properly to use the brushes in her right hand to apply eye shadow and the like on both eyes. After creating a few Picasso-esque faces, she came up with a solution. She would do the left side of a woman's face with her right hand and then turn the woman to face the mirror, hand her the brush, and, like a wise teacher, say, "Now let's see if you can do what I just did to the other side of your face."

Women loved the attention and instruction and were empowered by learning a skill from the expert. They bought copious amounts of products, and everybody was happy. Management thought Mom was a genius, and she was soon promoted. Lila was Mom's boss in the beginning but soon Mom was practically running the place. It was a gift she had—how she could turn her weaknesses into seeming strengths. People looked up to her and thought she could do anything, even though she was technically not trained. She was a person who would never admit to not knowing something.

Mom was now meeting a more uptown crowd and soon had many new friends. She was exposed to the fabulous fifties in New York City and all it had to offer. Mom befriended many gay men who were hairdressers or in fashion, and she beguiled many members of the New York social set. Her usually brown-red hair was blond at this point.

She was a five-foot-nine bombshell with a narrow waist; long, gorgeous legs; and a sexy hourglass figure. She seemed to celebrate her physique and had no issues wearing a bikini or minidress. She had a friend named Joanne who was a fellow blond. Joanne had a mean parrot that Mom taught to curse. Jo and Mom often wore one another's bathing suits and always took fun pictures on various boats and with various men suitors. The same leopard one-piece has shown up in many photos of Mom as well as Jo.

Mom loved to have her photo taken and always had a glimmer in her eye and a glass in her hand. In photos of her with other people, your eyes are always drawn directly to my stunningly beautiful mom. The men were either handsome or rich, and you could tell they wanted to shower her with the good life—the life she so coveted.

One particular gay couple became Mom's closest friends. They had a place on Fire Island and often repeated the story of how one day Mom was walking one of their poodles on a leash on a boardwalk. The dog wrapped the leash around Mom's legs and she got totally tangled up and fell head over heels on the wood planks. Her dress flew up over her head and she was wearing not a stitch of underwear.

Mom never parlayed her many talents into a profession but kept starting jobs, excelling in them by sheer street smarts and innovation, and moving on. She seemed to be searching for some kind of recognition or social status and an escape from her roots.

It wouldn't be long before Mom met a man to whom she became engaged. I never heard much about him and was shocked and saddened when I found out why they never actually got to take a walk down the aisle together. Mom told me the story of his death every time she took me to have a cheeseburger at P. J. Clarke's original Fifty-Fifth Street and Third Avenue location.

Turns out Mom and her fiancé, who I later learned was named Morton Gruber, were on a double date with a girlfriend of Mom's and her boyfriend. They all were in the car together on the way to have drinks and dinner at P. J. Clarke's. They were having trouble finding a parking spot and didn't want the ladies to have to walk far. Mom's fiancé was behind the wheel and suggested he drop the three passengers off at Clarke's to get a table. He would find a spot for the car and meet them inside. Mom and the other couple went in and waited the normal ten minutes for a table and sat to order a cocktail. Some more time passed, and the group began to discuss how bad parking had gotten lately. Even more time passed and they began to get a bit curious and even slightly concerned. Did her fiancé suddenly get cold feet? This joke ended up being a terrifying and morbid premonition. Moments later, sirens were heard and red lights flashed through the paned windows. Everybody rushed outside and was horrified by what they saw.

This was at a time in New York City when Third Avenue was a two-way street. Evidently, Morton had parked the car on the opposite side of Third Avenue from the restaurant and was crossing the street when he was hit by a car. His body was thrown thirty feet. He was dead on impact, and by the time the ambulance came his watch and wallet had been stolen. The whole story was shocking to me. I couldn't believe that people would steal off a dead or dying bloody man. And if he had lived, I would have never existed.

According to my mother, the next day Third Avenue was converted to a one-way street heading uptown. It turned out to be a bit later than the next day, but the day after sounded more dramatic and appealing to her. This was just another one of my mom's slightly lying truths.

I can only imagine the sense of loss my mother must have experienced. I believe that because she lost her dad as a kid and then her fiancé, a deep fear of abandonment began planting its roots in her heart. Mom was a tough cookie in many ways, and she did what she could to move forward. She was never one to talk about her true feelings but suffered inside and alone.

Her life continued and she found other suitors but no proposals she wanted to accept. She wanted to date, have fun, be entertained, and, I am guessing, drink. She was the life of every party and I don't believe her drinking had done more at this point than help her maintain her fun-girl status. At one point Mom did meet another man with whom she was rumored to have been very serious. But it wasn't until years later that I would hear the truth about that relationship.

While she had plenty of tragedy in her life, she also had a great deal of fun. Mom loved Broadway and anyone associated with the theatre. Some years later she ended up dating a married (but separated) man named Murray Helwitz, who was treasurer of the Shubert Theatre.

They dated for a while, and Mom fell right into the world of premieres and late-night cocktails, dinners, and dancing at various dinner clubs. Social hobnobbing like that made my mother come alive. She befriended all the local bartenders, coat-check girls, and restaurant managers. This seemed to be the beginning of a lifelong pattern where Mom gravitated toward those she called the underdogs.

While seeking her fabulous and glamorous future, she always seemed to hover on the fringe. It appeared she meant to inhabit two paradoxical worlds. It was an odd paradox because she wanted to be accepted into a more elevated social status, but she held tightly to a darker and more troubled socioeconomic echelon. She was seeking some kind of recognition and a level of improvement in her life but fought it at the same time. It seemed that she was longing for, craving, an escape from her roots. Yet she could never quite give them up. She'd revert to a tougher type of talk if she felt intimidated. I always said she wore being from Newark like a badge, flashing it when necessary or threatened. Whenever she felt a crack in her armor or felt a moment of social ineptitude, she'd counterbalance with a brash declaration of her Newark upbringing. She often outwardly credited Newark as the reason she couldn't be beat. I always loved visiting there with her because it felt uncomplicated. But I also loved leaving because I would get bored, just as she did.

The bartenders in particular seemed to look out for her. Once, while Murray and Mom were in a fight, a bartender spotted Murray with another woman, sitting at what had been "their" table. The bartender reached under the counter for the phone and called my mom. He quietly informed her that her beau was currently at the joint with another gal. Mom thanked him, took a quick shower, and put on the new mink coat Murray had purchased for her as a gift along with a pair of high heels. Decked out in *just* a fur and heels, Mom cabbed it to the restaurant, walked to the back of the place, stood in front of the table for two, and looked right at Murray but angled herself slightly more toward the other woman, who turned out to be his wife. Seems like they weren't so separated after all! She asked him if he liked her new fur coat. As she asked, she proceeded to open it up and do a full twirl before wrapping her naked self back up and continuing out the restaurant. On the street she may or may not have cried, but she had made a point. Mom liked to make such scenes, and her various dramatic antics would become legendary.

The fur-coat story aside, clothes paid an important role in my mom's life, and she chose them carefully. Early on, she recognized the power of certain labels. But she also realized she was unable to afford them. She knew how to dress for various social environments and would not let her lack of finances infringe on her wardrobe. In the late fifties and early sixties Emilio Pucci had become wildly popular. Mom loved the bright colors of Pucci and thought it ingenious how he wrote his name throughout the patterns. But she was unable to afford the famous print mini shift dresses all the uptown ladies were wearing. So Mom once again had to be creative.

And that she was. Mom bought some fabric in a print that was practically indiscernible from the now famous Pucci patterns and fashioned her own shift dress. She sewed it herself and then in pen she wrote her own name, "Teri," in cursive on all the same areas one would find the esteemed signature "Emilio." She recalled many socialites coming up to her at a cocktail party and commenting on the specialness of her dress. "I just love your Pucci, Teri!" Mom said she made a point of saying thank you and walking away so her secret stayed safe. She would joke that she was fine as long as she wasn't caught in the rain, because then if she had been unlucky enough, her dress would begin looking like a fashion by Rorschach test, with ink blots developing where her name had been previously so neatly placed.

Mom coveted the clothes she saw the rich women wear, and eventually learned to hunt them down in various Upper East Side thrift shops. She knew those were the places that the Park Avenue women were likely to deposit their old Gucci, Courrèges, or other designer labels. She combed through the racks and stacks and over time, and with her keen eye, was able to procure and savor a wardrobe that any proper Upper East Side WASP would deem appropriate.

It was thanks to this wardrobe and her recently, intently, avariciously learned rules of etiquette that Mom began dating more and more well-bred men and being invited into communities previously reserved for high society, for the educated, wealthy, and elite. Mom felt at ease and if she was at all insecure about her level of education, she made up for it with her humor, her style, and her astute ability to read a room. Mom's wry wit and her keen human observations made her a welcome dinner date or companion to anyone lucky enough to have her at their table. When you added alcohol to these characteristics, she was hard to resist. Her drinking at this point in her life, although probably necessary for her confidence, was still not a negative. Mom dated senators and theatre owners, bankers and trust-fund kids. She was wined and dined by them all. Mom began being recognized around town as the beautiful and vivacious "Teri Terrific."

Mom looks happy in the photos I have from this time. I believe that during this period of her life, she might have actually been. There was no sadness in her eyes yet. This may have been the happiest I had ever seen her. She was on the ascent and having fun. She looked the best she had ever looked and was celebrated for all she wanted to be. I held on to the fantasy that one day I'd be able to help Mom return to that feeling in her life.

She seemed gorgeous, carefree, and very alive. She was living the life of a single woman in New York City in the early sixties. But she was getting a bit older according to the current social mores, and I believe she began wanting a bit more security and a more substantial relationship.

Well, such a relationship was around the corner, and although it may not have been what she had expected, it changed the entire course of her life.

Chapter Two

Shields and Co.

I f asked, Mom always boasted that late '64 and '65 were a very good and very busy time. Over the course of a year my mother met my father, got pregnant, married my dad, had me, and got divorced.

As the story goes, Mom was nursing a broken heart at a local watering hole called Jimmy Weston's with an equally sad buddy who had just been dumped by his lady friend. His name was Jack Price and he evidently knew my father from around. Together Mom and Jack ventured out to commiserate and drown their sorrows. Evidently my twenty-four-year-old dad, still wet behind the ears and newly graduated from the University of Pennsylvania, walked into this particular bar on the Upper East Side by himself. He stood six foot seven with thick black hair slickly side-parted and combed over like a little boy's. His strong jaw and Roman nose gave his face a regal appearance—to me, his face always looked a bit like the Statue of Liberty's or like one of the Greek gods. According to my mother, Dad was wearing shined Belgian loafers, a crisp shirt, and a navy blazer. He was beautiful.

Mom claims she took one look at him and thought, *I want that!* Somehow introductions were made as they often are in these bars filled with regular customers. Friends of friends introduced everybody all around and Mom quickly devised a plan. She proceeded to focus on getting her drinking buddy hammered so as to unload him. Once Jack began to stammer, Mom made her move. She asked my father to help put her friend in a cab. She told the cab driver his address and then stood on the street with my dad, open to suggestions.

"Can you believe he just left me!" Dad offered to take her home.

Here she was, the five-nine blond beauty with legs like Cyd Charisse's, the attire of a well-bred New Yorker, and a riveting wit. These were her most beautiful years, and when you add in some inhibition-erasing cocktails, she became captivating. How could he resist? This was all I got of this part of the story, but evidently she went back with him to his apartment on East Fiftieth Street and there it all began. My father missed his flight to Los Angeles the next day and had to make up a story to tell the girlfriend he had intended to visit. Mom claims they didn't leave the apartment for three days. I did not need to hear that particular detail, but I got the impression things went well. Mom and Dad began dating (and finding out about one another).

My dad came from a very, very different background from that of my Newark-born mom. His mother was Infanta (Donna) Marina Torlonia, an Italian-born aristocrat and daughter of the 4th Prince of Civitella-Cesi, Marino Torlonia, and Elsie Moore, his American wife. Marino had been the first private banker to the pope and was the primary administrator of Vatican finances. Mussolini even claimed one of his properties for his summer residence, paying him only one dollar.

Dad's Italian mother, Marina, married New York City–born tennis player Francis Xavier Alexander Shields. "Pop-Pop" or "Big Frank," as people referred to him, was president of the Davis Cup and a finalist at both Wimbledon and the US Open. (This was his second marriage.) Pop-Pop was also an actor under contract in the old studio system. It was said that his contract had been used as collateral in a poker game and because of a loss he was forced to switch studios.

Mom and I would see some of his movies later, particularly *Come and Get It*, which was directed by Howard Hawks and starred Pop-Pop and Frances Farmer.

My grandparents divorced after having my father, also named Frank, and his sister Marina. His mother then married Ed Slater, another American, and divorced him after having a son and daughter. Pop-Pop had two more children with his third wife, Goody Mortimer. It was always interesting to me that in almost every case, there was an aristocrat marrying outside the social boundaries, and to an (American) commoner. My royal grandmother married a tennis player–actor from New York City, my dad married a woman from Newark, and I first married a tennis player from Vegas. Dad would comment on this when I was about to marry Andre. (Clearly, none of the couplings ended well.)

A few years later it was said that my grandmother was in love with a married man. While on her way from the wedding of her nephew in Italy to the reception, she was killed in a horrible car crash. It was rumored that she purposely did not ride in the same car with her secret love so as not to create a scandal. The sad irony is that this man's son, Roffredo Gaitani Lovatelli, would die the same way. More grim, however, was that Dad's mom was decapitated and her only son, who was just eighteen years old, was forced to identify the body. In Italy, the firstborn son is considered the next of kin, and because she was divorced at the time, he had to fly over from the University of Pennsylvania, where he was a freshman, to Italy to identify the body.

It must have been a very sad time in my father's life. I don't think he was ever the same after his mom died. Even though he had been at boarding schools and often not with his mom, she was a prominent figure in his life. She lived the life of a royal and jetted all over Europe. Mom once claimed she saw postcards from Dad's mother from places like Gstaad, where she wrote she was sorry she could not be with him for Christmas but was skiing and would see him soon.

Like Dad's mother, my mom was tall and statuesque. His mother would be considered more of a "handsome" woman rather than the beauty my mother was, but they each had a strong presence. Marina was strong and obviously in control. Maybe my dad saw something of his mother in my mom? I'm sure he was drawn to her power and seeming confidence as well as her beauty. He did not seem to have any qualms about my mother's age. She was eight years older than he was and this was not common in the sixties. I guess he couldn't resist the gorgeous spitfire who made him laugh. However, Mom's upbringing and background would later be a prominent obstacle.

But at the time, even though she wasn't a college graduate or an upper-class society debutante, I'm sure Dad found Mom's charisma and humor refreshing. She was known for her energetic personality and game attitude. It appeared that she could converse with people from all walks of life and could blend into a variety of different social settings seamlessly. But he wouldn't have known at first that she was also quite volatile and frequently prone to drama in her relationships. He was no doubt going to be confronted with his own version of the fur-coat incident if he stayed around long enough.

Soon Mom discovered she was pregnant. When she told my dad, he must have felt a sense of panic—and rightfully so. He wasn't ready to be a father. He was just starting his life in business and was forced to travel a lot. He had less money than one would think, and he was still a baby himself.

Dad really did not know how to handle this. He must have told his dad, who took it upon himself to try to persuade my mother to terminate the pregnancy. I was told my grandfather called my mother to meet with him to discuss the situation. Mom met Pop-Pop at his apartment and he sat her down to talk. He requested that mom terminate the pregnancy, explaining that having a child out of wedlock would risk my father getting kicked off the Social Register.

Mom explained that she hadn't meant to corner my father into marrying her and would not hold him accountable for the child. Personally, I believe my mom really did want to be married to my dad but would never have purposely gotten pregnant to do so. She wanted a baby. Period. She craved unconditional love. Pop-Pop (rather hypocritically) alluded to the fact that because Mom and his son Frank came from such different social backgrounds and social status, it seemed an inappropriate coupling. Basically, it just wouldn't look good for my dad to father a child with somebody from Newark. He discreetly slid her an envelope and asked her to take care of the "situation."

According to my mother, she nodded in agreement, explained that she fully understood the state of affairs, took the envelope, and departed. She had no intention of getting an abortion but saw no reason not to take the cash. Instead of going to a doctor, she proceeded immediately to a favorite antique store. There she used the money in the envelope to buy a cherrywood oval coffee table whose four sides folded up with brass brackets to form a sort of connected tray. She was not surprised or angry but defiant as always and knew she wanted the baby and that was that. It's funny—that table would become a favorite standing tool for me as I grew up. I remember teething on it and loving to repeatedly fold the sides up and down and up and down. The table saved my life and helped me to stand.

I didn't learn the truth until recently, but Mom, after buying her new coffee table, suddenly decided to play hard to get. She stopped talking to my father entirely. She said she didn't want anything from my dad but just wanted the baby. She refused to see or even speak to him. Mom was trying to get Dad to realize that he could not live without her. My father, distraught by the pregnancy, and afraid for his future, went to Mass (for the first and last time) and received communion the day he found out about the pregnancy. He was heartsick. He was evidently so in love with my mother that he sent her flowers galore and even sent my godmother, Lila, a cactus garden because she was from Arizona. As much in love with my mom as he was, my father was still not ready to get married or be a dad. He knew Mom would not terminate anything except their relationship, but he was extremely conflicted. Mom cut him off for a few months and hoped he would miss her enough to propose. She made it very clear to everyone that the baby was here to stay, and both my father and grandfather knew it.

When my mother originally told me this story, she had altered it entirely and decided to tell me that my father had left the country during this time. She claimed that when he returned and saw that she had not had an abortion, he proposed. She said that she just calmly waited for his return and enjoyed the life growing inside of her.

My mother's version of the story has my dad going away for a few months and eventually not being able to stay separated from her. Like a comic-book detective, she loved declaring, "Your dad couldn't stay away from me, and I knew he'd eventually come sniffin' around again."

Mom continued on with her altered story, adding that when Dad did return to rekindle, he was shocked to see her big belly and immediately demanded she marry him. Mom loved the dramatic addition of saying that Dad thought he'd return and she would be thin again and without child, but when he saw that she was hugely pregnant, wanted to be a family.

In her version of the story, she opened the door and he turned white as a sheet. "Jesus Christ, Teri. . . . I thought . . ." Not ever being one to be told what to do, Mom reveled in the idea that she could be so in control and shocking.

But the truth was Mom avoided him until he said he wanted to marry her. I guess she broke him down. He did love and miss her, even though he wasn't really ready for any of this. In the end, Mom happened to be desperately in love with my father. Once he claimed he wanted to get married, she ended his solitary confinement.

Dad bought a small diamond solitaire engagement ring from Tiffany (that would eventually be thrown out the seventh-floor window during a fight between my parents, but that's another story). And one day in April, Mom, dressed in a gray wool gabardine maternity dress, went with my father down to city hall. Dad had forgotten his ID at home and had to cab back to retrieve it. For years Mom made up a story that my father was so young—and looked so young compared to her—that the city-hall official was forced to ask for his ID, fearing he was underage.

Sadly, it was not until I wrote this part of the story that I realized this was another little white lie. He had forgotten to bring ID, but it had nothing to do with how young he looked. Everybody is required to have a form of ID when applying for a marriage license. Ah, over the years how implicitly I have believed even the most outrageous mini-lies that my mother has told me. I simply took these fun facts as actual fact when Mom was just envisioning the movie that she wanted to create. You tell stories over and over enough times, and in a way, they become the new reality.

When Mom spoke of this time in later years, it seemed as if she had no worries whatsoever. She was feeling great and was taking so many vitamins that they filled a shoe box. She recalled standing on a corner waiting for the light to turn green one day and her hair—which was usually thin and sparse—had become so healthy and thick that she could, for the first time in her life, feel it swaying in the wind.

She enjoyed being pregnant and said she hardly had any morning sickness at all.

My parents moved to an apartment on East Fiftieth Street. I have only two pictures of my mom pregnant. In one Dad is lying on the couch and Mom is standing by a window holding a glass. This was probably the only photo of Mom holding a glass that did not have alcohol in it. Mom was extremely healthy while she was pregnant and I believe drank very little if at all. In the photo she is backlit and wearing a big yellow muumuu-like dress. She is smiling.

This time for my parents seems to have been a rather uneventful one. Mom prepped for the baby and Dad was working in New York City. In the other photo, they are at a restaurant where my dad is looking lovingly at my expectant mom, who is proudly displaying her diamond. They looked like such a beautiful and contented couple.

On May 31, 1965, my mother and father, along with my godmother, Lila, and a date, were on their way out of the city to watch the Indy 500 on a big-screen TV. The group stopped off at a diner to grab a bite to eat before the start of the race. Mom stood up to go to the ladies' room and suddenly her water broke. It was two months before my due date, and a wave of panic surged through my mother's veins. The only calm one in the place was the waitress who purportedly got immediately down on the floor and began mopping up the mess with her table rag. Mom would later remark at how nonchalant the woman was and how unfazed she was by what had just happened. By the time my dad got Mom to the New York Hospital–Cornell Medical Center maternity ward, she was in labor. Everybody was on high alert because of how premature I was. Mom said they gave her some medication, and from that moment on, she had no recollection of what took place. She awoke to my father leaning over her saying, "We have a perfectly formed baby girl."

Mom remembered thinking that Dad was a lucky bastard who always got exactly what he wanted—he had hoped for a girl and Mom had prayed for a boy. I never got to understand why my mother wanted a son over a daughter. I could speculate as to the psychology of losing her father, or having a less-than-stellar relationship with her mother, but for some reason Mom wanted a boy. She had picked out the name John and was *sure* I was going to be a boy. However, it was days before Mom got to see her perfectly formed baby girl because I had been whisked off to the nursery and placed in an incubator to be monitored. Days passed and still Mom had not laid eyes on me. She began getting suspicious as to why her baby was being kept away from her. She started experiencing late-night paranoia that it was all a lie and that there was actually no baby. She feared the baby had died and people were not telling her the truth. I would not learn until much later why Mom had such a fear of me dying. The doctors reassured her she had a healthy five-pound, three-ounce daughter who was safely tucked in her incubator, and they encouraged Mom to rest.

Mom desperately tried to sleep through the next lonely night but claimed an annoyingly squeaky door kept her awake. She summoned a nurse to request that the door be oiled so she could rest. The attending nurse looked right at my mother, with slight annoyance in her voice, and explained that the "squeaky door" was in fact Mom's newborn baby in the nursery next door, and nothing they could do would stop it.

Mom waited in silence after the nurse departed and, with mounting desperation, hobbled off her hospital bed and snuck out of her room. She was not convinced that any of these stories about her infant were true, and with increasing hysteria, she was determined to find out the truth. She snuck into the nursery and began frantically looking for her daughter's name on the cribs. Her fear and confusion became fueled by the fact that the manufacturing company of all incubators and cribs at that time was called Shields and Company. She went from thinking she had no baby to seeing every single crib with her baby's name on it. It must have been surreal.

Mom looked to the far end of the nursery and saw two cribs at the back a bit apart from the others. One crib was faced out and the other was faced to the wall. It was an unusually busy time for birthing babies and space was tight. In those days the children being placed up for adoption were put in cribs and then turned away from the glass so the birth mothers couldn't see the babies. It was thought to make the transition less fraught for the mother. It just so happened that I was in one of the two cribs against this back wall. Standing alone and looking at two cribs—one facing out and the other facing the wall, not knowing which baby was hers and fearing that somebody had put her baby up for adoption—my mother went insane. She began screaming and rushed to read the names on the two cribs.

A nurse burst in to calm my mom and asked her what she needed.

"I want to see my baby!" she kept screaming. "I want to see my baby!"

"Calm down, miss!"

"I will not calm down until I see my baby! You have all been lying to me about squeaky doors and perfect babies and I don't believe any of it!"

"OK, OK! Please relax. Here is your baby girl."

The nurse reached into the crib not facing the wall and, staring only at my mother, lifted me up. My mother gasped because I was totally covered in meconium. I guess I had not been checked on in a while and had managed to cover myself in the blackish green poop that comes out of newborns. This was, in fact, a sign that I was healthy, but the nurse almost dropped me the moment she saw that she was holding a slippery little, flailing dark-green monster.

"This is the squeaking door, Mrs. Shields. I'll clean her up and you can hold her." From that moment on, Mom never wanted to let me out of her sight again.

They released us from the hospital once I gained a bit of weight. Breast-feeding didn't seem to be popular in 1965, and I guess my mother never even considered it. I was put on Enfamil and sent home.

Evidently, Mom said that my eyes had remained closed since birth. She brought me home and waited but began to get worried because my eyes stayed shut. Well, Mom brought me back to the doctor, who said, "Oh, you want her eyes open?"

And with Mom's nod he took his big middle finger and thumb and flicked as hard as he could on the bottom of my feet. My eyes popped right open and I let out a wail and started to cry.

"There you go."

How rude! I had been born two months premature, so maybe I was just not ready to actually see the big world yet. You try getting out of a cozy bed two months before it's time to get up!

My father wanted to name me after his mother but Mom preferred the name Brooke. She had seen a beautiful photo of a woman in a field, and the photographer was named Christian Brooks. She thought Brooke with an *e* instead of an *s* would be a pretty name for a girl. When the time came for me to be baptized, the priest said that because there was no saint named Brooke, I could not be christened Brooke. Mom says she immediately responded by saying: "Well, put an *a* at the end of Christ. Is that Catholic enough for ya?" I assume the name Christa also had something to do with the photographer, but her reported response to the priest made for a better tale.

So I was born Brooke Christa Shields and baptized Christa Brooke Shields. After the christening my mom and dad went to P. J. Clarke's and placed me on the bar and toasted me. My husband and I have done the very same thing with both our daughters. Celebrating with a beer to the baby on the bar has become a bit of a tradition. I have never been called Christa but always liked it as a middle name.

My mother was terrified of SIDS. A politician's child had recently died of crib death, and Mom could not get the thought out of her mind. She slept with me literally strapped to her chest and repeatedly held up a mirror to my mouth and nose to make sure I was breathing. The steam from my breath became her source of calm. I was a terrible eater and ate only half an ounce every half hour. Mom said she would premake countless bottles filled with half-ounce bottles of formula in a cooler next to her bed and feed me accordingly. This went on for some time, and after about six months, I was transferred to my wooden crib. I soon started pulling myself up in my crib and used the rails as a teething surface.

Mom and I became obviously physically bonded and my dad remained seemingly less knowledgeable and comfortable with his baby. One day Mom passed by the bathroom while my dad was in the shower. I was in need of my bath and Mom suggested to my dad he shower with me and get me cleaned up at the same time. He took me and a bit later Mom passed by the bathroom again only to see my dad standing in the shower holding my little naked body but now wearing his blue boxers. Another time Mom went to church and left me alone with my father. We were using cloth diapers in those days, and when Mom returned I was lying completely naked in bed, and a huge pile of diapers lay on the floor. When asked what had happened, Dad explained he knew not how to clean the mess and that he had used the diapers like tissues. Needless to say, that month's diaper supply had been depleted. Clearly my father was in over his head with regard to being a dad.

Dad found out soon enough, though, that the mother of his child could be quite a troublemaker. During one argument between my mom and dad it somehow happened that Mom's bra had gotten torn.

For the first time ever, Mom had bought a sexy red-lace bra, which she was wearing at the time of the fight. In addition to the torn bra, a chair got broken. It was rare for my parents to fight in any sort of physical way, so this must have been a pretty big argument or Mom was the one to do all the damage. A broken chair and a ripped brassiere were hardly out of the realm of possibility for her to destroy. In any case, on this particular Saturday it all happened and my father stormed out of the apartment. Where he was going, she didn't know, which must have made her even angrier.

My mother was not satisfied. She wanted to have the final word. So she decided to tie the torn red-lace remnants of her bra onto the spindles of the destroyed chair and hand-deliver them to the Racquet and Tennis Club of Manhattan. Now, the Racquet and Tennis Club was one of the oldest all-male clubs in New York City. It is an incredibly old-school, traditional institution, complete with leather-lined libraries for cigar smoking and backgammon and huge oil paintings of elaborate foxhunt scenes or dead geese lined up under the watchful eye of a skilled pointer. Women were not allowed to be members and never set foot past the entrance.

Well, my mother marched right up to the club, walked through the doors, with the broken wooden chair strategically draped with red-lace undergarments boldly labeled "Mr. Frank Shields from Mrs. Frank Shields," and deposited it all right in the middle of the lobby.

I'm sure the staff had no idea of how to react. What was this? I guess they decided it was an art installation of some kind for one of their members. It was the sixties. Packages, evidently, were to be claimed during the workweek only, so, as my mother told the story, this symbol of public humiliation sat in the middle of the lobby for the world to see over the entire weekend. Dad's mortification would be witnessed by many an esteemed colleague. His shame had thus been initiated. It remained true that while Mom wanted to be accepted by high society, she equally loved challenging its social mores and sexist rules. My dad's version of the fur-coat story had arrived in full force; this should have sent up the proper red flags.

Looking back, I imagine that this incident was just one of many outrageous antics. It was not, however, enough to break them up—yet. I speculate that there was a power to her that he somehow could not resist. I believe that it was not dissimilar to the type of power his own mother wielded. No doubt my mother was unlike anyone else in his life.

He had relief, though, because he often traveled for work. Dad left once more for Europe and began writing letters to Mom from abroad.

What transpired over the next few months is documented by letters sent to my mother in very small, neat handwriting, usually on hotel stationery. In the letters from Dad, he expresses his confusion and sadness about the fact that his father had not been to visit Mom and the baby. His family was not the kind to have many family get-togethers. In his writing, Dad seems hurt by the fact that his father was not reaching out to me and Mom more. My father also worried that Mom was not getting any help. He said many times that he was concerned that she wasn't getting out enough and that she should really ask for some help so as to spend time on herself.

He also promised to give my mom more money when he could get it, and a real wedding in a church one day. At times he wrote of wiring money and wishing he could be sending more but Italian banks and the like were less than helpful. I am struck by the tenderness that Dad had for "little Brookie" and how sad he seemed to be away. He seemed quite sincere about wanting things to work out.

In one of his more vulnerable correspondences, he comments on the joy he felt receiving a Valentine's Day card from my mom and me. He said it made his day and he was sorry to be missing being with his "girls" on what had always been my mom's favorite holiday. It is heartbreaking to hear his vulnerable tone in the correspondences only to discover that he was about to experience a devastating blow.

Imagine my own shock at reading Dad's next letter, postmarked February 16, 1966, which read:

Mumsy, after receiving such a wonderful Valentine's cable, to receive your cable of this morning was a real shock and suddenly I am unable to think clearly. I have a feeling of loss, a sense of nothingness, no aspirations, no idea of what to do, and as a whole a very sick feeling inside. Up until this morning I didn't consider the impact of the meaning of divorced, which I have brought on myself, my wife, and baby. I am trying to reason that the decree is merely a legal document and not an emotional state which cannot be reversed or resolved. I wanted to start clean but I didn't see the necessity legally of anything more than a separation. . . . I want to be happy with the two of you as a family and I am not going to change my thinking. I think of you as my wife this time away from New York, and I hope to God that I can redeem myself in your eyes so as to bring us back together. . . . I am trying to put out of my mind the trip to Mexico. I just don't know. . . .

He was clearly confused and did not know how to continue. He did love my mom and they did have a child together, so maybe he believed a separation would help. But he seemed to be fooling himself. My mom was not going to wait for what she was feeling would be the inevitable. She feared they would not last, and although convinced my father wanted to try to do the right thing, she thought he would not be happy in the long run.

I have no letters from Mom to my dad during this time, but I found some diaries in which Mom wrote about how ashamed my father was of her: "I am a burden to him financially and especially socially," one entry read. "He's ashamed to be with me in public for fear I may say something that might embarrass him." Another one read, "I am too opinionated and don't act right in public. I give a cheap appearance. 'Cheesy' was the word he used."

She told me Dad would get exasperated with her and her "deez, dems, and doz" way of speaking. She felt my father was ashamed to be with her. She writes that he wanted her to be a different person with a different background. I believe Mom was afraid he would eventually reject her, and she wanted to save herself the pain.

She knew deep down that my father loved us but wanted a different life. Maybe she really was doing this for him, to set him free. I can't say what is actually the truth or what my mom's real insecurities were, but for some reason, she made a preemptive decision. My mother probably heard my father use the word *separation* and just made a rash choice.

She flew to Mexico, where it used to be the very easiest place to obtain a divorce on your own. Mom left me with Lila and got the divorce by herself. By the time Dad returned from Europe, my mom had declared herself a single mother.

What is so shocking and sad is how stunned my dad appeared by Mom's pronouncement. I don't think he was quite ready to be free from my mom, but I wonder if he was secretly a bit relieved.

Mom's actions often had an impulsive and self-destructive quality. She saw herself alone, and although I believe she craved love and partnership, she feared she was not worthy and therefore often jumped ship before she could get too hurt.

Now, however, she had this little baby who couldn't leave. She had a baby daughter who was completely dependent on her.

My mother explained to my father that she wanted neither alimony nor any kind of child support other than an education for me. She said she could take care of the two of us somehow but insisted that he send me to school all the way through college.

I doubt Dad talked about marriage again but they definitely took time to fully disengage with one another. They seemed to find a way to still spend a lot of time together because of me. He helped out when he could and they celebrated some holidays together for a couple of years. In fact I have many photos of us all together while I was a toddler and a young kid. It was as if without the pressure of being married, my dad could relax and love us both. They lived separately but eased out of one another's lives. I have no idea if it was painful for my mom during this period but I am sure his getting married again would have stung when it happened.

My father kept true to his word and paid for my entire formal education and was present and beaming on every graduation day.

So, although the whirlwind of life and the emotions that accompanied the events of 1964 and 1965 were fraught, they did not seem void of love and some version of respect and understanding.

Chapter Three

She Could Make It Rain

Having never really known my parents as a couple, I had no feeling of loss or guilt surrounding their divorce. I would grow up knowing, or at least trying to know, them each independently. From the day I was born, whether they were a couple or not, my mom always made sure that my dad saw me frequently.

It was clear that my mother wanted my father to have a relationship with me. Even if she herself could not be with him, she wanted me in his life. She would invent ways for him to be forced to see me. Sometimes, if Dad hadn't seen me in a while, Mom would dress me up in a fancy dress or romper, complete with bonnet or bow and Mary Janes, and take me to the building in which my father worked. She'd do this at the end of his workday. Mom would wait with me just around the corner but with a good view of the building's entrance. She would watch for my dad to leave, and as he came out of the building, she'd push me out alone and say, "Go, go see Daddy!" She told me she'd duck out of sight and I'd toddle over to him. Slightly surprised and a bit nervous for my safety, he'd scoop me up in his arms and search for my mom. When she popped out into view, he'd use his naturally booming voice and exclaim, "Jesus Christ, Teri, what the hell are you doing?"

After the ambush, I'm not sure if we all spent some time together or they just chatted on the street for a bit. I'm sure my dad usually had some place to go, but Mom was satisfied just knowing she made him see his baby girl. There was never a doubt in my mind that he was my dad.

I even have pictures of both Mom and Dad strolling me down Fifth Avenue during the Easter parade. In the photos I'm about two or three, and we look like a perfectly intact, happy family. Mom is chic in her black-and-white plaid skirt and cropped jacket with a white pillbox hat. Dad looks dapper as always, in a suit and tie. I am in a navy wool double-breasted coat and a white hat. My white tights were a bit twisted or saggy and dirty at the knees, but my black patent-leather Mary Janes are shiny. Together, they were a stunning couple and always turned people's heads. They didn't look divorced.

But even though the photos make us look as if we were just like any other family, the truth was very different. From the time my parents divorced, my life with my mother was very unique. Surprisingly, being a single mom in New York City proved to be more convenient for Mom than one would think. I did have occasional sitters, and my godmother often watched me, but for the most part, I was portable and a welcomed accessory to any of my mother's fashion-forward outfits. Sporadically, she brought me by bus out to visit her mom and siblings in Paterson and Newark but, for the most part, we remained in good old Manhattan. Mom took me to parties with her various fashion-industry friends. We went to dinner clubs and movies and even the theatre, and I would either play or sleep and was obviously happier being with her than with a sitter. I was simply most comfortable being physically around my mother.

Although my mother managed to stay in contact with many of the friends she made while with my father, she also maintained the friendships she had cultivated outside his Waspy circles. She made new friends as well, many who were in the fashion industry or entertainment of some kind. She befriended photographers and stylists, designers and artists. She was developing a very colorful group of talented people from diverse walks of life. In any given week we would be visiting a huge mansion out in the Hamptons as well as going to a downtown evening in a jazz club or performance-art space or photo exhibit. She frequented all walks of life, with me in her arms and then on her hip. It appeared Mom began forging her own path.

I was one of those babies you see out late at night in restaurants and being passed around the table to be cooed at or brought into the bathroom to be changed on the sink. I slept soundly, lulled by the low din of voices and silverware clinking. Everybody made sure to write "Don't forget to bring the baby" on invites to dinner parties and cocktail gatherings. I had very little fear of new people, and although most bonded to my mom, I would gladly go smile at a stranger. Some things never change. . . .

Mom always dressed me like a little doll. I wore smocked dresses and pressed cotton bloomer outfits with matching bonnets. I was always spanking clean and all dolled up. Mom put extra effort into my looking a girl because I had no hair and people repeatedly asked, "Oh, what's his name?" Mom taped little homemade pink mini ribbon bows to my head to ensure people knew I was a girl. But that still didn't work much of the time. Once, in an elevator, a woman scoffed to my mother, "Why would you do that? Why would you put a pink bow on a little boy's head?"

Mom told stories about my babyhood just like she used to tell stories about her own life. Some were true, some a bit embellished. One example of this happened while we were living on Fifty-Second Street. Mom let me crawl on the sidewalk before I learned how to walk. Evidently, one day, on one of these jaunts, we passed Greta

Garbo's apartment building. Garbo herself just happened to be out on a walk, and as the story goes, she stopped, looked at me and then to my mother, nodded her head, and continued on her way. Mom took this as a literal nod of approval from a legend and believed I had been blessed and sanctioned as one destined to make a mark in the world. I do believe Garbo was walking and perhaps noticed this little kid crawling on her knees on the pavement and made some gesture to me, but the real meaning of the nod is open to interpretation. For all we know, the regal Garbo could have been looking disdainfully at this careless mother who was allowing her baby to rub her soft knees on cement streets. Or maybe she was, in fact, envisioning the future?

Mom and I were rarely apart from each other, and I'd do anything to make her happy and get her attention. When I was around four, she took me to a piano bar and I asked if I could go to the bathroom alone. The bathroom was a small place and tucked into an alcove. When I did not return quickly, Mom started to rise to come search for me. As she stood she started to hear my voice over the sound system. She looked at the piano and I was seated atop it, legs crossed and singing a cappella. I don't remember if the piano player accompanied me or not, but according to my mom, my voice was heard throughout the club. I knew "Embraceable You" and "My Funny Valentine" were my mother's two favorite songs. She would often sing them to me, so I knew the words to both. I was offered the mike, chose "Embraceable You," and serenaded her. This particular club would later become La Cage aux Folles. We'd someday be among their favorite patrons, but I never did sing on the piano again.

Even before I could talk (or sing), people often remarked to my mother about my looks being rather extraordinary. My mom would boast that when I was an infant, people often stopped us to comment on my "beauty." Of course Mom thought her child was the most beautiful child in the world, but doesn't every mother think that?

One day, while riding in a checker cab, Mom was given an idea that may or may not have occurred to her previously. It was about her baby's looks and the possibility of using them to make a living. The story she told was that one spring day in 1966 a typical New York cab driver was driving her and her ten-month-old baby girl uptown in his cab. The driver glanced in his rearview mirror a few times and then exclaimed in an old New York accent, "Ya know dat liddle kid a yers? She should model!"

Evidently he had a two-year-old niece who had become a model. "Now the kid makes more than I do by the hour. Figure dat."

Mom thanked the cabbie for the compliment and the suggestion, gave him a nice tip, and exited the cab. But the idea stayed with her, and as fate would have it, a few weeks later one of her photographer friends phoned in a panic. "We need a baby who can kiss!" He was shooting an Ivory soap ad and was seeing countless babies for the campaign. The client was not happy with the selection. Not one baby out of hundreds he saw was the one. They were either not similar enough to the model chosen as the mom, not cute enough in a unique way, couldn't kiss, or they were simply hysterical. The baby had to know how to kiss, but that was the *last* thing any of these kids wanted to do at this moment. It was mayhem. Kids were screaming and the client was on the verge of tears.

The photographer begged my mother to bring me down to his studio. I vaguely feel like I can remember being carried through the chaos and cries. It could be that I have been told the story so many times that I imagine I actually remember. But as the story goes, it was midafternoon and I had already had my afternoon nap, so I was in great spirits. Being, as usual, comfortable and acclimated around adults, I was all smiles, and kisses, and curiosity. I got the job on the spot and was shot for the ad, holding a bar of soap out to my "mother"—no kissing involved after all. During the shoot I reportedly sat on the floor of the freshly white-painted set and opened twenty-four cases of Ivory soap, each containing twelve bars each. The client was thrilled and everybody was happy.

The relieved photographer scooped me up in his arms and hugged my mom for saving the day. To the world, that photographer was the already famous Francesco Scavullo. But to me, he was just "Uncle Frankie."

My modeling career had begun.

So by the ripe old age of eleven months I already had a major national ad under my belt. Mom realized that she had an opportunity and should follow up. I was not with any agency, so we had no percentage to give away and the money from this first job went solely to my mother and me. Mom had periodically worked part-time at Brentano's bookstore, but the salary would not cover child care and living expenses. Though not required, Dad did help out with the rent, but the chance for additional revenue being generated by us was clearly appealing.

Mom found me a manager named Barbara Jarrett, although it appears as if I did not have another big modeling job for a while. By the time I was two or three, however, I began to get jobs for catalogues and I spent the next few years being managed by both Mom and Barbara. I find it interesting that both my mom and I began working at a very young age. Cleaning houses and modeling are very different, but a certain work ethic was instilled in us both early on. Mom was imaginative and gutsy as a child and now she was being forthright and creative as a mother. She was turning chance into an opportunity.

I still had hardly any hair, so for the first two years I modeled primarily as a boy. Once, right before leaving on a location shoot for a catalogue in Jamaica, Barbara took my mom aside and said: "For God sake, don't take her bathing suit off around anybody. They think she's a boy."

As child models, we got paid to do the activities that we might not have always been able to afford ourselves. The trips were always a blast. The moms and the kids would meet early in the A.M. on a street corner and all load into a huge camper. They had fun drinks and snacks, and the drive was crazy, with kids playing and singing songs. I loved being on locations or checking into various tropical resorts and chasing lizards and being in the sun. It was usually the same basic group of kids who eventually became close and even longtime friends. These were some of my earliest and fondest memories of being a model.

I thought my mom could do no wrong. I believed she could even change the weather.

One day, when I was about four, she bought me a red patent-leather raincoat and matching rain hat. It was a sunny day but I still wanted to wear my new coat and hat. Mom insisted that it was unlikely that the rain would fall and that I'd be hot and uncomfortable. The way my mom told the story, I walked out of the apartment, and turning to her over my shoulder, I declared, "Don't worry, Mama, you'll make it rain." And, as the story goes, as soon as we went outside, the skies opened and there was a torrential downpour.

Around the time I was nine years old, my mother and I moved into an apartment on Seventy-Third Street between First and Second Avenues. It was on the seventh floor of a white brick building called the Morad Diplomat. I was close to my dad, but it was my mother to whom I was incredibly bonded. She was my everything. When we moved in, we had very little furniture. Our first night was spent on a queen-size mattress on the floor, pushed up to the wall. We had sheets, one down pillow, and a large multicolored neon crocheted blanket that my mom had taken from a visit to her mother's apartment in Newark.

Mom slept with her back to the wall, and I was the inner spoon. I will always remember that I fell asleep peacefully and comfortably. It was one of the best nights' sleep I can ever remember. To me, being spooned has always been an instant sleeping pill. This closeness with my mom gave me the utmost feeling of comfort and safety. In a way it was like being tied to her chest once again, only this time we were side by side. I think we both believed that we would forever exist within this dynamic. I loved the bed being up against the wall and spooning with Mom and being able to see the door. I was in a warm cocoon and had not a worry in the world. We were conjoined and content.

On those first nights I would say, "Hug me!" and my mom would wrap me up and drape her left arm over my side. She would always ask if her arm was too heavy. It never was, but even if it had been, I was too afraid she'd remove it if I said so. Instead, I always said it was fine. I'm not sure Mom ever gave me her full weight until she knew I was asleep.

I was becoming so enmeshed with my mother that it was as if my taste buds were affected. I liked Yodels until the day my mother tasted one and said it tasted "waxy." After my next bite, I concurred and never ate another Yodel again. Actually, I'm not even sure if she disliked Yodels at all. She may have just wanted to get me to stop eating junk. But in any case, her opinions were strong enough to influence how I actually tasted my food.

I know she was drinking even then, but the effects weren't clear to me at such a young age. If anything, it seemed to make her more fun and more creative. My mother was always such a great artist and creative crafter. Each Halloween she made elaborate costumes for me. Starting from about three years old and for many years after, she did get off easy because I always went as Charlie Chaplin. I often won first prize for that costume and for my ability to imitate his recognizable waddle and circular cane swing. But as I grew up I began wanting to wear more fun or feminine costumes. One year she crafted me into a huge blooming red rose. My head popped out from the middle of a layered red crepe rose. She dressed my body in a green leotard and tights for the stem, and on each hand she gave me cuffs of green crepe-paper leaves. I wore the tights over my penny loafers and by the end of the night had worn through them by walking around. Another year Mom made me an exact replica of a tube of Crest toothpaste. She perfectly copied the tube onto cardboard and even included the cap. I was transformed into a dental delight. I was thrilled with the precision of her rendering but it was extremely hard to walk in. I had to take geishalike steps and the edge of the cardboard cut into the front of my ankles. The pain didn't bother me, though, because it was such a creative costume, and I was proud my mom made it by herself.

Mom put so much time into my costumes I began to expect to win the contest at the gymnastics space, Sokol Hall, where we'd attend their annual party. Because we lived in an apartment building, trick-or-treating was easy and I could go alone with a friend. I'd invite

a school buddy and we'd begin on the penthouse floor and work our way down. It took hours, and our pumpkin-head buckets would be overflowing by the time we got to the lobby apartments. This was the height of the razor-blade-in-the-apple panic, and I was never allowed to eat any of my loot until after Mom had done a thorough check. It was always fine because we knew every inhabitant in the building. I never actually ate all the candy I got. It usually got stale before I finished even half the bucket.

Another story I love was about my doll, Blabby. Blabby was a doll similar to the amazing Baby Tender Love dolls of the seventies that I adored, but she was more unique. She used to make a sound like a baby cooing when you squeezed her rubber stomach. I took her into the bath with me so many times, however, that the coo soon turned into a bark. Later, with my kid scissors, I cut off almost all her hair. She looked rather punk and ahead of her time, but soon, because of the baths and the brushing, it all fell out.

Blabby went everywhere with me. When we traveled by plane, Mom would strap her in with me in the seat. The seat belt went around us both and was fastened only when Blabby gave a "nod" that it was tight.

When I was around six years old, Mom and I had a layover in some city on our way back to New York. I had left Blabby in the terminal while waiting for our connection and playing some Pac-Man–type game. We hadn't noticed until Mom was strapping me into my seat and realized Blabby wasn't on my lap. The plane had begun its taxi on the runway when my mother suddenly and frantically called for the flight attendant. She told me not to say a word and then looked straight into the stewardess's eyes and calmly and emotionally, but deadly seriously, said, "We must get off this plane! It is a matter of life and death."

This was way before 9/11, and security was much more lenient. The flight attendant must have been alarmed enough, though, so she went to the cockpit and they stopped the taxi and returned to the gate to let both of us off. Mom and I deplaned without saying another word and I went directly to the game I had played before boarding the plane. Blabby was not there, so we tried lost and found. We reported Blabby's physical profile and had been waiting for over an hour when, from a distance, we saw a male airline official walking toward us, holding something behind his back. He was hiding my doll with an air of embarrassment and was, no doubt, relieved to return her to me. Well, he could not have been more relieved than I was. I knew my mom would fix the situation.

I still have Blabby. But because she is bald and now has a large split down the middle of her head, my girls say she is "creepy." I don't agree. I have never before, nor since, seen a doll similar to her. Mom had given her to me, and after she died I put her necklace on Blabby. Creepy or not, she still sits in my room and reminds me of the time my mother stopped a 747 on a runway to retrieve my baby doll.

Mom probably loved the fact that she could wield that type of power. She always said that as long as you remain firm in your opinions and in their delivery—even if you're not telling the entire truth or you're not completely clear—you'd be surprised at what you can achieve.

Mom has been an unconventional person her whole life, and she wasn't about to change just because she had become a mother. She continued to take me to bars even as I got older. I remember when she taught me to shoot pool from behind my back. I couldn't have been older than eight and I learned fast. When I'd excitedly called my father and said, "Dad! I just learned how to shoot pool from behind my back," I remember him saying: "Where are you?"

"At a bar," I said.

"Jesus Christ."

I'm sure Dad wasn't thrilled with any of this, but I was seemingly safe and having fun, and my mother seemed in control. The argument was tough to have.

The most useful bar talent I acquired—before learning how to tie a knot in a cherry stem with my tongue—involved holding up twelve sugar cubes stacked in between my thumb and pinky finger. It was this skill that I would use as the beginning of a conversation with the one and only Jackie Onassis.

Mom and I were at her long-standing favorite bar, P. J. Clarke's, when Mom spotted Jackie and Aristotle sitting at the tiny window seat in the empty middle section of the restaurant. It was their table! Mom said, "Brookie, that's the mother of the boy you are going to grow up and marry." Without waiting for permission, I leapt up and went over to the table to politely introduce myself.

I evidently went right up, said, "Hi, when I grow up, I am going to marry your son." Jackie said, "Oooh . . . ," as if the thought of her little boy growing up was too much to think of. I then showed her how to hold as many sugar cubes as she could between her two fingers. I simply showed her how to do this trick and then returned to my table. My mom claimed she was embarrassed, but it made for a great story and she loved to tell it.

Mom's version of discipline was unconventional. She was creative with punishments. I once begged her to let me have Devil Dogs for dinner. I cried, pleaded, and threw a tantrum, wanting this cakey, creamy, artificially made dessert snack for my meal. Mom finally conceded but said that if I really wanted Devil Dogs for dinner, I'd have to eat twelve of them. I thought I had hit the junk food jackpot until the third one brushed the roof of my mouth. I started to feel sick and ended up throwing up all over the bathroom. Mom simply asked if I ever wanted Devil Dogs for dinner again. I don't believe I have ever had one since. (Two major cakey junk foods crossed off my list!)

She wasn't afraid to embarrass herself, if necessary, to make a point. She once took my cousin Johnny to see *Godzilla* (which he called *Godzillabones*) and he threw a tantrum when leaving the theater. She immediately got down on the floor and threw her own tantrum, shocking Johnny and showing, once again, how creative—and effective—her discipline could be.

Some of the stories Mom thought were funny could also be scary. She was great at imitations, and most of them I loved because they made me laugh. But the one I did not enjoy at all was her imitation of the Witch in *Snow White*. In the animated movie the witch had this horrible and terrifying cackle that my mom could copy flawlessly. She would do it randomly and it unsettled me horribly. I'd beg her to stop; she'd continue the imitation for longer than I would have liked. I loved her ability to mimic and I consider my talent in this area a gift from her, but the minute Mom started with the voice, I'd start chanting, "You're my mother, you're my mother!" She simply wanted to do what she wanted to do and loved the attention. I don't think Mom ever knew I was actually, honestly scared. She would later tell this story and beam with pride at the fact that I kept repeating that she was my mother.

During these years my modeling career really began to take off. Mom was my manager, but she was hardly the typical "stage mother" one would have expected. She'd ask if I wanted to go in for a job and then simply let me do my thing. She never grilled me on how it went inside the rooms and instead waited for me to volunteer information. I am sure she would have loved getting feedback, but I don't remember her ever pressing me. When I did not get the job, she would just brush it off and we'd discuss what we should do with that free time. There were many times we'd hear parents through the elevator door screaming at their kids or even slapping them. We often heard the sound of crying getting fainter as the elevator descended to the first floor. I never understood why moms promised their kids things like bicycles if the kids agreed to go in on a "go see."

If the kid didn't want to model, I thought he shouldn't have to. My mother never bribed me or forced me to audition or work on things or on days I didn't feel like it. Granted, I was quite young and hardly ever stood up to my mom, but I don't recollect feeling pressured, like I was being forced to do something I didn't want to do. Mom made me feel that it was all my choice. She'd say I could stop anytime I wanted to. I, of course, wanted nothing more than to please her, so I rarely refused to do anything. On any particular day, if I ever expressed not wanting to go in for a job, Mom would unplug the phone or we would escape the house and go to Central Park.

This infuriated clients and agencies, but it ironically made me more sought after. *No* is a powerful word.

Strangely enough, I got only a few jobs in commercials. I was cast in a Johnson and Johnson Band-Aid ad and a Holly Hobbie doll commercial, but it quickly seemed that my looks were not considered all-American enough, and I was often turned down and labeled "too European." Whenever I did get a job, I knew I'd have fun no matter what, and my mom would feel happy. It was a win-win situation.

I learned early on that the sweeter I was to the adults, the nicer they treated me. It was all just for fun during those years, or at least it seemed that way to me.

I stayed at my grade school in Manhattan while working and rarely missed a day to model. On some of the bigger trips, I might miss a Friday. Even as I got older, Mom maintained this rule. If the agency phoned to say I had a shoot for 10:00 A.M. on a Thursday, Mom would respond by saying that was great and we would see them all at 3:00. If they pushed, she'd claim that if they didn't want me, it was fine to choose another child, but I would not be available until after school let out at 2:40. Basically, while other kids were involved in after-school sports or playdates, I was shooting for various catalogues. I can't say I minded not playing sports or being forced to spend any time separated from my mother.

I have a lot of great memories from these early years. I was once cast as Jean Shrimpton's daughter in an ad. Mom always said that I looked more like her than any other model or actress. Mom thought she was beautiful and had a face with perfect symmetry.

Over the next few years I modeled in ads and catalogues for Macy's, Sears and Roebuck, Bloomingdale's, Alexander's, McCall's, and Butterick. Whenever I had a "go see," Mom remained in the background. On set, Mom was not one of the moms who made her presence imposing. She never hovered over the creative team or offered unsolicited direction to me. She saw everything and had her opinions about everybody, but during these days, she was more subtle and did not share her judgments with me.

Our life was active and fun. We basically each had a full-blown career. I modeled and Mom managed.

By the time I was ten, it became obvious that I was in need of larger and more credible representation. Mom looked around at the various available children's agencies for models and was evidently dissatisfied with what she found. Even then, she had high aspirations and was not content settling for anything she deemed commonplace or plebeian.

Because she frequented many photographers' studios and artists' lofts socially and had friends who worked at cosmetic and hair care–oriented companies, she knew the best in the business. The models she loved all seemed to be represented by the Ford Modeling Agency and she knew the top ad agencies looked to them for their talent. Ford was an agency with such prestige and power that Mom decided it was the only suitable place for her baby girl.

In 1974, Ford Models did not have a children's department and had no plans of incorporating one into their already thriving business. But we had an in. Eileen and Jerry Ford, who had started Ford Models, knew my father from various social circles and from supplying models for Revlon ads, and my dad was now working for Revlon as a sales executive.

I remember that my mother had met Eileen and Jerry many times. They had all remained friendly, so Mom decided to approach Eileen personally. She loved to tell the story about how one day she opened the door and marched up the three flights to Eileen Ford's spacious and bright office. Mom said she stood in front of Eileen's desk with her hands on her hips and explained to Eileen, "This agency doesn't have a children's division, and it should. Brooke will be your first child model."

Eileen was initially against it because she did not want to represent children. She turned my mom down. I am sure my mother did not appreciate being told no and would never admit it happened that way. Mom instead intimated that it was on that fateful day that she changed my future and helped make Ford a success. Ford did eventually begin a children's division that remains today. I was *not* the first child model to join, as I had been led to believe. Mom always claimed credit for being the woman who convinced Eileen Ford to start the Ford children's division. But did she at least plant the seed?

Somehow, as time went on, I began thinking there was something wrong with my mom's drinking. We were so busy that it was easy to overlook, but looking back, I see that although I would not have had the vocabulary to articulate it at the time, I realized that Mom was a highly functioning alcoholic.

She kept it hidden for years, but the signs were there, even if I was too young to see them. I recently met a man at a funeral who said that when I was two or three he lived in an apartment on East Seventy-Ninth Street and Mom lived temporarily on a floor above him. He had met her with my father and they had become friends. He told me that Mom would sometimes knock on his door in the evenings and say, "I'm going out for a drink. Here, just take her for a bit."

She would leave me there and we would hang out. It would be 10:00 or 11:00 P.M. He and I would just climb into bed and fall asleep. He said he never knew what time it would be, but Mom would eventually return and take me back upstairs. It is a bit sad to think that Mom just dropped me off so she could go drink, but at least she wasn't keeping me out all night.

Still, Mom was the world to me, both at home and when I was working, and we had wonderful times together, but they were increasingly tempered by alcohol. She managed to keep our lives going for years before it would become a more obvious and debilitating problem; the negative effects becoming undeniable. In addition, it's equally surprising to see how humorous the results of her drinking actually were early on.

Mom went to church every Sunday, no matter where she was. I was raised Catholic and completed catechism to receive my first Holy Communion and was also later confirmed. Every Sunday I accompanied her to this little church on Seventy-First Street and Second Avenue. It was there that I sang my first song on stage, for the Saint Patrick's Day concert. I sang "When Irish Eyes Are Smiling" and was so nervous I twisted the bottom of my green velvet dress into such a balled-up knot that I showed my white big-girl pants to the entire congregation. I won first prize but will never be sure if it was for the song or my early attempts at striptease.

Mom and I were once at Mass and I was not aware that she was hungover. I was still rather naïve about such a thing as a hangover and she must have done a lot of her drinking alone or while I slept. Mom dozed off during the sermon and I did not even realize it until the moment when the congregation stood up. We all stood up, as did my mom, except she began to start vigorously clapping. She must have thought she was at the theatre and tried to cover it up by pretending she was brushing dust or lint off various articles of her clothing. It was a scene worthy of a Lucille Ball sketch and we would retell it for decades. It just seemed funny then.

But at some point, her drinking stopped being funny. One day when I was in third grade my mom and I were walking to school and chatting. I remember thinking that I wished I knew my mother only in the mornings. She was never drunk before school. She may have been hungover but I never knew it. I realized she never drank before school, but, come 3:00, I knew I'd find her in an altered state. It became inevitable that when school was out and she came to pick me up, she'd have the look in her now slightly glassy eyes. I needed only to see the dryness of her lips to know she had been drinking.

Once at night, soon after detecting her pattern, I blurted out how I felt. I don't remember her response, but even when I declared in anger how I wished I knew her only in the mornings, her behavior had not altered. I can't imagine having an addiction so powerful that a comment like this from a child would leave me unchanged.

If Mom wasn't at home for some reason and I had been at a friend's apartment, I knew where to find her. There was a bar at Seventy-Third and First Avenue on the northwest side of the street called Finnegans Wake. I could either locate her there or farther down Third Avenue at an Italian restaurant called Piccolo Mondo. It was always such a physical relief to see her that I began overlooking the fact that she was on her way to being drunk, if not already there. Usually either I convinced her to come home or we sometimes had some food and then returned home to watch some TV. Mom was rarely violent, and it

Dear Mom,
I just want to say thank you for being so very good about drinking. I love you for that (not only that). I also feel that we are happier together when you are not drinking. We don't fight as much, we laugh more and have much more fun. I love it, I really do. I wish you could see yourself and me when you are in that state, it is real hateful.
Mommy I beg of you please stay without drinking and also PLEASE can we not go to the rice and beans place tonight it takes so long and I love it when you eat at home. I admit I don't help at all with dinner but I promise from now on I will set and clear the

would probably have been easier for me to admit to her disease if I was ever physically abused.

My particular abuse was much more subtle and created a longer-lasting impact. Because every time Mom drank, she left me. I was not able to articulate this until years later and only after a great deal of soul-searching and therapy. I felt abandoned by her when she drank, but as long as I wasn't hurt and she was accounted for and alive, I could justify that everything was all right. Never really knowing what I was going to come home to established a constant underlying sense of anxiety in my gut. I remained unrealistically optimistic that every day would be different. Mom would keep her promise and not get drunk at that birthday or that particular function.

More and more, I began to understand the blueprint of my mother's drinking on a deeper level. I remember not knowing how to complain to her about it. I always felt taken care of and deeply loved and she had not yet become as verbally abusive as she would in years to come. I tried to find ways to show her that her drinking was becoming an issue. It started off subtly: I would suggest Mom just drink ginger ale with me at dinner, for example, or I'd say, "Hey, Mama, maybe you don't have to drink tonight. And we can watch a movie." She assured me it was all fine and then simply did as she pleased. Sometimes she was smart enough to curb it for a while, and then when I had seemingly relaxed a bit, she'd resume more heavily.

Mom was never one to enjoy decorating the Christmas tree. One particular Christmas Eve, after going to midnight Mass and a local diner that served alcohol, we came home. I needed to finish decorating, and while I was focused on the tree, Mom must have fallen asleep. When I turned to ask her what she thought, she responded only by snoring. She basically passed out on the couch, and at that moment I immediately saw a way to show her she had a problem. I chose not to awaken her. It was a risk I had to take. It all had to do with trying to catch her in some way, so that I could legitimately blame her drinking for my unhappiness. In earlier years I would have just awakened her and pretended, both that the guy with the red suit was real and that her drinking was not a problem.

If Mom woke up on her own and dealt with Christmas presents under the tree, then it was proof, I told myself, that Santa existed and her alcohol consumption was, in fact, not that bad. If she stayed asleep and could not rally to play Santa, I could accuse her of passing out and ruining Christmas. I could say, "See, there is *no* Santa and because you were drunk, I now know and I am crushed. I hate you and I hate your drinking." This was the year reality hit me, and the blow was threefold. Mom was a drunk, there was no Santa, and Mom's drinking ruined Christmas. And, in a way, everything.

Chapter Four

If You Die, I Die

Throughout both the closeness and turmoil of living with my mother, I always had something else, which was my relationship with my father and his family. I spent quite a lot of time with him in the Hamptons, where my Pop-Pop, the former tennis champion, was something of a legend at the Meadow Club of Southampton. Mom and I would spend the summers out there, visiting with my dad and enjoying the beach club where my father was a member. We didn't have a house of our own, but Mom wanted me to know my dad and be a part of the privileged existence that was available via his upbringing.

We at first stayed at friends' houses or with relatives of my father's, but we also rented a room above Herrick Hardware in the town of Southampton. I attended day camp and spent my days at the beach club, where I learned how to swim in the large, rectangular, seemingly Olympic-size pool. There are many pictures of me and my little friends eating hot dogs or ice cream, wearing our little Lilly Pulitzer floral bathing-suit bottoms and no tops.

When I was a baby, Mom took me to the Meadow Club when

invited, and as I got older she would drop me off at the club mid-morning and I'd be watched by various mothers and families who welcomed me as their own. I am not sure what my mom did during the times I was at the beach club, but I don't remember her being with me there all the time. She would have had to have been specifically invited, because she was not a member. Mom managed to stay busy. She befriended a bartender at a place called Shippy's. It was in town and a popular joint for food and drink. It basically became Mom's go-to watering hole. She had her haunts in every town we inhabited. I imagine Mom spent many hours at that particular establishment sidled up to the dark wood bar.

There is something tragic in the thought of my being introduced to and accepted by a part of society in which my own mother existed solely on the periphery. She never let on if she felt like an outsider or if she coveted a closer membership to this more rarified world.

Looking back, it seems that once again she enjoyed straddling the fence that separated the Waspy culture from her Newark roots. She enjoyed knowing the locals as well as the wealthier set.

At the end of the beach day, when all the other kids returned to their big houses by the sea, I was either picked up or returned to the small rented walk-up room over Herrick's. It was a very modest space. The tub stood in the kitchen and was covered by a long wooden lid. In order to bathe, one would lift the wooden countertop and fill the tub. My father stayed with various friends and relatives who had stunning properties a short distance from the ocean with rolling lawns, pools, and guesthouses. I was happy anywhere and bounced between the mansions and our single room. I have to believe I welcomed the proximity of my mom in this tiny space. I felt uneasy, sometimes, in the vastness of these other homes and felt safe in our insulated shell. I was also still so young that I didn't recognize the disparity in socioeconomic status evident in the varied living arrangements.

One night when I was a bit older, maybe five or six, Mom and I were with my friend Lyda at a dinner party at a friend's house way out in the potato fields. My mother and Lyda's mother had been pregnant at the same time and were both single mothers. They had a special bond, and in turn, "Lydes" and I became the closest of friends. Her grandmother had a house out in Southampton and much of our summer was spent with them.

On this particular night Mom had been drinking pretty heavily throughout the evening. The adults were all sitting around in the living room after dinner, and the kids were playing on the floor. Mom commented on one little girl's beautiful head of hair. She then reached out to touch it and, in doing so, lost her balance. Mom always wore many rings, sometimes on all her fingers except the thumb. One of

Mom's rings got caught in the little girl's hair and she got yanked down with Mom's hand. The girl's mother got very angry and accused my mom of purposely pulling her child's hair. She said she wanted her to stay away from her daughter.

Mom, uncharacteristically, did not put up a fight. The plan had been for all of us to spend the night, but the ring incident shook us all up. Lyda called her grandmother, who soon arrived. Lyda said to me, "You know, Brookie, you can come to my grandmother's if you want."

I explained that I had to stay with my mom. I needed to make sure she was OK.

Even then, I realized something wasn't quite right. "You're so lucky, Lyda, that you have someplace to go," I added.

I was a young child, but I was more worried for my mom's safety than for my own. Sure, I would have preferred the warmth and comfort and safety of the cozy and beautifully decorated guest room in a drama-free home, but I had a deeply embedded sense of loyalty and obligation to my mom and her well-being. I could never abandon my mother by choosing to stay with my friend over her. I was the only one around to take care of my mom and I was constantly worried that something would happen to her. I had made an unspoken promise to continue to be by her side and protect her from harm, and I wasn't going to let this episode change that.

I am pretty sure we never socialized with that particular family again, and I imagine that this incident fueled gossip about my mother's drinking and her conduct. I never understood why Mom did not convince others of her innocence. It had begun as a warm gesture toward this little blond girl. Also, why would a grown woman purposely yank a little kid's hair? It all seemed kind of unfair to me, and I felt embarrassed and sad for my mom.

Over the years, I also had fun memories of both the beach club and hanging with the year-round local community. I remember being welcomed by the polarized world and not really even noticing the differences.

For many years, I was too young to understand social barriers. I had been taught very strict manners by my mother. Other mothers would comment on how polite and well-behaved I was, and I was always invited for playdates. On one particular playdate I brought my plate to the kitchen sink at the conclusion of the meal. I was quickly reprimanded by the mother and informed that I needn't do such a thing.

"But my mommy said I should always bring my plate to the sink."

When I returned home, my mother got a phone call from this particular woman, who said, "Please tell your daughter that we have people working for us who clear the table. When she visits, she does not have to bring her plate to the kitchen sink."

"Well, we *don't* have people who do that for us, and you need not worry about her doing it again in your home, because my daughter will not be returning there again for a playdate. Good-bye."

Mom laughed when she told the story later, loving that a woman from Newark had taught her daughter better manners than people who had more money than we would ever have.

When I was five years old, Dad married Didi Auchincloss. It was on May 1, 1970, in Manhattan. Didi was from a prominent New York family and had been traditionally educated. She had been married previously but was divorced from Tom Auchincloss, who was Jackie Kennedy's stepbrother.

I don't remember them meeting or dating, just that one day I was told Dad was getting married. Because I had never experienced my mother and father as a married couple living together and as a bonded couple, I felt no jealousy toward my dad's new bride. In fact, I thought she was very pretty and that everything in her house was always so neat. She was petite and reserved and kept her life in strict order. She was a brunette, well-bred, and well-educated debutante who reminded me of Jackie Onassis. Dad had chosen the antithesis of my mother. This, without a doubt, must have killed Mom. There is a beautiful photo of a smiling Dad and Didi coming out of an Upper East Side church and crossing the street. Dad is in tails and Didi has flowers in her hair. To me, it all seemed beautiful and perfect. I used to stare at every detail of this photo when I visited their Eighty-Sixth Street apartment. It all just looked so classic and beautiful.

Didi had two children from her first marriage. Her daughter, Diana, was six years old, and her son, Tommy, was nine. I suddenly had an instant family, and I was excited by the future. It wasn't long before another baby was on the horizon. My stepsister, Diana, and I were very lucky that our parents married, and even though we did not know it at the time, we were to become partners, allies, confidants, and lifelong sisters.

Didi gave birth to my first half sister, Marina, when Diana and I were seven and six, respectively. Imagine the joy of knowing I was an older sister and that there was now a baby to play with! I had wished that my mom would have another baby, but it was not possible. I vaguely remember her going into a hospital and having a "female operation." I suggested we adopt: "Just get one from the foundling home." I didn't want her with a man, but I did want a baby sibling. Now I had one, and Mom was off the hook.

Over the years, Diana and I began spending more and more time together and unabashedly laughing the whole time. Diana even became quite attached to my mother, and Mom often introduced us as her daughters. Talk about unconventional! Didi seemed to have no qualms about her firstborn daughter being in the company of her husband's ex-wife. She allowed Diana to spend time—a great deal of time—in our company and in our small-by-comparison apartment on Seventy-Third Street. Later, she even traveled with my mom and me all over the world. Diana and I became extremely close, and my mom loved us both. All parties involved seemed to support our being together. The three of us became a real team and we all benefited. Diana confided in my mother, who authentically loved her. I now had a partner with whom to commiserate. During the times Diana stayed with my mother and me, it seemed like we were always having fun and laughing.

Soon Dad and Didi moved out to the North Shore of Long Island. They bought a beautiful house in an area called Meadowspring. The house was huge and the backyard ample. I shared a room with Diana during my visits, and Tom and Marina had their own rooms.

Over the next seven years, little girls would be born into this growing brood. Cristiana next and Olympia "the baby."

Sometimes Diana would stay in the city with my mom and me. The three of us would drive around in our silver convertible, with the top down, eating cherries or peaches from the fruit stand. We would park outside Dad's office with the radio blaring, eating our fruit and awaiting my father, who would drive Diana back out to Long Island. It was slightly reminiscent of when Mom used to wait to surprise-attack my father outside his old office building. This time it was slightly more intended to create a stir. Picture an old silver convertible, its top down, loud music and laughter blaring from it, parked in front of a Park Avenue office building filled with investment bankers and CEOs.

Sometimes Dad picked us both up and sometimes just Diana. I spent many weekends out on Long Island with Dad's family and accompanied them on spring breaks in the Bahamas. I had two totally different lives and seemed to go in and out of each with ease. At my dad's there was routine and a schedule we strictly adhered to. There were three meals each day, served at roughly the same times. Kids washed up for meals and often ate with the nanny. During dinner parties, the adults ate in the dining room while the kids stayed in the big kitchen. On days that Dad came back late from work in Manhattan, Didi or the nanny would create a plate for him that he just had to heat up. There was very little in terms of surprise. At the end of the day you could always find my dad sitting in his study watching the boob tube. Bedtimes were set in stone, and only late-night whispering delayed actual sleep.

By stark contrast, Mom had no set mealtimes. We often ate out at various Chinese or Italian restaurants later than conventional mealtimes for children. We rarely cooked breakfast but instead went to the corner deli for a buttered roll with coffee and copies of the *Daily News* and the *Post*. We'd read each other our horoscopes and enjoyed the taste of the sweet butter on a hard roll. There was always the perfect amount of crunch on the outside and soft on the inside. My coffee was mostly milk and sugar but I loved being able to order "The regular, please."

That was our routine and we craved it. With Mom I never had a nanny and only rarely a sitter. Mom and I went to see movies and off-Broadway shows. We'd stay up late and didn't always get up on time for school.

But by the time visits to my dad's rolled around, I welcomed the change of pace. I loved having the option of varied and contrasting lifestyles. The structure that my dad's world provided was a tremendous relief from the adventurous and more Bohemian existence I lived with my mother. In the same way, the lack of routine and spontaneity with Mom served as a welcome reprieve after living under my stepmother's roof.

This duality, however, would create confusion later. Not clearly adopting any one side would later prove to be perplexing. Where did I really belong? It was as if I were living two parallel lives. The environment my father provided was the antithesis of that in which I lived with my single mom.

However, I was so enmeshed with my own mother that even though I looked forward to the order I felt in my father's house and knew how included I was as a family member, I was not open to my stepmother as a symbol of anything maternal. I once put ice down our English nanny's shirt and ran from her only to fall and split open my knee. I was rushed to the hospital and definitely needed stitches. Didi came in with me as I lay down on the bed to be sewn up for the first time in my life. She warmly tried to hold my hand while the doctor stitched me up, but I refused. Gripping the side of the bed with one hand and holding a clump of the hair on the back of my head with the other, I defiantly stated, "No, thank you. You are not my mother."

I did not dislike my stepmother—not in the least—or that my dad had a new wife. But I was simply not attached. I made it clear that nobody in the universe could fill my mother's shoes. And with all due respect, Didi never tried. My stepmom was the antithesis of my mother. She was tiny, systematic, and never prone to drama. She believed in protocol and lists. She was fastidious and was even known to alphabetize her spices. I used to do anything I could to unsettle her. I loved screaming and having her run into the kitchen, worried I had been hurt again, only to greet her with "Ahhh! Does the cayenne pepper go with *C* or *P*?"

She always smelled good and maintained her own nails. I'd often smell the enamel from down the hall and knew the color she picked would be a subtle one. I made sure to paint my nails black whenever I visited. Didi always wore an array of yellow-gold bangles and bracelets. To this day, if I hear a jingling of bracelets, she comes to mind.

By contrast, my mom was larger than life, disorganized, and often incited chaos. She was frequently boisterous, she drank and cursed like a construction worker, and she wore red lipstick and fire engine–red nail polish. She was clean but often disheveled. Mom's idea of order was writing important phone numbers on tiny scraps of paper and losing them and tying up her credit cards with one of the thousands of rubber bands she had saved from delivered newspapers.

My mother never seemed outwardly resentful about the other life that I had at my father's, but there were signs that she wasn't fully accepting of all it represented. She tried to control it. For instance, at the beginning of every summer, Dad took me to get my annual pair of Top-Siders and a few Lacoste short-sleeve shirts. I loved these outings and couldn't wait to wear what I knew the other kids would be wearing. Mom shopped for me only at thrift stores and would never buy me brand labels. In fact, every time I came home with a Lacoste shirt, Mom would painstakingly cut out the little signature alligator. This was not an easy task because the thread was a sturdy plastic, and a hole would inevitably be left. Mom would then sew up the hole with the same color of thread as the shirt, and even though they were brand-new, they looked secondhand. Only then was I allowed to wear the now no-name item. It amazes me how much she coveted the world of privilege yet thwarted its symbols. It was a confusing time for me, but I knew I was loved by both sides. They were each protecting me and caring for me in their individual ways and from their unique perspectives.

Overall, there was a good relationship between the two families. I have always been pleasantly surprised and deeply relieved that neither my mother, nor my father, nor my stepmother ever spoke ill of one another. Nor did they try to pit me against the other family or try to prove their superiority. I went back and forth frequently and never felt like a traitor.

One thing that never changed was my devotion to my mother and the feeling that our lives would be forever intertwined. The brakes on our new black Jeep once went out while we were traveling across the George Washington Bridge heading out to New Jersey.

Mom screamed for me to get in the backseat and strap in because we had no way of stopping. I refused. I remember feeling strangely proud and looking straight ahead and saying, "No! If you die, I die." I was steadfast.

We veered off the bridge, onto the Palisades Parkway, and up an incline, eventually slowing to safety. We shut off the engine and were fine, but that Jeep model and year was soon after recalled. I am sure I remember the event so vividly because Mom herself loved telling the story of how her daughter would rather die than be without her. She got to hear me pledge my undaunted love for her. What more could she ever want?

I continued modeling throughout my childhood. I was getting a few more commercials and did one for Tuesday Taylor, a Barbie-like doll whose ponytail grew when you pushed a button. This one was fun because I got to keep one of the dolls while the other girl got to take home Piper, her sister. I also did a Susie Q's spot, which was not nearly as fun because I had to eat Susie Q's all day and got supersick. It was a commercial with Mason Reese, and I remember thinking his mom was a real character.

When I was nine years old, I was cast in my first film, then titled *Communion*, which was later changed to *Alice, Sweet Alice*. The film was a horror story in which my character gets tortured by her older sister and is eventually murdered. It mostly takes place inside a church and during the young sister's first Holy Communion. The casting process was an odd one, and the story of my audition became an anecdote my mother loved to repeat to anybody who'd listen. As usual, I went into the room by myself while Mom waited outside. I was then asked how I would pretend I was being strangled. Funnily enough, I was at the age when my friends and I did this crazy thing with our breath that always made me laugh. We'd push all the air out of our mouths and then do this deep, guttural, crazy machine-gun laugh until our faces got completely red and puffy and we became hysterical. Because our faces were so red and our eyes filled with tears, it looked kind of disgusting and scary. So I was very ready to pretend to be strangled.

I was told that in the pivotal death scene, my character was to get strangled with a candle, stuffed in a deacon's bench, and set on fire. A deacon's bench most commonly found in churches and chapels is where the deacon or priest sits during the Mass. It's usually wooden, with a spindled back and arms. During the audition, in a room full of people, I proceeded to do the demonstration of my suffocating red face. I held my breath, bore down, and let out a huge fart. I was incredibly embarrassed and quickly mentioned that during the actual filming I would not do that.

Later that same day, after having gotten the part, I showed up for rehearsal. A group of actors were discussing astrological signs and asked me when I was born. I said I was a Gemini, and one lady said, "Oh, that's an air sign."

"We know!" added the director, laughing. My face got really red, and not intentionally this time. Mom thought this was incredibly funny, and we would laugh about it for years, saying that maybe I should fart in auditions more often and I'd get more movie roles. Needless to say, the movie (later retitled again and rereleased as *Holy Terror*) was not a box-office hit but went on to become a bit of a cult classic.

Soon after filming *Alice, Sweet Alice*, I was brought in and cast by Woody Allen, to appear in a new movie he was directing that was titled *Annie Hall*. I was going to play the focus of the young Alvy's obsession. In one of the scenes I was a sexy pilgrim in a flashback of a Thanksgiving-themed school play. I filmed for only two days, and although singled out briefly, I was one of many kids in the scene. I did stand out because I was dressed all in white with flowing hair while the others had mismatched clothing and seemed uncomfortable. Woody had chosen every odd-looking child he was able to find in New York City. The scene was filmed in a gymnasium and we were all given box lunches. During this time my mother and I had adopted a husky puppy, and Mom had brought the dog to visit me for lunch. I didn't wish to finish my box lunch and asked Mom where I should put it. She said, "Give it to funny face."

I went to a little boy who was very short for his age, had black greasy hair flattened down on his head, and wore Coke bottle–thick glasses. I handed him my lunch. Mom blurted out, "I meant the dog!"

I felt so bad for having thought the kid was "Funny Face" and prayed his mother didn't hear the conversation. Thankfully, neither the kid nor the mom heard a thing. But, embarrassingly, Mom and I did laugh pretty hard about it later that day.

The strangest part about doing *Annie Hall* was that Woody Allen asked my mother out on a date and she went. I think it was only the one night and it was just dinner. Mom left the apartment, and our close friend Alice from across the street came to babysit. Alice was young and blond and like a big sister to me. While Mom was out, Alice and I made crazy-funny signs that said things like "Oooooh, how was your date?" Or "Did Woody get smoochy smoochy?" Or "Hope you had fun, Mom."

We stuck them all over the hallway on the seventh floor. When Mom got off the elevator, she was faced with all these funny signs leading to our apartment door at the far end of the hall. It turned out the date was uneventful. She explained that Woody was too neurotic and was in too much therapy for her liking. It is fitting that that was her take on the situation: a woman who would never fully be able to examine herself honestly, criticizing a man who appeared desperate to examine his neurosis. I get the phobic piece being unattractive in any person, but self-reflection, in my mind, is never a bad thing.

In the final cut of the movie, the flashback of the school play was edited out. My sexy pilgrim ended up on the cutting-room floor. I am pretty certain this had nothing to do with the date, but it was fun teasing my mom and accusing her of doing something that made Woody cut me from the film.

Mom and I were the closest when we were laughing. Our comedy and innate sense of timing created our deepest bond. We had the same sense of humor and it would carry us through many a difficult period. Mom kept her wit basically until the end.

Even though things didn't work out with Woody, Mom did have two other notable relationships at the time. The first was a man named Bob, whom she began dating on and off when I was about three. I don't think Mom was ever really attracted to him or was in love with him, but he was a very generous man who loved us very much and he embraced me fully. He worked in oil rigs and shared with us substantially. I think Mom accepted him as a temporary provider but never wanted to remarry. He was around—and a very strong source of support for me—for many of the more tumultuous years, when Mom's drinking escalated to disruptive heights.

Mom also met a man in Brazil one summer named Antonio Rius. We had traveled to Rio when I was two, but we went back to visit several times during my childhood. Their relationship was intense. She was never more beautiful or happier than when they were together. But he was separated (though not divorced) from his wife, who said he'd never see his children again if he left her to marry an American. Mom was devastated but said if he was the type of man who could abandon his kids to be with her, then he would not have been the man with whom she fell in love. She said she would wait for him . . . and she did.

During these years my parents had very different reactions to my growing career. My father was uncomfortable with my fame and was intent on its not being a part of my life with him. I know he didn't approve of my being a model or an actress and never went to see any of my movies. He liked my TV work better and in later years enjoyed watching me on the Bob Hope specials and then on *Suddenly Susan*. But back then he really wasn't comfortable with my other life as an actress and model. I remember once when we were taking the annual family photo, Dad stepped out and looked at me and said, "Now, Brookie, don't pose!"

I was embarrassed and hurt but would later understand his fierce desire to keep me "normal."

Even though my mother always believed in me and pushed me to take risks and never give up, she was also familiar with rejection and abandonment. She was concerned with how I'd deal with it. It wasn't that she discussed it with me on an emotional level; she just tried to prevent me from feeling pain and rejection from others. But, ironically, over the years and thanks to her continued drinking, she herself would end up abandoning me the most and causing me the most emotional pain.

But in the moment, she could be wonderful. Right around the time I was starting to make movies, my mother took me to see the musical *Grease*. It starred Adrienne Barbeau and Jeff Conaway. Our seats were close to the stage. They were the seats we could afford, and back then Mom told me the closer the seats the better—something I would later learn was not true. We had not planned it, but we were attending the hundredth performance of the original Broadway production. The preshow for *Grease* usually consisted of some fifties music and the DJ revving up the audience members and inciting them to clap and dance in their seats. To celebrate this particular show and momentous occasion, the producers decided to hold a Hula-Hoop contest. Any audience member could join in on stage. Mostly people from the *Grease* era—the actual fifties and sixties—began volunteering to enter. The prize for first place was a signed album, a chance to take photos with the cast, and an invite to their cast party celebrating their one hundred shows. I had never Hula-Hooped in my life but wanted desperately to meet the cast. I jumped up and raised my hand. Mom smiled and through a somewhat clenched mouth reminded me that I had never Hula-Hooped before. I didn't care. Mom was always supportive of anything I wanted to try, but this was the first time I had ever volunteered to do something completely foreign, and in front of a packed and rowdy theatre. This was a far cry from singing in the church basement. She was nervous for me but encouraged my participation and urged me on.

"I'm going up there."

"OK, then. Knock 'em dead."

Well, I went up on stage and was given a Hula-Hoop and began to wiggle as if my life depended on it. It was nine adults, who had been teenagers in the fifties and had Hula-Hooped many times before, and me. I was blindly determined. My jaw was set, I looked at no one, and I made no notice when a contestant dropped the hoop and was eliminated. Before long, it was down to one older man and me. I would not give up. My hoop would go all the way down, almost touching the stage, and then suddenly go all the way back up, each direction eliciting a different-toned "Wooooooo!" from the crowd.

My mom could not believe her eyes. Then, in one amazing moment that I did not even register, the old man's hoop dropped to the floor. I kept going until the DJ stopped me and said, "Well, little lady, we might need to make you a part of our cast! Congratulations, and I'll see you at the party."

I didn't even hear the thunderous applause. Back in my seat, the show began. From the overture till the finale, I was riveted. After the show I met the cast and got their signatures on my vinyl cast recording and attended the celebration. They presented me with a small trophy that said "Hula-Hoop Winner 1976." From that day on, if I ever expressed a fear of failure, my mom would simply say, "Remember the Hula-Hoop!"

Part Two

I've never left her as a daughter, but everytime she drinks and hurts me, she leaves me as a mother. It's been like this all my life.

—*Brooke's diary*

Chapter Five

Pretty Baby

My mother never had any clear plans regarding a career path for her daughter. We kind of just kept rolling along with whatever came our way. One day I could be doing some print ad for the epidemic of young pregnancy and the next I could be doing an amazing ad for the inside of *Life* magazine, standing in a bathing suit next to Lisanne, a fellow model and close friend. I did some commercials and had two movies under my belt, but we had no idea if I was an actress, a model, or a spokesperson for good causes. As a side note, I feel that this multifaceted approach has always been both a blessing and a curse. I am in a business that loves to define and categorize talent. Being multifaceted suggests that there is a jack-of-all-trades-and-master-of-none quality. It has made for an interesting and extremely versatile career but at times has been strangely and frustratingly limiting.

But back when we were just beginning, each job meant Mom and I could buy something. As we worked and I earned, Mom and I began to be able to buy things like cars, homes, jewelry, or vacation trips. We went from job opportunity to job opportunity never really thinking in terms of how each project contributed to my career as a whole, or how it fit into the overall representation of me as a talent. Mom also never had specific goals that we reached for. Basically, the criteria for whether I took a job or not was this: Did it fit into my school schedule? Was it going to be a fun and different experience? Would it pay well?

I don't remember it ever really being about the type of film, or caliber of people involved, or even if a particular film or project propelled me into any particular category as a performer. Mom and I never considered if any one project made sense in the context of the future of my career. She never really considered nurturing my talent or pushing me to study acting. Rather, it seemed that success was measured in property and popularity.

Early on, it became evident that there were not many actresses who looked like I did. People kept saying that I had a unique look. As much as I was working in print, I still often didn't fit into the all-American type that was popular in TV and film. I was frequently turned down for not looking like a freckled-face kid from a farming town. I was still "too European."

How weird is it that I would eventually be labeled "America's sweetheart"? Did Mom consciously commit to changing these early impressions? I really don't think so. I certainly wasn't Shirley Temple, and although I had always been compared to Elizabeth Taylor, I had no *National Velvet* to identify me as the next "girl next door."

So when an acclaimed French filmmaker called me in to meet him for the lead role in his first American film, Mom thought I might have a fighting chance.

Why not? Mom loved European films and directors and had exposed me to films by Fellini and others. She seemed to understand the level of artistry they represented, and she always said women like Catherine Deneuve, Ingrid Bergman, and Sophia Loren were the classiest and most beautiful and most talented actresses out there. I also think she wished she resembled them a bit in style and stature and looks. Personally, I thought my mom was even prettier than any of them.

A meeting was arranged, and, thankfully, Louis Malle was not interested in an all-American look for his star. The film was to be titled *Pretty Baby*. It told the story of photographer E. J. Bellocq, who became famous in the early 1900s for photographing women living and working in the bordellos of the red-light district in New Orleans. In this movie, based on his real life and real stories, he falls in love with a young prostitute, Violet, who had been born and raised inside one of these houses.

Meeting with Louis wasn't an audition in any typical way. We didn't work from a script. I went into an office somewhere in the middle of Manhattan and chatted with Louis Malle and the film's producer, Polly Platt. Polly and a guy named Tony Wade were the unit production managers. Polly had been married and divorced from director Peter Bogdanovich and was currently in a relationship with Tony.

I don't remember too much about the "audition," except that we spoke for quite some time. My mom was not a part of any of the conversation. She wasn't even in the room. I have always been under the impression that Mom never wanted to be thought of as a stage mother who hovered and interfered. She wanted to be the un–stage mother who was part of the team. In actuality, Mom was much more of an emotional hoverer who affected me internally.

However, I realize now that my mother was likely very distracted by what had happened much earlier that day. The night before, Mom had taken me and my model friend Lisanne out to a bar. Lisanne and I were very close friends and Mom always thought she was one of the most beautiful girls in the business. This particular night out, not only had we stayed out very late, but also Mom got pretty drunk. Lisanne spent the night but needed to be taken to Penn Station in the morning for a train back home. The next morning, Mom, still kind of tipsy from the previous night's imbibing, piled us in the black Jeep and drove to downtown Manhattan for my big movie meeting. Mom told me to go into the meeting room and she'd be back to get me. After basically leaving me with strangers, Mom left and took Lisanne to the station. Evidently she had two fender benders on the way, but Lisanne made her train. Mom came back to pick me up and didn't say a thing. I didn't know that it had happened at all until Lisanne told me years later.

But back in the room, I was having a wonderful time. The team showed me photos of inspiration for the film and I was completely enamored of the clothing and the culture of the period. It all seemed beautiful to me. Like an old-fashioned fantasy world.

The world seen through the eyes of E. J. Bellocq reminded me of paintings I had seen in museums my mom had taken me to. We chatted about the subject of the film. They asked me how I felt about a love story that takes place in a world of prostitution. I don't remember if they phrased it with such articulation, or as if they were talking to an adult, but I understood the gist of their question.

I replied that my mother had told me about the part and that I had already known about prostitution by living in Manhattan. Mom and I often talked about the different choices people make. I added that it always seemed sad to me that the prostitutes I saw on Forty-Second Street had to walk on the streets in all sorts of weather and did not have nice homes. My mom always said we should pray for them. I assumed it was because they did not have a safe place in which to live. In the movie the prostitutes all lived at home, which seemed a much more protected setting.

I don't remember if the question of nudity came up in the meeting, but I was later under the impression that my mom had discussed it with the producers, and they had agreed on no explicit nudity. She was promised it would be filmed in a way that I would be protected.

I honestly didn't give it any thought. I think I assumed that it would all be OK. Somehow I had no qualms about any of it. I was eleven. I'd go to the bathroom with the door open in front of people and have full-on conversations. I was not conscious of my body. Never young but somehow youthful.

Even though I was such a young girl, I always had mature and evocative looks. I was far from precocious, and that was what Louis Malle wanted. I was not in any way what Nabokov had called a nymphet or a Lolita. That wasn't what Louis Malle envisioned for his Violet. He believed that her power rested in her wise innocence. Louis wanted a sense of duality and contradiction in his lead character. He saw the woman/child as someone with real naïveté and innocence coupled with intelligence and emotional maturity. He didn't want savvy provocation. I was what he wanted—at once a little girl and an emotionally mature adult, all the while lacking shrewdness or a cunning persona.

The audition/meeting didn't last very long. I was surprised it was so easy and fast. I worried that I should have done more. My mother picked me up and we left. As I remember it, we got the call later that same day. I was offered the role. Mom asked if I wanted to do the film and I said it sounded like a fun movie to make. We would get to move to New Orleans for a few months—we had thought it would be over summer vacation—and I'd get to dress up in period clothing. We would have a whole new adventure. We accepted the part.

Another reason Louis said he chose me was that I was not a trained actress. I had never studied acting, and he felt I would be able to just respond to situations once I understood the scene. This has always felt like the smartest approach to me.

Production was pushed back and what was supposed to be a summer shoot ended up starting around mid-February. This would be the first time I would miss school to work, but we had signed on and the money was good and this was a famous director. It was an opportunity not to be passed up. Mom and I felt we could make it work with a tutor and homework assignments. Plus, I knew in advance and could try to get ahead in school before leaving for New Orleans, which I was able to do.

The entire movie was shot in and around New Orleans. It had all been storyboarded and was seemingly meticulously planned out. The majority of the filming took place in a big white house on Saint Charles Avenue, which has since been converted into the Columns Hotel. The house had a big porch, a beautiful winding staircase, and stained-glass windows. Inside and out, the film's creative team built the world as it actually existed during E. J. Bellocq's time.

But once we arrived, everything was more chaotic than I imagined. The cast and crew were a rowdy bunch. They became known for their loud partying and drug usage. Every night, crew members would either take over the bar or use their rooms to party. Complaints from visitors would be lodged but never seemed to cause change. A lot went on and there were many on-set romances, including a pregnancy (my mother went with the poor girl when she had her abortion). We had all left our real lives at home and had entered a somewhat altered universe.

I enjoyed life on the set, but it could be very difficult and tense. There was a mystique surrounding Louis. He was making his first American film and there was a great deal of pressure, and he was often a man of few words. He watched more than he talked. He was not one to praise his actors. At first this scared me because I was like a Jack Russell puppy jumping up and up and up, asking, "Do you like me now? Do you like me now?" I wanted to do anything for a treat and a nod. Louis's reticence made me nervous, but I always believed he was kind.

He could be difficult with me but he was never mean or overtly demanding. I learned to navigate his often distant manner, and even though he seemed removed, I came to trust that no words were good words. I never fully knew whether he was ultimately happy with my portrayal of his lead character, but I had to believe he was getting what he wanted from me.

At times I craved more direction and felt awkward not being constantly told what to do and how to be and sometimes even how to feel. I began the movie by asking questions or if I was OK, but as time went on I, too, quieted and trusted my instincts a bit more. Sadly, this would be one of the last films in a long while during which I was learning my craft and experiencing hints of self-confidence. I believe it was because of the quality and artistic caliber of the director. He had vision and he expressed himself quietly and without unnecessary chatter. He could say, "Just be defiant." I knew exactly what that meant to Violet.

The cinematographer, Sven Nykvist, was a genius. A gentle, beautiful soul whose art came out through his eyes and his heart. He was incredibly sweet and had a shy little laugh whenever I did or said something funny. I remember how quietly he worked and how thorough he was. If Louis was revealing what he called "a slice of life," then it was Sven who simultaneously stripped away facades and illuminated the honest truth.

We were all working long hours every day on the film, and sleep became my most coveted commodity. The amount of work I was required to do was staggering. The shooting days lasted between twelve and fifteen hours and included early calls, late wraps, and all-night shoots that began at 5:00 P.M. and went until at least 5:00 A.M. the next day. The weather was at times excruciatingly hot, and when we worked near the rivers the bugs ate us alive. Occasionally it was miserable, but none of us complained.

Because it was a period piece (my favorite thing in the world to do), all the costumes were authentically from the era. Nowadays many of the undergarments are remade in new materials, and shoes are copied in the style of the 1900s but with more comfortable modern technology. But on this film we were working with the legendary costume designer Mina Mittelman, and she had warehouses filled with period costumes. Her stock was plentiful and she was insistent that even the undermost petticoats be from the actual era.

I adored how beautiful the clothes looked but the shoes created a real problem for me. They were old and dry and I got a terrible case of an eczema-type rash that made my feet crack and bleed. I had waited to tell my mom how much they hurt and hoped it would get better on its own. I was never one to admit a discomfort and did not want to be a problem. There was work to get done and I could deal with the pain.

They were the shoes I had to wear the most, and when not wearing them, I was usually barefoot and running across broken shells. Neither option was a good one. The shells were used in the backyard to create a sort of driveway, so to protect me from getting badly cut, the wardrobe person taped moleskin to the bottoms of my feet. This helped and tickled when I peeled them off.

I never asked my mom to run lines with me the night before; I was happy to memorize and do the work on my own. I liked hearing it in my own head before getting the input from anybody. This meant that I was experiencing much of the filming on my own and within my relationships with actors and the creative team on set. I loved having this entirely separate family and life to the one Mom and I lived together. It felt safe and fun and we all had a common goal.

But things began getting difficult and I was becoming run-down and tired. The schedule had been extended, and we were overbudget and tensions were high. Mom intervened and insisted that whenever my feet were not visible in the frame I could wear other shoes or go barefoot. She called a doctor and he prescribed a medicinal salve I was to use nightly. Mom would coat my feet in this ointment and then wrap them in bandages or athletic socks. Each morning it was a relief for them to be soft and a bit less cracked. My feet eventually healed, but Mom remained displeased that it had gone on for as long as it had and that nobody on set had bothered to address the issue. I had never told anybody else how bad it really was. I tried to explain that to her, but she said they still should have been more conscientious when using worn period items.

Up until this film my work environments had always been very controlled. We knew what to expect and Mom had been fine leaving me at a bit of a distance to do the job at hand. On this set she was more around, but contrary to popular belief, she was not always intruding; I never saw her giving her input to the director. She knew call times and locations, but I honestly felt she didn't want to interfere with the creative process.

Tensions were mounting between Polly Platt and my mother, and if it were up to Polly, Mom would have not set foot in New Orleans at all. Everybody wanted control of his or her own domain. When it came to me, my mom had no intention of relinquishing any. I was eleven years old.

I liked knowing Mom was near, and I was glad she intervened, but I never wanted her too close to me when I acted. I hated it when she watched me perform, and would get distracted if I saw her out of the corner of my eye. I never thought I was good enough, and her watching me would make me too nervous and I'd freeze. I felt I was good enough for basic strangers but feared my mother would be somehow dissatisfied. I was embarrassed and nervous about not being perfect for her. I just wanted her to think I was good, but I feared I might not be.

What was strange was that Mom always said she was proud of me and that in her eyes I was perfect, but she'd also make little comments that seemed like jokes or throwaways but made me feel less than. I couldn't get past the self-doubt and the insecurity of wanting to always be the best for her.

I am sure it made her feel sad and left out when I told her I didn't want her to watch me, but she found other ways to feel needed and important. I'm also sure Mom spent a good portion of her day drinking. She had a favorite bar she frequented during the days and nights and quickly became a regular. It was sort of near the St. Charles Hotel, and if I wrapped and the van dropped me off at the hotel and she was not there, I could usually find her at Igor's Lounge. Teri Terrific gravitated to seedy bars no matter where we were. She always had her favorites and loved being a regular. She often met our tall, slightly disheveled hippie of a boom operator at this famous bar they called "EEEEYYYOORRRSS." His name was Ringo and he had an unkempt sex appeal about him. He was tall and had muscled arms from holding up the heavy boom all day. He was very sweet and protective of me and I know Mom had a crush on him. I don't know if they ever hooked up. To be honest, I didn't want to know. It made me squeamish and jealous and angry just thinking about it.

Pretty Baby was based on a real story, and Violet was modeled after an actual person. The real Bellocq was rather unattractive, however, and was said to have had an enlarged head caused by hydrocephalus. (Obviously our version of Bellocq was the very handsome Keith Carradine.) It could have been because of his deformity that the girls in the brothel trusted him, but they also believed his intentions were pure. He was an artist with no ulterior motives who wanted only to capture the girls beautifully and with their individual personalities.

The still photos we took of the actresses were direct duplicates of the original Bellocq photographs and were remarkably similar. There was a scene, adapted from the actual historical photo, where Violet's image was being taken while she lay naked on a chaise lounge. I had been given a G-string, but it was determined by all of us that it wasn't necessary. My legs were slightly crossed and Louis did not want it to be pornographic in any way. The shot was quick and represented the snap of Bellocq's lens right before my character jumps up to petulantly destroy some photo plates.

We copied the famous photo and I was unself-conscious and unfazed by what was an extremely short scene. I remember only being slightly disappointed that I had no real breasts yet, but neither did the young girl on the photo plate. I didn't feel violated or compromised. I put the G-string back on once I was standing and was also only photographed from the shoulders up. I had not yet learned how to use my sexuality as any type of tool and was therefore able to play this scene with the calm quality it called for.

Mom again didn't watch the filming of this scene and no one seemed to fret. It was quick and I was so young and innocent. Mom was crucified for permitting any of it, and in many ways I understand the criticism, especially now that I'm a mother. But the world and the industry were markedly different back then.

I have been asked this question over and over in the press, but I have always maintained that, at the time of the filming and thereafter, I did not experience any distress or humiliation. When the movie came out a year later, the press was up in arms about the whole thing. There was a sense of fury and a need to assume that I was a victim in this circumstance. The press wanted me to have shame and regret and could not handle my being cognizant and wise and self-possessed. There was a firestorm and Mom took most of the heat. My poise, whether innate or earned, gave me a certain adult perspective, and I remained clear in my convictions of the scene and of the film in its entirety.

As a mother of an eleven-year-old today, I am equally clear that I, myself, would not allow my daughter to be photographed topless. But it was a different time, and not only did my mother really believe we were creating art, but this film was special, too, and the scene was one of the shortest ones in the entire film.

I was not yet a sexual being, and this was how Louis Malle wanted it to be. He was more interested in showing my emerging sexuality through my attitude rather than via gratuitous nudity. We simply did not make a big deal of it. I was never scarred in the way the press wanted to speculate and hope.

I was, however, deeply concerned by a much more innocuous scene. Later in the film, once Violet and Bellocq have gotten to know each other a bit better, they're playing a game they call "sardines" and find themselves alone in an attic and kiss for the first time. During the filming, I kept scrunching up my face right before a first kiss. Louis kept saying "Cut" and I could tell he was getting slightly disturbed. He wanted it to look tender and beautiful, not like I had just sucked on a lemon. All of a sudden Keith, who played Bellocq, whispered to me, "You know it doesn't count, right?"

"It doesn't?"

"Of course not, it's fake."

This was the first time I had ever kissed anybody on the lips except my mother, and I was so relieved that it would not count as my first kiss that I totally relaxed and the scene went on without another hitch. In hindsight, I feel that the director, or at least my mother, should have shared this sort of insight with me before Keith had to do it. I was very lucky that Keith was so kind. He was such a gentleman and was lovely to both my mother and me. I am sure he was struggling by having to film romantic scenes with a young girl, but he showed me such gentle respect that it made it all easy.

I would not be quite as lucky when it came to Susan Sarandon, who played my mother, Hattie. Hattie and Violet had a difficult relationship, and the scenes Susan and I had together were very challenging. Her attitude toward me ran the gamut, and while she could be sweet to me off set, she sometimes approached me during filming in a manner that seemed to cross a line. It would always be in the guise of staying true to her character but also hinted at something I did not quite understand. Now, she was extremely talented and beautiful and maybe she was just really being a serious actress who chose to stay in character for the duration of the film, but there were inconsistencies in this theory.

My mother seemed to understand early on that there might be some discomfort between Susan and me. Mom actually warned me that there might be some jealousy between us. I didn't get it. Susan was young and very sexy, and it was obvious Louis liked her. Why would she have a problem with eleven-year-old me? But I will admit that I felt something was up. Something was uncomfortable and I got the feeling she did not like me very much. I am almost positive she would not interpret any of it this way, but it was a vibe I was constantly trying to navigate.

Mom hinted that Susan may have been threatened by me because I was the lead in the film. In addition, it turned out that even though it was not yet public knowledge, everybody on set knew that Susan and Louis were involved in a romantic relationship.

Susan was breaking up with her then-husband, Chris Sarandon, and would be divorced within two years. I don't remember how Mom alluded to this, but where Mom lacked in maternal advice, she seemed to make up for with regard to a woman's mind and her actions. Mom was pretty intuitive when it came to other people's internal emotions. Which was funny, since she usually wasn't particularly in touch with her own.

One day we were filming a scene in which Hattie tells her daughter that she is getting married to a respectable man and leaving her daughter behind, at least temporarily. She has told her fiancé that Violet is her sister so he would marry her. Violet stands stoically, and instead of commenting, she just cocks her head, raises her eyes slightly, and smugly offers her mother some lemon custard she had been eating from a little bowl with her index finger. Hattie immediately and violently slaps her daughter across the face. The slap conveyed so much. Before shooting the scene, Susan explained to Louis that she would be unable to fake the slap. She would have to actually slap me in order to act her most convincing. She literally said, "I can't do this unless I actually slap her."

I remember thinking: *Is this being a real actress, or does she really not like me? Oh, well, I'll show her she can do what she wants. She won't hurt me.*

It was in this scene that Louis's direction to me was simply to be "defiant." In any case, I decided to act as if I couldn't care less what she did. So I stood there and took repeated slaps across my left cheek without flinching. I remember feeling stubborn and resilient and that I was showing her how she couldn't affect me. This reacting was also telling and was equally appropriate for Violet and for Brooke. There was something hurtful yet empowering about standing up to her in this way and in response to her trying to rule how the scene went. It was perfect for the scene, so maybe Susan did this on purpose, but I'll never know.

The funny thing is that in truth, although seemingly polarized in life, Violet and I were not that different. I had been supporting my mother's sometimes distant or angry attitude with a similar approach for years. When Mom drank, she would get flippant, and hurtful verbal attacks were not uncommon. Nasty barbs and inappropriate insults could fly out of her mouth without warning. I often chose to remain stoic and unaffected by her change in behavior. She would often impatiently bark orders at me to "sit up" or "say thank you" or "don't do that" or "God, Brookie, wise up." "Move your ass. Stop being such an ingrate."

I actually learned to thrive by adopting the attitude of "I don't care, you can't hurt my feelings." As Violet, I summoned a jaw-jutting, smug, steely gaze that felt very familiar from real life.

It took a minimum of nine takes from each angle to complete the coverage on this scene. Oddly enough, I got a smidgen of a payback when I saw the finished movie. As I closely watched this scene on film, I noticed red finger marks on my cheek from a previous take. This may have been wrong for the film, but I felt privately avenged.

This particular incident excluded, for the majority of the time, everybody involved with the making of *Pretty Baby*, including Susan, treated me quite well and with genuine kindness. But, as time went on, and the movie went overbudget, things got more intense. I always felt Mom was there to protect me against whatever threats existed.

My mother and Polly Platt had begun as friends, but this friendship rapidly deteriorated. Polly and Tony were at the helm of a ship that had found itself in troubled waters, and they would stop at nothing to get their film made.

The long hours started really getting to me, but I still would never complain. I was never a quitter and would keep that proverbial Hula-Hoop up around my waist for as long as necessary. Mom began outwardly commenting that she couldn't believe a minor was being allowed to work as much as I was working. I had made only one small independent movie and Mom and I were still relatively new to the film industry. We had no idea how big studio movies were made. She made a call to the local labor board to find out their rules regarding working minors. She was just trying to get basic information and find out what the local laws were. As a model in New York City, there were some protections for models, but not many, and nothing like those protecting TV and film actors. I was already a member of SAG because of my first movie, so we thought the same protection that was provided elsewhere had to apply in this case.

But, because I was a New York hire and not a Louisiana hire, they led us to believe that the same rules didn't apply to me. The producers were hiring mostly union actors for their film, but they wanted to work them as much as they needed to complete the project, so they just kept stretching the rules. That was until my mom began sniffin' around. She had no idea what rock she had just overturned.

Apparently the union that represented the film's crew was working together with the local authorities and therefore also "collaborating" with New Orleans organized crime. The powers that be got wind of Mom's call and spread the word that my mother was trying to shut down production. This wasn't true, but they wanted to put a stop to anything that threatened to delay the filming of this overbudget and overdue film.

As I remember it, the night after Mom called the labor board, she and I returned to our hotel room to find the lock had been broken and the door left ajar. In my adjoining bedroom, written in Mom's red lipstick on the mirror over the dresser, were the words: *This is to let you know what we can do!*

The next day, when we picked up the room phone we heard clicking on the line. Mom said she feared the lines were being tapped. I had no idea what that meant, and when she explained that somebody might be listening to our conversations, I immediately thought only of my potential romantic life. I became terrified my calls to the Bodack boys back home would be listened to. Naïvely, I didn't know there was anything else to fear.

Mom had befriended the cleaning lady in this hotel and showed her the writing on the mirror. The woman said that there was clearly something going on in the producer's room because she would find blood splatters and needles in the garbage baskets. Outwardly, Mom seemed unruffled, and I continued to work the long hours. Mom had a plan, though. Mafia or no mafia, drugs or no drugs, she was going to do something about it. Whoever was causing trouble didn't know my mother.

But the opposition was ready to play dangerously dirty. One day my mother took the same hotel cleaning lady out to lunch for her birthday. Mom drove to meet her on her day off from the hotel. They went to a restaurant off a highway a bit away from town and had a celebratory birthday lunch. After the conclusion of lunch, both women got into their cars and began the drive back. My mom was driving a rental, and as she entered the highway, she lost control of the car. The brakes failed and she swerved and was only able to slow the car on a truck incline. Mom told me that within seconds, a patrol car's lights began flashing and a cop was out of his car approaching my mom. There was no doubt that Mom drank during lunch, but it was a sad (and unfortunately true) fact that my mother was capable of driving drunk and avoiding being pulled over for being beyond her limit. There was something suspicious about her losing control of the vehicle and how quickly the cops arrived. It was as if the cops had been waiting for her and they weren't the only parties involved. Something seemed suspicious about all of it. Mom was arrested on the spot for drunk driving and was taken to a holding cell at the police station.

From the cell Mom called her lawyer in New York City immediately. Being a tough broad who could fight, Mom and her lawyer came up with a plan to deal with how we were being treated. She had only a lucky nickel she kept in her Levi's minipocket but decided to save it for now. She decided to call a friend from the set and reverse the charges, asking the friend to tell me that she was fine but that she would not see me tonight. Mom then used the actual nickel to call my French tutor, who was also on set, to come and bail her out.

All I remember is this friend telling me to come directly to her room in the hotel after work and not to tell anybody where I was going. It all seemed kind of exciting to me and I played along. In the room I spoke to Mom on a phone that had evidently not been tapped. She told me that some people were not happy with the fact that Mommy had had lunch with the black cleaning lady and that something strange had happened to her car. She said laws were different down in New Orleans and it would all be OK. She insisted I not let anybody know where I was but to report to work as usual the next day. Now, she was not wrong about the racial tension in New Orleans at the time, but something quite big was going down and she wanted to spare me the truth.

Mom was going back to New York for a few days. I loved Mom's friend and welcomed a sleepover. I had no idea what was really going on. At one point I remember somebody banging on the hotel door. I hid in the tub and Mom's friend opened the door. Someone—it may have been Tony Wade—asked if she had seen me. She calmly replied no. I remained undetected, had some room service, and went to bed.

The next morning, at call time, I went down to the lobby as usual. The moment I got off the elevator, Tony was waiting for me. He quickly hustled me into the stairwell, and on the cold, gray metal stairs, he very seriously looked me in the eye and said: "Your mother has been in a very serious accident. There was a lot of blood and you may never see her again."

Somehow I knew it was time to be defiant again. Head slightly cocked, with a slightly curious scowl on my forehead, I said, "Oh, that's funny because I spoke to her and she sounded fine, so if you'll excuse me, I have to get to work."

I don't know if I was channeling Violet at that moment, but I didn't like Tony Wade anyway, and I loved knowing I was doing what my mom needed and that we were a team. I was unflappable and enjoyed being a good soldier.

I continued filming while Mom remained in New York for a few days. During this time she managed to get a mechanic friend to come check out her vehicle. He deduced that the brakes on my mother's car had undoubtedly been manually cut, and that the whole thing was a setup.

After Mom returned from New York, things changed for me. First of all, we moved out of the St. Charles Hotel and into the Fairmont

Hotel, which was a beautiful old hotel in the downtown area of New Orleans. It was safe and quiet, and because we were separated from the rest of the crew, it meant fewer parties. It was, however, closer to Igor's and therefore easier for my mother to stop in for a nip more often. I tried to look on the bright side by justifying that it was also easier for me to find Mom on those nights she went missing for a bit. It was a beautiful, fancy hotel, and I honestly don't think Mom picked it for its proximity to booze, but I wouldn't put it past her.

Suddenly I wasn't working such long hours and I had more breaks on set in which to study. Things got so much better for me that I remember frequently feeling guilty. I even felt kind of like I was missing out by not working the same hours as everyone else. I loved being with these people, even if it meant all day and night. They had become my family. Even when we were waiting on the light or moving locations, I wanted to play games with them and enjoy our inside jokes. Sometimes it was sticking a KICK ME sign on a big gaffer's back, or doing arts and crafts with the wardrobe people, but it felt like home. I loved the actresses and would entertain them on the big porch of the white house by singing Barbra Streisand's "Queen Bee." The girls loved it, and Mom loved that they loved me. One day I wasn't called in until later in the day, but I got up and ready to go anyway. My mom said I did not have to go in.

"Oh, but I have to, Mama."

"Why?"

"Because I am their bubble."

I found out later that Mom had been able to alert the proper people and fix the situation legally, so I would actually get the benefits that I was meant to by being a member of SAG. I remember a welfare worker–type person being brought in and the tone on set changing. Production was on alert and no longer allowed to abuse the rules as they had been for almost three months.

The production company was less than overjoyed by this new

state of affairs and I am sure it made my mother even more unpopular with Polly and Tony. But it worked. Thankfully for everyone, we only had about a month's worth of filming left for completion of the movie, and I don't remember these rules adding any days to the schedule.

I enjoyed my new freedom, but not fully. It was too much of a change and I felt isolated. I kind of wanted to let the crew bend the rules at times, and I'd beg the teacher to let me stay on set to finish an uncompleted sequence, but she rarely complied. We all wanted to get this movie finished.

Finally, the wrap was upon us. The last day of filming was surreal. This had been my first starring role in a film. I loved the feeling of being part of a film family and I had grown very attached to everyone involved. I was even, in a way, attached to Polly and Tony. Something happens when you share an experience with people. A bond is created, and whether it's a positive or negative experience, connection is made. Because of my youth and maturity I bonded easily.

The day we shot our last shot, the cast and crew erupted with applause and hugs. It was the applause of collective relief. Four months of hard work, tears, pain, fear, insecurities, and rough conditions. We had survived together. We had created something we all felt was important.

At the wrap party, back at the St. Charles Hotel, my mom asked me what I wanted as a wrap gift. I said I wanted to cut my hair all off. I wanted a haircut partially because my hair had been destroyed during the making of the film with irons and teasing and techniques that were used to make it look frizzy and of the era. My main reason, however, was that I thought that if I chopped off all my hair, they would not be able to call me the next day and say we had reshoots or a scene had been added. As sad as I was that it was over, I was so relieved that I did not have to actually film anymore. I wanted to make sure that I would be unable to, if called. My mom gave me money then and there and said I could go do what I wanted.

"Surprise me," she said.

I was thrilled with that freedom and went to a local salon. I told the woman to cut it all off and she gave me a shapeless bob. I really didn't care what my hair looked like. To me it was liberating to be able to turn my head from left to right and have my hair swing back and forth past each shoulder. I was excited about how light and released I felt. This was a seeming act of rebellion and I felt freed. I would not follow up this act in any way for decades.

Two days after we wrapped, Mom and I boarded a plane to New York. I cried the entire plane ride "home." I instantly missed everyone and felt I had not said good-bye to everyone enough. It felt like a death. I had never felt more disoriented or homesick in my life. I was confused by my feelings but knew they were quite real. Going back into the real world and my real life would be like reentering Earth's atmosphere after going to outer space.

Once in New York City I couldn't shake my depression. Mom tried to comfort me by saying we would keep in touch with people, but somehow I knew that would not be the case. I felt drained and tired and a bit confused. Together, Mom and I made the decision that we were done. I would not be filming any more movies. The entire experience, and the toll it took to endure and then readapt to real life, was too much to take.

Chapter Six

Fuck 'Em If They Can't Handle It

O nce I returned to New York it was time to go back to school. This year I was starting junior high in a brand-new school. I had only attended schools so far on the Upper East Side. I had gone to the Everett School through the second grade until it closed. From third through sixth grade I went to the Lenox School. It was an all-girls school and would stay that way until 1974. It was a wonderful school and academically superior to my next school.

Mom, however, did not want me to continue at an all-girls school because she said she believed it was important for girls and boys to be friends and not socially intimidated by one another. I adored Lenox and still have a friend I hold dear to my heart from those years. But Mom insisted. The natural progression for me—especially because my dad was paying my tuition—was for me to go to a Spence, Brearley, or Chapin, all legendary and traditional girls' schools, but Mom wanted me to have a coed education. So after wrapping *Pretty Baby* and right after returning to New York, I enrolled at the New Lincoln

School. New Lincoln was a coed school known for its diversity. I remained there and floundered for two years. We had no uniforms and the curriculum was characteristic of the seventies.

Going to a new school was both a relief and in ways frightful. The frightful part came first in the form of a pair of gauchos. Because I was attending a school that did not require uniforms, a first for me, I needed practically an entirely new wardrobe. Mom took me shopping and we picked out clothes that would be fitting for a school in England. She took me to thrift shops for my clothes and proceeded to amass a wardrobe of wool vests, tweed jackets, corduroy gauchos, plaid skirts, white shirts, and of all things . . . dickies! She might as well have included a cabby hat.

I followed her lead, as usual, and got excited about looking smart and stylish for my first day of school. I chose the gauchos and a white shirt and vest, finished off with penny loafers. I walked proudly into my first day of seventh grade in an outfit straight out of the musical *Newsies*. I took one look at the jeans-clad, ripped-T-shirt-wearing hippie kids and wanted to run. I couldn't believe Mom let me go to this school dressed like I should have been on a street corner yelling out headlines. I was so embarrassed and mad that when I got home I said I looked stupid and that everybody made fun of me, and I refused to wear any of the clothes Mom bought me ever again. She didn't fight me and even bought me the Frye boots I eventually begged for and wore almost every day. I'd tuck my blue jeans into my Frye boots and I finally fit in.

During this time Mom and I began putting together a book called *The Brooke Book*, which consisted of photos of me, my writings and poetry, and various tidbits about my mother's prized baby girl. She worked on the book with her longtime friend John Holland, who was a hairdresser in the city. I loved John and laughed a lot with him. He and Mom believed I was "special" and that a book about me would actually sell. They worked on it a while, found a publisher, Pocket Books, and planned to release it around the time *Pretty Baby* hit the theatres.

The first few months of school, I made some very good friends but I struggled in my classes. The school was way too progressive for me, and the kids were much more mature. We were still living on Seventy-Third Street and I would walk to school every day with my mother. Just like the years before, mornings with my mother, before she started drinking, were once again the best times. She would pick me up in the afternoons, and the moment I looked at her face, I could tell. She'd look at me as if I were accusing her of doing the exact thing that she was doing. But I didn't have the guts to say this to her on the walks to school because I didn't want to ruin the one time a day I knew she would be most lucid. Even a hangover was a welcome relief from who she was when she drank.

Enough time had passed and the negative parts of *Pretty Baby* had all but been forgotten. I remained sought after for movies. I soon got an offer to be in a movie called *Tilt* starring Charles Durning. I would be playing a young pinball whiz who runs away from home to gamble by playing pinball.

Even though my mother and I had sworn I was done with movies, some time had passed and this project could not have seemed more different from *Pretty Baby* in terms of tone, time period, and duration of filming—only a few weeks in November and December 1977. Plus, this one sounded fun and we could use the money. But was it the right move for me, careerwise? My mother had no real long-term plan for my career, nor did she consider the quality of the projects or the directors. She appreciated the beauty of *Pretty Baby* but seemed unable to turn down projects just because they didn't carry the same artistic weight.

Did it not occur to her that following up a movie of the caliber of

Pretty Baby with one being guided by a first-time American director might not have been such a smart move? There didn't seem to be a great deal of thought put into any of it beyond the question of money and the possibility of adventure. It seemed that my mom made many of my career choices based on everything but the creative factors.

To this day I remain shocked at her lack of commitment to craft. She truly had exquisite taste in the cinema we watched, but those parameters never seemed to consistently apply to me and the work I was doing or could be doing.

This absence of commitment to becoming a cultivated actor was perpetuated and supported over the years. It was easy to do because I was always busy working on something, so we could justify that I was successful and getting better. Two prominent film directors hired me because they did not want a studied thespian but an untapped resource. I had been labeled a "raw talent." Was raw talent supposed to become "studied"? Wouldn't that contradict the situation? And yet how was it supposed to be nurtured? Mom did not have a clue.

When working with directors like Louis Malle or, later, Franco Zeffirelli, I would trust them completely to spend time actually directing me. I knew they would not finish a scene until they were satisfied.

Later, I thought that because I knew I wanted to be an actress, Mom's goal was for me to be a cultivated one. She convinced me that work led to work and it would all come together, but I believe people became confused as to what I was. In high school, while I was dreaming of being in Merchant Ivory movies, Mom seemed to have had little focus beyond keeping me in the public eye and maintaining a name the world knew. I think Mom's goal was for me to be a movie star and for us to earn enough money to be wealthy. Fame to her was not a bad thing but it opened doors. She associated it with power. We both worked very hard for the money we had but not for the clarity of a career.

I am rather conflicted by it all. I appreciate that my work did not take precedence over my young life. Yet this attitude also seemed to keep me from committing to my work in a way imperative for growth and to cause a lack of clarity as to what I really was.

As a result, I never researched or deeply contemplated the characters I played, either. I learned my lines right before bed the night before and sometimes even on the day. I have a photographic memory, so memorization came easily. Mom never discussed the lives of the characters I portrayed. I never studied acting or took it very seriously. The moment the director yelled "Cut," I would jump out of character and back into silly kid-Brooke mode. I resented scenes in which I had to feel deep emotion. I wanted to pretend but not actually be affected by the emotions.

This was in a way healthy for a girl my age with my acute innocence but would take a toll on my talent. I just didn't take any of it too seriously. I thought all the actors who moped around or stayed in character all day were missing out on the fun it was to make movies.

But in the end, I feel my talent suffered. It would not be until years later that I recognized that I deeply wanted to be an actress and that I saw the beauty in identifying with the characters I played. My focus shifted slowly toward wanting to improve my ability. As I grew older, being respected for the quality of my work became my priority. As I matured, it all became a matter of perspective and balance. Whereas I had previously thought it a waste of time and embarrassing, I began to value the deeper levels of acting. I found freedom in detaching from everything to focus on a character. This would not happen until years later, however.

But back in 1977, I was too young to think in terms of a creative next move filmwise. But the sound of spending two months in sunny Santa Cruz, where I'd be eating Butterfingers and playing pinball, sounded a lot better than staying in New York, getting C's on tests, and being still somewhat socially awkward. Plus, I'd heard I'd have two pinball machines in the house we'd rent. It sounded like a vacation. I reconsidered my original position of never again doing another movie.

It's funny how Mom's stringent rules on my missing school changed just as I was entering my most important years of education. Just when my actual presence in school should have mattered, Mom decided that it made sense to leave for a few months at a time. But I didn't mind—I wasn't doing that well in my classes anyway! On set I would have a social worker and a tutor and I could get my assignments from my school. It might even be a positive thing, almost like being homeschooled. In addition, as an A-plus student in ACOA (Adult Children of Alcoholics), the only class in which I seemed to currently excel, I was secretly hoping that being away from New York would inspire my mother to curb the booze. Oh, how I continued to hang on to that persistent dream.

Mom and I packed up and headed out to Santa Cruz, California, and settled into a big wooden ranch-style house on a quaint street. Inside the living room sat the promised two pinball machines. One was Bally and the other a Williams. I was thrilled. I played during every free moment I had and became quite good. I had the mechanic set my tilt feature to be very delicate so as to make the game harder for me. I started to get very competitive but it was never against anybody else. I was always going up against my highest score.

I'd practice and practice, but at the time I had a bad temper in general and had always been a sore loser. I hated not winning, and if I made what I considered a stupid mistake, I often took it out on the machine. I once got so mad at myself for not playing well that I smashed my flat hands on the surface of the machine and screamed. Can anyone say "projection"?! Mom got so angry at me for displaying such a temper that she sent me directly to bed.

Even then I found it funny how conventional ways of parenting seemed so ill fitting on Mom. She typically didn't just ground me or send me to my room. No, she'd pour Yoo-hoo down the toilet or wake me up in the middle of the night and get me out of bed for no real reason. And on this particularly frustrating pinball evening, that was her exact punishment of choice. After sending me to my room, she continued to drink with friends, then suddenly decided to wake me up and force me into the living room. By now it was extremely late and I had fallen asleep on the top bunk of the dark-painted pine bunk bed. She threw open the door and told me to come out *now*. She told me to sit on the brown velvet couch in the living room and stare at the pinball machine. She wouldn't allow me to play but made me just sit there, looking at it and thinking about how not to get so angry. Well, this just made me angrier, quite honestly. It felt crazy to me, but I admittedly never smashed my hands on top of the machine again. Once more Mom's behavior was reinforced.

Mom prided herself on her particular methods. She practically gloated at the fact that she never spanked me. She preferred controlling my mind and my emotions. She honestly believed it was a genius approach and effective in ways that quick physical punishments weren't. She thought she was really doing the best thing for me. Simply discussing things might have been a nice change of pace. Mom also found that instilling the fear of potential punishment proved effective. I never got the belt, but she often left a wooden spoon on the kitchen counter where I could easily see it. Every now and then she would pick it up and smack the palm of her hand with it so it made a loud cracking sound. Each time I went near the spoon, I offered to put it away for her.

"I put away for Mommy?"

"Nah, that's OK. You can leave it out."

It was never unclear as to who held the power in my house. As I got older I sometimes wished I had been hit in order to be done with it. But I knew Mom would never hit me—she knew it would be wrong, and it wasn't in her nature to be violent. It could be in her nature to be nasty and hurtful and to emotionally unravel—but not to be phys-ically violent. Mom would sooner come at me wielding a butter knife than a sharp one, dramatically crying about what I had done to her. I think Mom wanted to prove her prowess as an authority by manipu-lating my brain, not by hurting my body. She was creating and form-ing me and I was dutiful.

But back on set, filming was a lot of fun, but much to my dismay, Mom did not show any signs of quitting drinking. She treated the movie like a permission slip to drink. She drank and I played pinball all the time. We worked mostly in and around Santa Cruz and then went to various locations in Texas. We traveled to Corpus Christi and heard country music (my all-time favorite at the time), and I even got to ride the mechanical bull at Gilley's Club in Houston.

This was a great couple of months and not a great movie. I can't say I really cared. We had had another very different experience. I returned to school in January a very different student. It turned out that tutoring was immensely positive. Not only was I ahead of my class when I returned, but my study and organization skills had im-proved dramatically, too. Despite the fact that Mom's drinking didn't get any better while we were gone, and she showed the first signs of how truly volatile she could be, I'd had a good time and we both had a better taste in our mouths concerning filmmaking. Once home, I again tried to forget how difficult it could be when Mom drank. Every shift in location seemed to give me hope. Back then I didn't know how irrational that sort of thinking was. I just craved what I felt was the safety net and avoidance tool a movie set was.

By the spring I had another movie offer. I was called in to meet Italian producer Dino De Laurentiis, who was producing a movie called *King of the Gypsies*. The film was a family drama about present-day Gypsies in New York and the reluctant rise to power of the eldest son. I was playing Susan Sarandon and Judd Hirsch's daughter. Shelley Winters and Sterling Hayden were my grandparents, and Eric Roberts played my brother. The director was Frank Pierson, who had written the Oscar-winning screenplay for *Dog Day Afternoon*. The movie shot in New York City and I had to film only during April and May of 1978. Because of the large cast, I had a very light shooting schedule and much less pressure than had I been the star. In hindsight, this was a good next step in my career. The cast was strong. It was a big Paramount production and had a reputable Italian producer at the helm.

I was a bit surprised that both Susan and I were cast as Gypsies because we both had very light coloring and sandy hair. She was completely lovely to me during this experience and I think she actually liked me. I was a bit older this time and clearly not the star. We were not isolated on a location together, and it was a totally different experience. We also never had a one-on-one scene together like the traumatic slapping incident during *Pretty Baby*.

It was rather cool to cast us as mother and daughter twice, because it almost seemed as if it were true. (The craziest thing is that now I would be too old to play her daughter. I'm not sure how I caught up, but now it almost looks like it.) Susan actually dyed her hair black for the film but Mom insisted on a Roux rinse for me. It was a temporary color that washed out. Every time I stood in the shower to wash my hair, the black dye would blanket the tub. I was glad not to have to dye my hair black, and I read later that Susan resented actually changing her hair color while I was allowed to use a temporary one.

I have to admit that her hair looked much more natural than mine did, and in hindsight, I feel her choice was the better one. Here again Mom made a choice that may have protected me personally but that compromised the integrity of the piece and my portrayal. It doesn't feel right to blame her. It frustrates me, but can I really say I'm angry now because she wouldn't let a production team do anything they wanted to my naturally highlighted blond-brown hair? It is interesting where she chose to draw the line, however. Consistency, except in drinking, was never one of my mother's strong points.

Shelley Winters was also fair skinned and lighter haired. She was a piece of work to navigate. I am not sure she liked me too much, but I can't say I liked her, either. We had only a few scenes together, so I knew I would survive. However, there was one scene in which my character was skateboarding through the hallways of the hospital as my grandfather lay dying in bed. I was supposed to be eating a sandwich that Shelley was going to rip out of my hand as I skated by. She insisted I eat ham on white Wonder Bread with ketchup. Who eats ham with ketchup?

I was the one who had to eat almost all of it, and Shelley was just supposed to take it from me and have a bite. I hated ham and ketchup. But I couldn't complain because she was an Academy Award–winning actress. Take after take I ate that disgusting sandwich, not ever being told that I could spit it out once the director yelled cut. I had not learned many of the tricks, such as asking for a bucket near you to spit in once the camera had stopped rolling. I was getting sicker and sicker each take, but Miss Winters insisted that she could not act the scene unless it was a ham-and-ketchup sandwich on untoasted white bread. Slight flashback to *Pretty Baby*, but at least this time I was a moving target. I vowed never to do that to somebody else when I grew up. I never let on how sick I felt but passed on lunch that day.

Something dangerous and shocking happened while filming the final scene of the film. Eric Roberts's character saves me from my fate in the family by kidnapping me and driving away with me in his car. A wild and violent car chase ensues.

It was very late at night and the rain had just stopped. Right before we shot the scene, the stunt coordinator told me it might be a good idea to buckle my seat belt. Before Standards and Practices insisted that for legal reasons seat belts had to be shown fastened, we shot scenes unbuckled all the time. I found this recommendation from the stunt guy a bit strange but followed his advice.

We planned on driving and filming continuously down one long road. There was really no place set up for people to watch, so only the very necessary people were involved in the filming of this sequence. It was just the director, cameraman, Eric, and me in the car. The director was crouched down in the backseat to listen to the scene. The chase began and we accelerated to eighty miles per hour—easily—in just a few seconds as the other car began to gain on us and drift over to the passenger side. I have no idea if it was planned, but all of a sudden Eric wrenched the wheel to the right and slammed our car into a car speeding next to us. This happened repeatedly and on both sides of the cars. He began smashing into whatever side was closest to him. We smashed into the other car so hard each time that my side of the car dented in on me and I was bruised and terrified. We suddenly came to a halt, and our vehicle was so destroyed that the director's door was bent shut, and to free him they needed to radio for a Jaws of Life. I was shaking and crying and begged the director not to have to do the shot over again. Well, we couldn't even if he had wanted a second take because we had only these two cars.

I was shocked and scared that it had happened because up until then I assumed I'd always be safe on a movie set. Eric was not a stuntman and was not supposed to have done this stunt entirely on his own. We could all have been killed, and I was hurt that it had been allowed to be so real.

Today that would have caused quite a stir and legal actions would be taken, but they all just thought the scene was amazing. Because Mom couldn't watch the scene from anywhere, I think she must have been either back at base camp or at a bar. When I told her what had happened, I am sure she must have gotten upset, but I don't remember if she spoke up or not. This was very different from the way she acted during *Pretty Baby*. She must have been drinking much more during this movie to have let this incident slide. I am surprised that she did not make a big deal out of something that had resulted in a much more dangerous situation than long workdays or cracked feet.

Mom sometimes had small roles in my movies. In *King of the Gypsies* Mom played a hooker who leaves a party on Eric Roberts's arm. They stumble out of the building and stagger arm in arm down the dark street. Mom had to get drunk before she could do it. She never seemed to do anything pressured or important without drinking first. I remember thinking that Mom would have probably dated Eric. She was that sexy, boozy blond who flirted. She had a sharp wit and a provocative vocabulary. There seemed to be some guy on every set who had a crush on my mom and ended up asking her out. She managed to keep the details from me, and I never saw her be overtly romantic with anybody. I imagine she met people from the crew later after I was asleep. I hated anybody she had a crush on and she knew it.

The crash scene was one of my last on the film and I wrapped earlier than most. Soon the rest of the film was complete. We had a big wrap party at Regine's on Park Avenue. But something even more exciting was about to happen—within days we were on our way to the Cannes Film Festival. It was to be my first trip to France.

Pretty Baby premiered at the Cannes Film Festival and received the Palme d'Or. The film created a frenzy at Cannes. One that would scar me for life. The press both ripped us apart and could not get enough of the controversial nature of the movie. Certain members of the press called it pornography. I was being called the next Lolita. The very thing that Louis wanted to avoid was rearing its ugly head.

I was shocked and overwhelmed at people's reaction to me. The fans and press went insane. During the premiere of the film—before it won the award—the crowd was so big and disorderly that I was almost trampled. I was walking in flanked by my mother; her "companion," Bob; and some guards. Mom was holding on tightly to my arm as we pushed through the immense crowd. Out of the corner of my eye I saw a hand and a glimmer of metal. A fan had reached out to me and grabbed a clump of my hair and was just about to cut it off with a pair of scissors. Bob karate-chopped the arm away and I escaped. In trying to block more people from actually gripping on to me to touch me and get some kind of piece of me, Bob had to stretch his arms around me like a dome. As he did this, the buttons on his tuxedo shirt all popped off. He had only the one at the top and the one at the bottom remaining. We eventually got inside the theatre, and Mom used her eyebrow pencil to draw black dots on the buttonholes where the buttons would have been. Poor Bob had to suck in his belly as far as he could and maintain perfect posture the entire evening in order not to have his hairy chest exposed. We would eventually laugh at this but it would take me twenty years to even consider returning to the Cannes Film Festival.

The frenzy surrounding *Pretty Baby* in Europe would never be matched in America. Europeans savored the controversy and what they saw as the titillating aura surrounding the film. Most American audiences and critics recognized the film's artistic merits, but they still trashed it. It was called pornography, especially by people who hadn't even seen the film. I was labeled a nymphet whose mother pushed her into inappropriate situations. Canada banned the film. It was fascinating—some of the media were disappointed that I was not more of a Lolita, while others thought the character too provocative and highly inappropriate.

I was shielded from much of the controversy, but I remember being appalled that most people did not see the film's merits. Smart art and film journalists appreciated the film's artistic value, but the controversy meant I had been thrust into a type of cinema purgatory.

I never read any of the reviews of my work, and my mother wanted to keep it that way. If I hinted that I had heard negative comments from the press during interviews, my mom's response was "Fuck 'em if they can't handle it. Are you proud of what you did?"

"Yes."

"Well, then fuck 'em. That's all you need to think about."

Mom kept every single article written about me, my entire life. She had the originals and the duplicates and had them stored in hundreds of banker's boxes. It was not until over twenty years later, as I was writing my first book, *Down Came the Rain*, and cleaning out my storage, that I came upon the enormous collection of reviews. I began reading them and was quickly shocked and immensely hurt. I could not believe the vile way that people wrote about my mother and me. The amount of vitriol directed at us both was devastating. My talent was skewered and my mother's character harshly attacked. I felt relieved that I had not been privy to any of these reviews as a child. I am not sure I would have been able to handle it.

Mom had kept me in a glass case. At first I was content there. It was almost like I was Rapunzel in an enclosed tower, and just as in the fairy tale I was safe, pure, and kept away, at least in my mother's eyes.

Back then, people noticed how naïve I was about everything and found even more to criticize as a result. The press kept asking and speculating about how my mother could allow me to play such provocative parts while keeping me so sheltered. Sometimes even during press events she could be loud or slightly disruptive if she was drinking (which she usually was). And although she was often correct in her judgments on people or situations, she handled almost everything inappropriately. She thought she was the only one in the world who knew better when it came to her daughter. Only she could guide me and give me advice, and anybody who crossed her, in any way, would get written off or not-so-subtly verbally attacked.

In reality, I know Mom was just trying to protect me, but in the long run, she may have gone too far. You can't protect your kids so much that they have no emotional antibodies. She tried to continue to strap me to her chest my entire life. She was undeterred, and as a result many people thought the worst of her. People either decided Mom was the enemy or they appreciated her courage and her ferocity when it came to protecting her daughter.

Thankfully, the negative press did not hinder my chances of working. I did not know how bad and personal the press actually was. I just wanted to keep doing what I was doing. We needed money, of course, and I really loved making movies.

The offers continued to come in, and we now welcomed them all. We began talks with Peter Fonda about a western called *Wanda Nevada*. The movie would take place in Arizona and would star and be directed by Peter Fonda. I played a girl who gets won in a poker game by Peter and travels with him through the Grand Canyon in search of gold. I had to know how to ride horses and be willing to withstand the extreme temperatures of Arizona in August. I told my mom I wanted to do this movie because it was funny and it would be fun living in the Grand Canyon and the remote area of Page, Arizona, that housed the amazing man-made Lake Powell. It sounded like a great way to spend a summer.

We left hot New York City for an even hotter Arizona. We began the trip in a raft on the Colorado River in the Grand Canyon. Because it was summer, I had no teacher or homework. The film schedule was limited because of daylight. We spent more time traveling than we did working. It was like a vacation. There were rides through rapids and campfires and singing and ghost stories. We filmed scenes all along the river, then would pack up, put life vests on, and raft down farther to camp out for the night. We climbed rocks and swam in calm sections and I had a blast. These trips often have steaks and lobsters and other delicacies included in the package. We were feeding a reduced yet still large crew and were traveling with four huge rafts.

At one point, we hit rapids so big that the boat with all the food supplies capsized and we lost all our fancier meals. The raft carrying the craft-service items remained upright, and we were forced to eat peanut butter and jelly, tuna salad, and junk food for the whole trip. Did I mention it felt like a vacation? I didn't mind one bit. Mom was drinking throughout the trip and many of the crew members were smoking weed and doing various drugs, even though I didn't realize the drug part at the time.

I did not mind Mom's drinking as much here in the canyon because we were all so happy and I felt so protected by this close-knit crew. She couldn't really get into any trouble. Morning came before sunrise and bedtime not long after dark. We were all on the same schedule, and even though Mom drank, she seemed happier and kinder to me. I don't remember her being flirty to any crew member or nasty to me at all, so for these ten days, for a change, her drinking was the least important part of the experience.

Every night we all placed our sleeping bags under the stars and settled in. The script supervisor would tickle my back until I fell asleep. Filming in the canyon concluded and we made it to the location for our departure out.

We were met by a pack of twenty or so mules that were to take us out of the canyon and up to the ridge. We loaded up the mules with camera equipment and people and headed out. I was up toward the front of the line near Peter and the cinematographer. It was incredibly exciting, and it was on this movie that I found my real love of moviemaking. It was here that I decided I loved being a gypsy and I loved living different lives and lifestyles.

Unfortunately, my mother had terrible asthma, an affliction I later acquired as well. While on these mules, inching our way along narrow paths that peered back down into steep canyons, my mother's asthma kicked in. They had placed her somehow at the end of the line of pack animals, and between the mule dander and sweat and the dust being kicked up by mules ahead of her, she had a full-blown asthma attack. In moments, she was unable to breath and had reached that frightening point when the attack switches from slight tightness in the chest to a debilitating blockage of the airway. She may or may not have had her puffer, but by then it would have been useless. She needed to be airlifted out of the canyon. We stopped and radioed for a helicopter evacuation, and Mom was loaded up and taken to a hospital.

I remember being worried, then embarrassed, then angry. I thought it interesting that it was my mother and not me who created the reason for the upheaval. I knew she did not do it for attention, for as much as she loved being dramatic, Mom did not truly enjoy or feel worthy of the attention. It was designed more to steer people away from her real self. But I remember a flicker of a thought—it seemed like my mother always managed to create a fuss of some sort. Maybe that is why I never did feel the freedom to upset any situation. Deep inside I knew my mom would do it for us. Mom was never too unruly in public if the press was around, but she'd get sloppy. At the birthday bashes she'd throw me, she'd hang on people and dance provocatively. She loved being the wild one and it made me even more reserved.

I was offered a ride on the helicopter to fly out with her, but I chose to remain on my mule. We never spoke about it again and I wonder if she was hurt that I did not choose to go with her. But I wanted to ride out with the team. It was fun and an adventure, and once Mom was safe, I was free to enjoy.

I was always worrying about Mom's safety. I never wanted anything to happen to her and I felt I always had to protect her. When she was asked to leave the Southampton home after pulling the little girl's hair, I thought something bad would happen to her if she were left alone. I would have died for her, as I showed I was willing to do when the Jeep's brakes went out on the George Washington Bridge. In the case with the mule, I relaxed once I knew she was in safe hands.

In a way my refusing the copter ride was one of the first times I chose not to follow my mom anywhere she was headed. This was the first time I can remember choosing myself over her. It is also true that I was able to relax more in this case because I knew my mother was in a professional's care. I knew she wouldn't come to any harm because she was not alone and she was going to be in a hospital. Basically, I found peace in knowing she was accounted for. This was a theme that would run throughout my life and up until the end of hers. As long as I knew my mother was OK, I felt freedom to relax and be present in my life.

Wanda Nevada felt like a camping trip. Because there was nowhere to go but the hotel or the desert, I worried less about my mom. She was drinking as much as always, but I knew where she was and knew she couldn't really get hurt. There wasn't even anywhere to drive, so I felt relaxed. Everybody looked after me and I was, once again, like a mascot. Even my godmother, Lila, who was born in Arizona, was able to meet up with us later in Prescott and stay for a lot of the filming. Mom made no enemies on this set that I can remember. In fact, we made some long-lasting friends. Peter Fonda gave me a chestnut two-year-old filly as a gift and we still speak to this day.

The movie wrapped in mid-September and Mom and I left immediately for Los Angeles. I had been offered a movie with one of my all-time favorite comedians, George Burns.

This movie was called *Just You and Me, Kid* and starred George Burns and a cast of funny and legendary old-time comedians. In the film I play a young runaway who is being chased by the mob. George's character takes me in and we form an unlikely friendship. The movie was shot entirely in Los Angeles and mostly on the Warner Bros. lot. I got my school syllabus and was assigned a tutor; once again Mom's old rule of not missing school had been pushed aside. I loved my tutor, though. She had a great sense of humor and made learning fun. We sent my work back weekly and I continued to do well. In the same way that filming movies gave me refuge from my mom's drinking, time in "school" gave me refuge from shooting. In a very unconventional way, there was a balance to it all. I had no reason to rebel against any of it because each provided a respite from the other and oddly enough gave me a very well-rounded existence.

I was on a roll now and was excited about moviemaking. To me movies represented new, fun, and safe experiences where my mother's drinking would take less of a toll on our lives. There was a safety in having to be responsible to my job and accountable to an outside obligation. It became easier and easier to avoid confronting Mom's drinking and go to a set. I had the excuse of having to work, and it became my ultimate escape. Mom may have been embarrassing or obviously tipsy on set, but there were always other adults, who felt like a sort of extended family, to take me away. They buffered me from my mother's drunkenness and served as witnesses to her behavior. I felt less alone. At home in our apartment I often shrunk from fear and felt isolated. But within the context of moviemaking, there was always somewhere to go and someone with whom to be. Movies felt, at least temporarily, bigger than her addiction. As long as there was a call sheet that outlined the day, I could avoid dealing with Mom's problem for a while longer.

George Burns loved my mom and treated me like a favored grandchild. He refused to light up his famous cigar when around me because he knew I did not like smoking, and we had ongoing inside jokes throughout the filming. Once again, I was treated like a favorite pet.

Filming on an actual movie lot was thrilling to me. The studios looked as if they did in the movies, and it was such a luxury to have a trailer and eat at a commissary or across the street at an old Hollywood restaurant. The SmokeHouse was George's favorite place to eat and he had a regular table. He always invited my mom and me to join him. There he would have fried fish fingers with a side of ketchup and never any alcohol to drink. I always ordered what he had and I wasn't even a fan of fish sticks. I remember Mom ordering her regular drink at the time, which was a martini straight up with a twist, and thinking I was so glad we had only an hour for our lunch break because she wouldn't have time to drink more than about two cocktails.

Mom and I rented a house in Bel Air. It sounds fancy, but it was a run-down ranch-style house with a cracked pool and rats that ate the kiwis we had in a bowl on the kitchen table. I thought it was a mansion and was very excited to live in such a posh neighborhood. Mom and I had fun, and although she was still drinking every night, her days seemed somewhat tempered. If she did drink during the days, I still did not have to get behind the wheel with her because teamsters drove me to and from the set.

It was a happy time. We were working in sunny California and Mom seemed untroubled. My stepsister, Diana, came to stay with my mom and me in our rented house, and, as usual, we all laughed a lot and enjoyed beautiful Malibu and going to Fiorucci or Heaven in Beverly Hills for our Candie's shoes and colored jeans. Looking back now, this seems like it was a bit of a golden era for all of us.

I realize now that I did an incredible amount of work at this time. Five movies in two years! But it made sense for many reasons. I was popular and directors and producers wanted me. But on a personal level, it was just the easiest and happiest way to live with my mother. I still felt incredibly connected to her, but her drinking had become scarier and more difficult.

Mom would not stop drinking for me. I could only believe I wasn't doing enough to make her stop. It took me about thirty years to realize that nothing I did could make her stop if, in fact, she did not want to or could not fight it herself.

But at the time, I still thought I could control things. That I could fix things. And as 1978 ended and I returned to New York, I thought I had finally discovered a way to fix her, this time for good.

Chapter Seven

Are You Finished?

The first thirteen years of my life were unconventional in every way. I lived two entirely different existences between being raised by a single mother and working in the entertainment business and spending time with my father's more conventional (but also more affluent) family. I was a star, but also a normal kid going to regular schools. I was the source of great controversy, yet a darling, an incredibly innocent bystander. The press both praised me and devoured me. Mom was the wild and needy one whereas I was the caretaker and adult. I went in and out of so many different environments and found my comfort zone in all of them. My world was ever changing and diverse, but I had no trouble adapting. Strangely the versatility did not unsettle me but instead fortified me. I grew to know that I could find my place anywhere. At times I did struggle with the question as to who I was because so many others seemed to be living in just one environment and could be defined as such. But I started to have pride in being able to put on a different hat and be a different person, each time learning and loving an undiscovered side of myself.

The circumstances of my daily life were definitely unique, but that was never the reason for my sadness or insecurity. There are clichéd ways of blaming the industry and the press and the public for some-body's demise emotionally, but I cannot ascribe my own troubles to them. I had enough love, good people around me, and a strong-enough innate sense of character to carve a path for myself and admit my own fears or insecurities without placing blame on the world or how unfair things were. I don't know why this was. Even if I had to keep changing directions, I just kept moving. Regretfully, however, I do have to acknowledge that the most damaging element in my life was loving and being loved by an alcoholic mother.

And the problem of my mother's drinking just got worse and worse over the next few months. It's ironic, but I believe that if it were not for the entertainment industry, I would have been a train wreck. I would have crumbled if I did not have a place to hide. I had to be pro-fessional because it was my job and I was getting paid. I couldn't fall to pieces.

My dad also provided safety and consistency and a conventional family. I appreciated it and him. I visited often, and even though it felt a bit too restricted and aristocratic at times, the knowledge that his home existed for me came to be a great relief. I found solace in know-ing that he was a phone call away. But he was only one part of my life. Most of my time revolved around my mother and what she created.

At work, I was always the good girl, the polite one. I got a good reputation early on because I was so easy to work with. I loved the responsibility because people liking me was the only real reward I sought. The pride I derived from my job stemmed primarily from be-ing liked and accepted. People praised me for being so well-behaved and I was fueled to continue being so.

With regard to my mother, it felt like it was never enough. Noth-ing I said or did seemed correct or could make her stop getting drunk or feel deeper happiness. I felt helpless. Why wasn't I enough to help her stop drinking? I felt much better about myself when I worked, so

I began to crave my jobs. I knew what to expect there. Come the end of my workday, however, I never knew what to expect. It did not seem abusive as much as it did claustrophobic, sad, and helplessly codependent.

In addition, the press wanted me to admit my mother and I had a *Mommie Dearest* type of relationship, but that was simply not the case. She also wasn't Mama Rose, the stereotypical stage mother. I didn't ever have the feeling that she was the one who wanted to be a star. Yes, as a young woman she wanted it all, but with me she was getting it without the risk of falling short herself. She never said, "I could have been . . ." Our relationship and my stardom satisfied all her needs in one. Except she would never feel fully proud of or satisfied with herself. My mother thought she had the most beautiful child in the world. She felt the attention I received was justified. I think she believed in my talent but she never focused on it. She saw people wanting me and that meant success to her. Buying homes and having possessions or traveling meant we were successful.

Looking back at these years I realize that our relationship was so scrutinized because it was so public. But ironically, it was also this public scrutiny that kept me somehow accountable.

I often thought of the private hell that many mothers and daughters were enduring, and I actually felt lucky. I justified my mother's behavior by saying I was lucky I wasn't like the kids out there who were beaten or had relatives who abused them. I just thought my mother was colorful and unconventional. Up until this point, it didn't occur to me that maybe it was unhealthy to live with a mom who drank as much as my mother did and was verbally and emotionally abusive. I believe I also saw how easy it was to focus on people in the public eye when there were so many private sufferers in the world. But I thought that because I was not physically abused or battered, my situation did not merit complaining about or even really fighting.

I knew that although the world thought I was living a crazy life, there were many others whose lives were more tragic. It was this type of empathy that kept me imprisoned by my mother's alcoholism. People assume that if somebody is in the entertainment industry, doom is inevitable. But then I believed those without a public platform were worse off.

The struggles I had never came from the entertainment industry. Stardom, and the fame or money associated with it, was not my issue. The business was my buffer. Stardom was a by-product. It was never the catalyst for my unhappiness. My unhappiness was rooted in my mother's inability to stop drinking. My sense of worthlessness stemmed from feeling insecure as to who I was and inadequate in getting my mother to stop drinking. I had lower self-esteem, not because I was a model but because I was a daughter. The movie business kept me afloat and sane. My mother's drinking superseded my stardom. I was a child of an alcoholic way before I was a star. I craved opportunity and I craved my mother's sobriety. I never understood the connection between the two.

In the end, I never got caught up in my growing fame or my public persona. My focus was always on what was going on at home. My mother's alcoholism tempered the positive and negative ramifications of fame and of being a "star." Between living in New York City, attending nonprofessional children's school, and navigating an alcoholic parent, there was little room for me to fuck up. Fame was easy in comparison. Fame was fake and fickle, but my mom's drinking was real and consistent.

I believed for a long time that I could affect my mother's drinking. Like many children of alcoholics, I thought if I asked a certain way, or made some type of deal with my mother where I promised something, it would be compelling enough to make her stop.

As I grew older, I started to notice the deeper change in her behavior and began to intensely feel the consequences of the booze. Once, when drunk, she got so angry with me for some little thing that she tipped over a full room-service table. Food went everywhere and one plate bruised the outer part of my eye. I wished it had cut it so I could show her the next day and make her feel bad. Another time we were driving somewhere in the car with Bob and she screamed for him to stop the car. She stumbled out and walked along the highway at night. Bob dropped me off with somebody and spent hours trying to find her. It was especially when I was not working that I felt increasingly unsettled by her drinking.

For years, I didn't know what alcoholism was or that my mother had it. I knew only the effects and I thought I could change them. But at the end of 1978, once we were away from the safety net of the films I had been shooting and back in New York, I was getting scared, both for her and of her. Her drinking seemed to be incessant and her mood swings acute. She had gotten sloppy. I had begged her so many times to quit but to no avail. I knew it was still up to me to do something. I had taken care of her in various ways my entire life and this was just another task.

I think I must have complained to my godmother, Auntie Lila; to Bob; and to my dad. It was probably Lila who introduced me to the concept of alcoholism and how there were people who could help. It is strange how hard it is for me to remember the details and the exact timing, but I distinctly remember walking Mom through the nondescript door of the Freedom Institute, a treatment center in New York that was founded just a few years earlier, in 1976.

It had been only a few weeks prior that I met with a counselor, also at the Freedom Institute, who had described to me what it was to be an alcoholic. She made it clear that Mom had a disease and needed treatment. The counselor explained that I had in no way failed by not being able to get my mother to quit. She clarified that while it was absolutely normal that I wasn't able to get my mother to stop drinking,

I was very much needed to help get her into treatment. This lovely woman exuded kindness and compassion as she took me through the necessary steps in getting my mother help. I listened intently and was resolved to do whatever it took. She kept saying it would be tough and I had to be strong and I was the only one to whom my mother might listen.

I knew I was important because I had been the one navigating my mother's behavior the most intimately and constantly for most of my life. I was the one who had run up the street to Piccolo Mondo in search of Mom and peered in the window at Finnegans Wake pub after school to see if I recognized the back of her head. I was the one who had pleaded with her to not drink on my birthday and made excuses for her when she was on a tear. I was the one who learned that there was no Santa because she was passed out on the couch on Christmas Eve. Of course it would be me who was the important piece in this whole thing.

My mom loved me more than any other human being on the planet. I could fix this—I knew it. Responsibility was a familiar feeling. I absorbed the information and the plan was set. We would stage an intervention and confront my mother. I knew it was a delicate situation and it could go horribly awry. But intervention was my only hope.

I had told my dad that I was going to give my mom an ultimatum. My plan was to tell her I would go live with him and his family if she didn't go into rehab. I remember being aware that I had to present this to my father in such a way that he didn't feel as if living with him was considered a punishment or something I dreaded in any way. I was very sensitive about his feelings as well. But we both knew that the thought of losing me was the only real threat my mother would respond to.

I had been told that in order for intervention to work, it would have to hinge on immediate rehab, because simply getting Mom to promise not to drink, without professional help, had already proven futile. Dad agreed to all parts of the plan; he would wait patiently to hear the intervention's outcome. I can't imagine how he felt hearing his thirteen-year-old child having such resolve.

Finally, the day had come. Auntie Lila had secretly packed a bag for my mother's impending trip. Lila picked me up from school. I somehow got Mom to meet me at the Freedom Institute offices to discuss something serious. It was a nervous, scary time. My mother was never one for surprises, or for any situation, for that matter, in which she did not have complete control. To this day I'm still shocked that she even showed up to meet us.

I remember sitting down with her in a small, poorly lit room. Maybe the lighting was fine or just fluorescent and unflattering, I'm not sure, but I do remember seeing darkness out the sides of my eyes. My vision was narrowing. Lila was there, too. All the sounds in the room, including our voices, had a sort of muffled quality, like we were speaking underwater. I assume now that this was the result of heightened anxiety; I was on the verge of the flight side of the fight-or-flight response.

I did not flee but instead sat down facing my increasingly anxious, soon-to-be-blindsided mother. Once settled, the counselor from the Freedom Institute began giving my mother some background on who she was and what the Freedom Institute was about. She explained that I had come to them some weeks ago to ask for help with my mother's drinking.

I remember immediately thinking that Mom must be getting mad that I went behind her back to discuss her with a stranger. The woman then looked at me and asked me to tell my mother some of the stories I had told her and explain how they made me feel.

I began talking. What could be going through her mind? I

imagined Mom saying, "Fuck this," and storming out and going straight to the closest bar. But to my shock, she stayed in her seat. I looked at her and mustered the strength to pretend that I would rather live with my father than with her drinking. For the first time in my life I didn't attempt to get her approval. I kept talking. I explained how mean she got when she drank and how it scared me. I told her I loved her and I wanted to have fun with her but when she drank she changed for the worse.

Her lips pursed and she was silent. One of Mom's go-to tactics in an argument was to keep silent while somebody ranted and then coldly pose the question "Are you finished?" When you said yes, she would basically shut the whole debate down by claiming she would do nothing you asked. How dare you question her?

I expected the same this time. As I spoke about how she acted when she drank and how hurtful she was to me, I had a sort of tunnel vision, the blurry haze that encroaches just before someone is about to faint. Lila chimed in to say that it was mainly for my mother's own benefit that we were doing this. We each had our parts to play. Mom scoffed at the idea of anything *ever* being for her.

The woman from the Freedom Institute said that there had been arrangements made for Mom to go to a place called St. Mary's in Minneapolis, Minnesota. For what seemed like an eternity, there was silence. Then I remember Mom saying she would "think about it."

I thought: *Oh no, we are losing her. I knew it wouldn't work.*

But I didn't give up. We explained that there was actually no time to think it over. That we had her bag ready and that the flight was in a few hours.

Even I felt this was harsh. If it had been me, I would have felt helpless, hurt, and angry. I couldn't tell how she was feeling. My mother's exterior did not betray her emotions, and I could tell she had decided to humor us and play along with this little game we were ignorantly playing, but had not yet decided to concede. She was steely, and I could tell she was upset and hurt and even scared but would never let on.

I knew she was also placating us. She was condescending to our lack of judgment. She was sure she didn't have a problem and would just prove us wrong. She could always turn even the most clear-cut situations into ones where she was calling the shots. She looked only at me and said, "Are you finished?" "Yes, Mama."

More silence and then: She finally spoke. "I'll go. But I am going for *you*. I'm doing this for you, Brookie, *not* for me. I don't have a problem."

She got into the car we had reserved, stoically turned her gaze straight ahead, and that was that. I honestly believe Mom hadn't seen any of it coming.

I didn't understand how I felt as I watched the sedan drive away. I was stunned. At that moment I didn't realize that I would only ever get one chance at such an intervention. I felt relieved Mom had not put up a fight. But I suddenly had the urge to run after the car and apologize and take it all back. I had a pang in my chest and immediately missed her like crazy. I was relieved she was safe. And I was thankful that, in this case, her absence didn't mean she was out at some bar. I instantly felt guilty for having ambushed her and knew she might never forgive me.

The woman from the Freedom Institute sat me down briefly and said we had done well. She said that the important thing was that she had gone. She told me that many people insist they don't have a problem and try to put the burden on the family members and friends doing the intervention. There was a certain pride in the idea that the drinker was taking the high road and doing a loved one a favor by giving in.

Afterward, I remember walking down Third Avenue in a bit of a daze. I felt like it had gone way too easily for total celebration. This should have served as a premonition. Also, with the constant preoccupation of Mom's drinking eliminated, I felt awkwardly unfettered.

There would be so much more time to devote to other things; I was suddenly at a slight loss.

Afterward, I went back to our apartment, where Lila would be staying with me for the next few months. I was glad that I didn't have to go live with my father. It wasn't that it would have been terrible, but it would have been inconvenient. I knew it was going to be a hard time. Even being back in the apartment near my mom's things felt suddenly unfamiliar. It felt a bit like a death because we would not even speak to one another for weeks. Phone calls were not allowed.

But life resumed, and Auntie Lila and I settled in to being roommates. I had a routine at home for the first time, which proved to be a welcome change. I started getting to school on time and eating at the dining table. I admit I loved the feeling of consistency yet felt equally guilty about preferring an ordered way of life compared to the chaos in which my mother lived.

The program lasted three months and included a family week. Auntie Lila and I would visit and engage in group sessions. I remember driving through Minneapolis, seeing big signs for addiction and depression and thinking that Mom had been sent to the right place. Within a day, however, I realized that the dreary place we were visiting was enough to make anybody want to drink. God, it was depressing. I really doubted that this environment would help my mom. But maybe it was supposed to be so bad that people wanted to be clean just so they did not have to return to godforsaken Minneapolis.

It had been a month since I'd seen my mother. During that time we hadn't communicated at all. The separation, the longest we'd ever had by far, felt violent and much like when animals are separated from their mothers for a forced weaning process. However, letters were permitted, and I had sent cards of encouragement. She sent letters back and in one explained how she had already been given the title of group leader and how her counselors continued to praise her. This immediately sent up a red flag to me. My heart sank at the thought that Mom had already seduced the therapy team. She kept alluding to her being the only person at the facility who was different and how, consequently, she was singled out and given more responsibility. I read "superior" as being the underlying subtext. Of course she was running her group. Of course she was not "common." Part of me thought it may have been the truth. Mom had always been unique and set apart from others. I would not learn until years later that this resulted from a sort of self-imposed exile. Mom could not admit to being like the other people in the hospital. They were "crazy" and they had "real problems." My mother's insecurities lay deeply embedded in her psyche. She would prove to be much harder to crack.

Maybe I saw the writing on the wall. Or feared she would outwit the people I had prayed would help. But in any case, I went to family week and resented the whole thing. I hated being there and despised going through the family sessions and lectures. Luckily, I wasn't quite a household name yet, so anonymity was relatively still on my side. I painstakingly stepped up and did what was asked. Ever the eager front-row, approval-seeking student, I completed the reading material and volunteered in class and spoke about hurt feelings. Yeah, yeah, yeah.

You were encouraged to cry and tell the truth, and for once and for all to come clean. I had already done that. I could not understand why it all had to keep being my problem as well as my mother's. I had done my caretaking and I wanted it to be her turn. When could I be done with it? I was angry that I had to spend my time in dingy Minneapolis, going to lectures on the effects of substance abuse when it was her problem. How could listening to how some redneck father hit his wife help me? Maybe I felt a bit superior as well but the people there were all extremely different from my mother and me. I was miserable, drinking weak coffee with disgusting Cremora. It was nothing like the buttered roll and delicious coffee in Anthora-patterned cups we'd had at home. In this place, I felt like a spoiled little kid who wanted to stamp my feet and storm out of the room.

I couldn't identify with any of these people or their stories. I had been told that I would meet people much like me in this environment and finally feel supported and fortified. It could not have been further from the truth. I could not have felt more isolated. I don't mean that the differences stemmed from the fact that I was a "movie star." The truth was that there was a cultural difference with regard to references and complaints. The people were actually lovely but I felt I was in a foreign country. The problem was that Mom was indeed savvier than many of the people at the facility; I could only imagine my mom reprogramming and manipulating each one of them. I had been told that once I realized that others had gone through the same experience I had by living with an alcoholic, I wouldn't feel so alone, but in this case, the booze seemed to be the only underlying similarity.

I honestly didn't fit in there, and I worried that Mom actually did not, either. Mom was one of those unbelievably sly, influential drunks who could hook you in, all the while cutting you down. It was borderline sociopathic, minus the murder. St. Mary's was, and is, a great and reputable institution that came highly recommended and regarded, but sadly it was not a good or effective fit for my mother. Had I made a mistake? Was Mom right, once again? I felt Mom really was smarter than most of the patients and even cleverer than some of the counselors. Why had I not been even smarter than she was for once? She was right again! Mom wasn't, however, smart enough to choose health over addiction. I wouldn't realize until many years later that my doubts were all part of my codependence. The venue may or may not have been ideal for her, but it was not necessarily because she was too much of a genius. It was more a product of her inability to be honest with herself or strong enough to choose to be healthy.

Aunt Lila and I completed our "family week" and left Mom to finish out her stay. Mom made one lifelong friend at St. Mary's. Except for one relapse a few years later, Mom's friend would remain sober for the rest of her life. I always wished Mom had been that type of a recovering alcoholic.

Overall, Mom played by the rules but never did the "steps." I don't believe she ever committed authentically, and the therapy never fully registered with her. She used the recovery catchphrases like a dutiful student. But all the while she was scoffing at how they didn't actually apply to her. She beguiled the staff with her humor and her street smarts. She was incredibly intuitive about the way others behaved and what their needs were. She could outwit almost anyone. But, sadly, she was still an alcoholic and hardly two steps closer to recovery.

I truly believe she thought she didn't have a problem and that she could control her drinking. But I'm not convinced she ever did the work that would help her get there. Vulnerability equaled weakness for my mom. One of the early steps in AA deals with admitting helplessness about your problem. Well, being helpless was never something Teri Terrific could cop to. I don't believe she ever fully admitted to the severity and authenticity of her disease.

Mom returned home after three months. I made a sign and got her flowers to celebrate her homecoming. Lila and I had taken a photo of us together and had put it in a little frame. It was the kind you get in a photo booth. Mom for some reason got so angry that it was of the two of us that she tore it up. I told her it was only supposed to mean we loved her. Shockingly that was where my sweetness ended. In the next few weeks and months I was horrible to her in any way that I could be. I may have been lashing out and punishing her for years of drinking. I may have been testing her to see if she would crack and start drinking again. Maybe I was just so uncomfortable with her sobriety that I was acting out.

I was putting her on trial for some reason, and I got a quietly maniacal thrill when I hurt her. I felt terrible about it, but in a weird way, I wanted to create a new dysfunction because that is what was familiar.

I couldn't stop being nasty to her. Yet she neither fought me nor began drinking just yet. It was all so awkward and foreign, and I realized I had no idea how to act around her when she was sober. I was so used to navigating her drinking and being sad, angry, or afraid, that without the existence of trauma, I was floundering. I hated her drinking but at least I knew what to expect. The protocol of being the child of an alcoholic was second nature to me, so without it I was again slightly lost.

I also realize that, in a way, I saw myself as a better person than she was when she drank. I liked that feeling. Most of my life I just wanted my mother's approval. But admittedly, when she was drunk, there was a type of freedom for me. I was justified in fighting her when she drank, but take away the booze and I just didn't know what to fight.

I could have never anticipated it, but I unexpectedly hated her for her sobriety. If Mom and I were not getting along for some reason or if I was feeling the growing pains that all kids go through, I did not have anything on which to place blame. It was very unsettling facing her insecurities and her behavior without accusing the booze. Having the troubles actually be a part of my mother's deeper personality was even more tragic. I even secretly wanted her to start drinking again so I could say, "I told you so. I knew you couldn't do it."

I was also so angry at St. Mary's and the Freedom Institute for seemingly having more control over my mommy than I did. It was all so fucked-up and confusing and I began lashing out at everybody.

The sweeter she was, the more I punished her. The more people tried to help me, the more I stomped and pouted. I even turned against Lila and cast her aside emotionally. On top of all that, I was getting my period for the first time and my hormones made me an emotional and irrational mess. I had been used to my codependence, and as much as I thought I wanted it, I was resisting the change. I wanted to hurt my mother. It was plain and simple. I pushed and pushed until I got tired.

I don't know how she did it, but my mother didn't crack. She stayed steady and loving. She was the most mature I had ever seen her. Maybe they'd told her at St. Mary's to expect difficult behaviors from family members. But for whatever reason, she waited it out, but it remained.

There was no alcohol to blame or to retreat toward. We all needed to adjust to this new dynamic.

The tragic part to me now is how idealized I had made her recovery. As a child of an alcoholic, I believed in a silver lining. One day it would all be better. I believed in the idea of a promise. Once this or that milestone was reached, then she would see and she could smile. One day she would be happy.

But the truth was that as kind as she was being, Mom had trouble being honest with herself about anything. How could she suddenly morph into this fully resolved and self-actualized being? I don't think my mother ever released her pain or her hurt, and therefore her healing was going to require more than just stopping drinking. I could not know this then. I was just baffled at how there was no rainbow.

I don't remember ever being told at the time what I learned later, which is that even if you remove the alcohol, there is still unresolved pain and hurt in a relationship. Damage has often been inflicted by both the drinker and those closest to the drinker. It must be acknowledged.

But just because the booze went away, it didn't mean the damage went with it. The term *dry drunk* means that the drinking may not be current but the precipitating feelings that drive the drinker to abuse alcohol have not gone away. People told me that drinking revealed a person's true personality, but I could never believe that. I refused to believe that, deep down, my mom was honestly that ugly. I did believe that deep down she could have been that damaged and hurt, but not ugly. There were wounds that needed to be faced and attended to for both of us. The problem was, however, that for me, I didn't want to ruin these moments of sobriety by stirring up my old hurts. It is so much easier to sweep them all under the carpet and pretend they never existed. This, unfortunately, took a toll.

My mother really did seem to try to stay sober at first. I could tell it was tough for her. I even dreamt of a world in which she could be able to drink moderately. Addicts must abstain completely. There is no such thing as an alcoholic being able to be a social drinker, but I secretly wished that she could find a way to reasonably drink so we could all be happy. This is how codependent my thoughts were and how much I wanted her to enjoy life and be healthy and happy. Because if she was happy, I did not have to worry. I never liked any part of her when she was drinking. She may have been fun for others but I really authentically enjoyed her only before she took her first sip. When she laughed sober, I felt oxygen in my blood.

I really thought everything would be better if she stopped drinking. But it wasn't. We fell back in the same patterns, just with different details. It was time to do something new and different. To go far away and get back to the golden age and good feelings we'd had shooting movies in the past and sticking my head in the sand about everything else. And as luck would have it, my next movie role would take us farther away than I could have imagined.

Chapter Eight

Blue

In early 1979, just as my mother and I were adjusting to post-rehab life, I got an intriguing offer. An author named Henry De Vere Stacpoole wrote a novel back in 1908, *The Blue Lagoon*, that had already been made into a movie twice. The first version was from 1923. It was black-and-white, silent, and filmed in England. Neither my mother nor I knew anything about the silent version, but my mother was a fan of the 1949 version, which was filmed in both England and Fiji and starred Jean Simmons and Donald Houston. Mom had loved Jean Simmons and thought the idea of a remake was wonderful.

The Blue Lagoon tells the story of two cousins, Emmeline and Richard Lestrange, who survive a shipwreck and grow up together on a tropical island in the South Pacific. Through most of the movie they're completely alone, eventually developing a romantic relationship and having a child.

Shooting this film meant we'd be on location again, this time for months. We'd leave for the South Pacific in June and not return until September. Mom and I had always loved being on location. It was like this great sanctuary in which I worked hard and Mom played hard. We were excited and I was anticipating feeling relieved because Mom had not been drinking and I believed her sobriety would continue on this deserted island. After all, there would be no bars.

The director, Randal Kleiser, who had just had a huge success directing the movie *Grease*, and the studio, Columbia Pictures, wanted Matt Dillon to play my character's cousin, a choice that thrilled me. But Matt's mother was against the idea and they turned it down. I was devastated because I knew Matt and thought he was cute and talented. He was very sweet about the whole thing and made it a point to tell me that his decision was in no way a personal affront to me.

The filmmakers began to search for someone to play Richard. This choice was, obviously, a very big deal for me, since the two of us would basically be the only actors in the entire movie. Minus some flashbacks it would be just us. By this time I had been in seven films and was very worried about working with an amateur. The studio finally found a kid with straight blond hair and a beautiful physique who had no film or acting experience and had spent his extracurricular time as an athlete. The director had called to tell us that they had found my counterpart, an eighteen-year-old student from Rye, New York, whose dream had been to go into sports medicine. His name was Christopher Atkins and I was going to love him! I was skeptical but had no say and his photo looked fine. I had worked with many veterans but this would be the first time that I was the actual veteran.

Mom and I packed our suitcases, sent our two rescue cats to a boarding house, and left for the island of Vanua Levu in Fiji. We had to fly to the mainland and to the city of Lautoka, via Australia, and then take a seaplane to Turtle Island, where we would be living for the next four months.

We touched down on water and taxied to the dock, where we were met by Randal and Chris and some Fijian men to help with the bags. Chris's light-blond, naturally stick-straight hair had been given a perm. I didn't understand why it was necessary for him to have curly hair but it was not up to me to decide. He looked different from his photo but cute. Once on the dock, I was instructed to leave my bags to be taken to where we would be staying and go directly to the tanning area. Some preparations needed to start right away. There was still enough sunlight to get color and I was told I needed to start to build up enough of a tan so that it looked as if I had been living on an island my entire life. The tanning space consisted of two small areas enclosed by mats of woven palm fronds. I was to take off all my clothes and begin that day by getting a base. Chris had already been on the island for a week so he was already darker than I was. I would have to catch up. I was told I could choose to live on the big sailing ship that would be featured in the film or I could remain on land.

At first, I was sure I'd choose the ship. I had this fantasy that I would have a quaint little cabin where I would write in my journal and be rocked to sleep nightly. I would stick pictures on my wall and write letters to my friends back home and it would be as if I was part of an expedition a hundred years ago. But after getting off the scary seaplane that sat only three people and being confronted with the real-life version of my fantasies, I took one look at the ship and changed my mind. It was ancient and had rats and creaking planks. I opted for a *bure*, or hut, as non-Fijians called them.

The bure I would share with my mother was right on the beach and basically consisted of a cinder-block square with a standing sink and a partitioned-off toilet.

The rafters were big palm-tree trunks and the roof was a thatched canopy with a peak. The shape of the roof enabled rain to cascade down the sides and not leak into the room. Our bure consisted of two connecting rooms, each with two twin beds. This was perfect for when I had friends visit from the States.

The first few weeks we rehearsed and prepared to film, and Chris couldn't have been sweeter. He was so excited, energetic, and kind all the time and took me on tours of all the special spots in our new home away from home.

He was really cute and I think everybody was even secretly hoping that we would become a real-life couple. I could tell that Randal, the director, really wanted it, and he enlisted my mother to be encouraging as well. Even though it was not overt, I felt people believed it would be good for the film. God forbid we just act! Chris seemed equally excited to become my best friend and possible boyfriend and was always around me. Anyway, if it was going to happen anywhere, this stunning island would be the perfect environment in which to fall in love. I, however, began to feel standoffish. I have never been good with people forcing themselves on me, or acting too gung-ho about becoming my closest buddy. The moment I sensed the push, I put up a wall so tall that my mother had to tell me to give the kid a break and not take it out on him. I would have none of it and their plan almost backfired. But he really was so sweet and happy that I would eventually develop a crush on him. It lasted only a very short time because Chris and I were really more like brother and sister than we were lovers. Strange that our relationship was actually closer to the essence of the film than even others could see.

Mom explained that Chris probably believed he had to fall in love with me to be a good actor. I was going to teach him otherwise. Even though Chris originally came across a bit strong and off-puttingly eager, I really did respect how he was committing to his debut role. Chris had learned to spear fish, skin-dive, build a thatched hut, and start a fire with sticks. He was trying to be as authentic as he could and I appreciated his approach. I, too, committed to learning whatever I could from the locals.

Like Chris, I set out to adapt immediately. Within two weeks I could climb palm trees in bare feet, dive for coral and shells without a tank and without making bubbles, and weave palm fronds into bowls and small boxes for catching rainwater. I had worked up to holding my breath for over a minute so I could do the underwater scenes more efficiently. I jumped right into being an island kid, rarely wearing shoes, and swimming whenever I could. Mom and I both chose to tie traditional *sulus* around ourselves instead of wearing shorts and T-shirts. A sulu is almost exactly like an Indian sari or a wrap you often wear at the beach. They are made of brightly colored cotton and can be tied many different ways.

We learned the difference between eating coconuts right off the tree and those that had fallen on the ground. One Fijian man in particular taught me to use a pointed stick and a machete to break open mature coconuts for their meat and young ones for their milk. Our crew consisted mostly of Australians and Americans, but included a few sturdy Fijians. The native Fijians spoke very little English, but with the few words they did know, and with the Fijian I picked up, we communicated fine.

I forget his name but the man who taught me about coconuts was the same man who made my mother a long sword from wood so she could beat away the rats that moved into our roof. The rats had moved in a few weeks after Mom and I began living there. They were really terrible and seemed to come out mostly late at night. I hated rats and slept with the blankets over my head. I pictured them landing on my head in the middle of the night and chewing my face off. I'd hear Mom leap up and start whacking at the thatched-roof ceiling after hearing a scurry. I don't think my mother ever slept.

We all got used to living on a deserted island and dealing with everything that came along with it, such as rats, bugs, sewage issues, mail once a week, storms, and sunburn. Only one man had ever lived on this island with his wife. He owned it, and his dream had been to eventually turn it into a resort.

The cinematographer, Academy Award winner Néstor Almendros, used only natural light and fire to light the entire film. In order to complete a day's worth of scenes, we needed as many hours as possible, so Néstor came up with the idea of pushing our clocks ahead. Everyone working on the film synchronized his or her watch to a new time. Each morning I had to get up at 5:00 A.M. or even earlier. So while my clock said 5:00 A.M., for my body it was actually 4:00 A.M. Mom was never a good sleeper and rarely slept more than five hours a night, sober or not. But the benefit of this self-imposed time shift, which we dubbed Bula Time, was that except for all-night shooting, which was lit by fire and candlelight, we would finish our days by dusk. Sometimes, immediately after filming for the day, Chris and I would go diving for shells. I was collecting white shells that had rays of red dots that fanned to the tip. It took me weeks, but I collected enough of them to make my mother a necklace for her birthday. Sometimes, if I was lucky, I'd find a piece of black coral and string it on to some leather for myself.

My skin had trouble holding on to a tan and I began losing all pigmentation. Patches of white began appearing, so to avoid looking like I was starring in *The Jungle Book* as a leopard instead of in a love story about sun-kissed teenagers, I had to get up even earlier than everyone else so I could be sponge-painted with makeup mixed with iodine. The makeup lady used big natural sea sponges and spread the liquid all over my body until I was the desired color. I was only allowed to take limited showers, and then only on days when we had finished a sequence the day before. The feeling of being painted by wet, cold sponges before dawn every morning was, to this day, one of the worst feelings I have ever experienced.

Our one day off a week was Sunday. Mom and I were getting along much better these days. My rage toward her had subsided and we were back in a routine we loved. Mom and I both loved to create new little lives for ourselves. Wherever we went, we would make it a home. We decorated our huts and wore traditional attire and played the music of the Fijian people. But we maintained some of our own traditions. Mom and I would wake up early and take a small motorboat to a mission on a neighboring island. It took forty-five minutes and we wore no life vests. For much of the trip no land was visible. Then, off in the distance, I'd see the outline of the small island and the steeple of a church. Mom and I attended Catholic Mass every Sunday with the nuns from the mission, who also taught the children their lessons. I kind of dreaded the idea of having to trek so far to go to church, but I loved being on the open water so early in the morning, and the service was always sweet and filled with singing.

One of our Fijian crew members enjoyed the ride and would come with us to do the navigating. At the conclusion of the shoot, my mother arranged for the film company to donate our generator to the mission. This generator enabled them to have electricity for the first time in their lives. The nuns loved my mother, who made them laugh and donated much of my per diem to them weekly. They needed it more. There was nothing else to spend the small weekly amount provided by the producers on, so it was no loss to me. My long hair fascinated the schoolchildren and it took me a while to get used to them wanting to touch it. I often had to remind myself I was not in Cannes.

We would return to our island in time to have a big breakfast or take a nap. Many Sundays and most nights, while walking back to my bure, I'd pass the local men having their nightly kava ceremony. Kava is a root that when crushed and placed inside a man's tube sock, and then soaked in water, makes a liquid resembling dirty dishwater that tastes like mud. It is served in half a coconut shell and if offered cannot be refused. It was considered rude, and unlucky, to refuse the call of "Kava, kava, *bula* kava!" Whenever I passed the ceremony, I'd try to go unnoticed, but I often failed and was forced to accept a cup. You were supposed to swallow the liquid from your coconut in one gulp. After ingesting this disgusting, lukewarm substance, you had to clap three loud, hollow-sounding claps with cupped palms, before passing it on to the next willing victim. I never learned what the claps symbolized but it was part of the ceremony. Kava numbs your mouth and throat and gives you a sedated feeling. The effects did not last too long, especially if you drank only one cup, but the taste was so disgusting and I hated it so much that I tried to avoid the torture whenever possible. Mom never got into it, either, because she said she didn't like the feeling. I was surprised they offered it to a kid, and I did not find it fun or cool.

It wasn't long before Mom began drinking again. The moment I saw the look on her face I knew. She got the usual flushed cheeks and familiar blurry eyes, and of course her lips had their signature brittle-looking texture. I always asked her to breathe out so I could smell her breath, and she'd come very close and open her mouth but never exhale. She despised the idea of my trying to control her in any way. I made it clear that I was aware that she had started up again. She had halfheartedly tried to conceal it from me, and then before long, it was every night, out in the open, and with zero remorse. I believe Mom simply felt drinking was her prerogative. If she wanted to get drunk, then she would get drunk, and as long as I was OK or fit her definition of *cared for*, then she saw no downside.

What I felt were the personal consequences of her drinking, consequences that she saw as insignificant. If I got hurt because she said I could be a "bitch" or in a rage that she hated me, she'd dismiss my feelings. Because she knew she loved me, and because she knew I believed she loved me, none of it mattered. She had no idea how deeply her mean comments, whether representing her true feelings or not, cut into my heart.

I was devastated at Mom's inability to stick to the program and her failure to stay clean. I felt angry that she did not keep her promise. Mom, however, never seemed ashamed by her choices—choices that I clearly regarded as displays of weakness. She would never issue forth any apology or justification. She just did what she wanted to do. I'd yell at her when she was drunk and told her I hated her, but she knew I loved her so she let the insults roll off her like water. I never talked to her sober about any of it. Why ruin the moment? We avoided all of it and all the rules of recovery, and I never expressed how deeply pathetic I thought it was that she could not control herself. But I had learned that accusing my mother of being even remotely inept in any way could easily result in disaster. She held a power over me. I mostly kept my mouth shut and instead pouted around her, hoping to give off an air of disappointment.

I felt like I lost my mother every time she drank. I felt completely alone and on edge all the time waiting to see if she had been drinking or was about to drink. I was always afraid of what she'd say when drinking. I was embarrassed by her cursing and flirting with crew members and was grossed out by everything about her attitude and appearance. I lived inside my stress and in a constant state of anticipation of the possible wreckage of the future.

Here, however, I wasn't concerned about her safety. There was nowhere my mother, nor anybody, could really disappear to on this island, so some of my fears dissipated. Unless she went swimming, the risks were fewer here than in a city. Mom didn't even know how to swim, so there was no worry of her going for a midnight dip and drowning. I guess she could have been trampled by the wild horses that roamed the island, or been nibbled on by the rats or the huge stone crabs that had invaded our camp, but this did not concern me. Soon, however, I began to compartmentalize, as I had learned to do years back. I just gave up emotionally. I hated her drinking, but I could not seem to do anything about it, so I buried my head and my anger in the proverbial (and fitting term for island living) sand. Once again, because I was on a movie set, and there was work to do and other people around, this was quite easy to do.

There was a real safety in being on an island that was seven miles long and a mile wide, with no roads or potential vehicle accidents. All this comforted me, but it especially helped that I had my favorite student-teacher and social worker on location with me, and I felt protected watched over by her. Her name was Polly and I requested her every time I got a job. She had been with me on many jobs and I adored being with her. We had the same sense of humor and had an incredible amount of fun together.

Mom must have felt confident knowing that Polly was watching over me, and was emboldened to drink even more. Often, at night, Mom would stay behind in the makeshift bar the crew had put together, and Polly would bring me back to our bure at bedtime. For this movie Polly acted as more of a companion and a caretaker than a teacher because it was summer vacation. She really kept an eye on me, occupied my time—which helped me not obsess about Mom's drinking—and even made sure the director did not try to talk me into doing my own nude scenes behind my mother's back.

Mom had insisted on a body double, and everybody was made aware of this fact. For the full-nudity scenes I would have a double, but for the seminude ones I would be somehow covered. I wore an extremely long wig, made from real hair, and it was long enough to cover my breasts. Even though my boobs were nonexistent, by the age of fifteen I had become self-conscious. The hair was long enough to cover them, but because of the wind, we had to secure the pieces to my skin with toupee tape. I called it tuppy tape, and every day when I took it off I'd stretch each strip as far as it would go. Toupee tape has a fun elasticity, and this activity became a tradition, bordering on an OCD tick for me. I'd have to stretch every strip or I got superstitious. I developed various mini-habits or neatening actions over the years and realize now that they were reactions to the frustrations and helplessness I felt toward Mom's drinking.

After all the controversy surrounding *Pretty Baby*, I am sure that Mom was even more adamant about not having her daughter be nude. Mom loved reiterating this fact to the press. Even though the producers hated the press knowing I had a double, because they said it threatened the integrity of the film, Mom loved telling the world. She felt it proved to people that she had my best interests at heart. I always found it fascinating that a Hollywood producer's idea of "protecting the integrity of a film" involved having a minor do her own nude scenes.

The company had trouble finding a suitable body double, so they ended up using thirty-year-old diver Valerie Taylor, who, with her husband, Ron, was responsible for filming the underwater shots. The couple had filmed all the water scenes for the movie *The Day of the Dolphin* and could hold their breath calmly and for minutes at a time. The first time Valerie dove into the water wearing my long, natural wig, the hair almost instantly matted up in a big mess. She came out of the water with a matted clump of hair worthy of Rastafarian status, and the shot had to be postponed. The wig, which came from England, was quite thick and cost thousands of dollars, and we had only one. Until we found another identical wig from England, we couldn't film any of my scenes. They ended up having to get a synthetic wig for all the underwater shots. Mom loved highlighting how ignorant these people were not to know a natural-hair wig should not get soaked.

As filming continued, Chris and I went through a myriad of phases in our friendship. It began with my resenting the pressure I felt from the director to actually fall in love; then we actually had short crushes on each other; then he annoyed me and I'd not talk to him for a while except on film; then we'd forget all about the fight and act like friends again. Maybe it was love! We were more like siblings, and midway through the filming I remember Chris even moving into our bure.

Mom insinuated that she saw something she thought inappropriate, and thought it best if he stayed closer to us because nobody would mess with him if she were around.

Then I had to face the relationship between the director and *his* tanned, blond boy. I am not saying it was romantic, but the director was seemingly infatuated. The boy was, of course, Chris, and it made me crazy. I was less jealous than I was frustrated by how obviously enamored the director was with this Adonis. I felt constantly disregarded. No matter what I did, or what my mom said to me to make me feel better, I hated it. The attention remained on Chris. Chris would be doing a take and the director would marvel at how extraordinary his talent was.

He'd say, "You, Brooke, you're the pro, but look at him; he's a natural!"

I could feel my jaw clenching and the jealousy mounting. I'd

complain to my mom, saying he was a rookie and thought he knew everything and the director just played into this behavior. She'd tell me to forget it, adding that the director was probably in love with the kid. Mom often made quick judgments about things like this. She would often say somebody was probably jealous of me or that that director "had a thing for" that actor or actress. She wanted to be the one who saw everything and knew everything. She was confident that I would believe her wholeheartedly.

At one point the tension got so bad for me that I began disliking how Chris even held his hands. I became competitive with him. I wanted the director to approve of my work as much if not more than he approved of Chris's. It was obvious that I was not going to succeed in this way. I found little ways to bug him and prove I was better than he was. I'd follow him around on set and sing the lyrics to Super-tramp's "Take the Long Way Home."

"So you think you're a Romeo, playin' a part in a picture show. . . ."

While filming water scenes, I tried to hold my breath longer under-water than he did and find more black coral than he did. I declared that I could drink more kava than he could and crack open a coconut faster. Truth be told, though, he could swim better and climb coconut trees faster than I could. I memorized my lines faster and I would correct him on his own if he messed up. I was basically being a brat. It never got ugly, thank God, and, over time, I got over needing con-stant approval from the director. Our angel cinematographer also no-ticed my needs and chose specific and necessary times to praise me.

Chris and I were never romantic, and because most of the intimate scenes in the film were between Chris and my body double, our rela-tionship stayed platonic. They had to be nude together, but all I had to do was kiss him a few times.

I find it interesting that, once again, I was able to uphold a certain sense of innocence in what had been considered a provocative envir-onment. My mom was with me on the island, but I was older than I was in *Pretty Baby* and I was rather self-assured. People really loved my mother on this movie. She was not viewed as a threat as she had been by Polly Platt, and we were in a very contained space. She may have unsettled Randal by her mere attitude and proximity, but for the most part they all got along. There was a raw quality to this movie. We were all isolated together and in it for the long haul. It was safe and we were all connected and we were a team. Because people genu-inely embraced her, I think she put up fewer defenses. There was something about the Aussies. They just knew how to meet people where they were, without judgment but with humor and a sense of adventure. Because they overlooked Mom's deeper insecurities, they were a perfect group for both of us.

Plus, the Aussies knew how to party, so my mom fit right in. Even

on this location, Mom was able to find ways to keep busy. She'd often try to make calls to the mainland or help organize parties and themed events for the cast and crew.

God knows Mom loved a party and enjoyed being a part of any event where drinking was practically a prerequisite. A few times she took a seaplane to the mainland and delivered mail or brought back film, magazines, and even pizzas. Although the pizza delivery came to a quick halt when we turned over a slice only to find rat droppings embedded in the dough!

By this time Mom was drinking as if she had never stopped. It was like it had all been a dream. It was such a shame, but there was so much alcohol at base camp and around this crew that it was evidently just irresistible to her. Excessive consumption was not out of the norm for this lot, and it was very accepted. It's amazing I never started then. I hated that Mom got drunk with the crew as much as she did, and I could not believe that after all the angst we went through for her treatment, it felt as if nothing had changed. Mom had started back up again as easily as she had gotten into that car on the curb waiting to take her to the airport to go to a facility. I tried to just remove myself emotionally and, when I could, physically.

But by the end of August, I had hit a limit with island life. As much as I had submersed myself in that sandy oasis, I was ready to go home. Mom was equally ready to leave. She never went in the sun and I don't remember her ever even going in the water. We were both ready for some of the tastes and comforts of home. We had become an incredibly tight-knit team, who experienced and suffered a great deal with one another, but I was homesick for New York. Shooting this movie had had an impact on all of us based purely on the long hours and sometimes intensely tough weather and living conditions, and we were all exhausted. We had lived through sicknesses, injuries, breakups, and even deaths of loved ones during filming. I still have scars lining my Achilles tendon from cuts that had ulcerated from swimming in water near a coral reef. It had been an intense, wonderful, and sometimes surreal experience, but it eventually got to all of us. Being away from home and from modern conveniences took its own toll, and we all needed an extended break from the island and from each other.

The first time I actually wrapped production, we were all packed and had taken off for and landed on the mainland of Suva. Mom and I went to a hotel to rest and wait the five hours necessary before catching our flight back to the States. After about an hour, we were contacted at the hotel and informed that some of the film had been damaged, and I was needed for an additional two weeks of filming. My heart sank. I cried when I realized I had to wait two more weeks before returning home. Cutting my hair all off would have had no impact on this movie because I wore a wig, so I felt even more helpless.

I'll never forget the real last day, when we were finally able to leave.

We were doing one last scene on the beach. Before it was over, the seaplane arrived. It coasted to the dock and waited. I remember looking at it and thinking that no matter what happens, the moment I start walking on that dock, I am not stopping. I told Mom I didn't care if the film blew up; I was going home. She concurred.

There was a part of me that also did not ever want to leave Nanuya Levu. Not because it had been paradise, but because on this island it felt easier to keep my mother alive. Losing Mom was a constant fear of mine, but these four months the panic surrounding her possible death had waned slightly.

We took off for the mainland, and as I saw our island getting smaller and smaller, my mind wandered to the impending future of my mom's drinking. Dread began creeping back into my stomach. Without the containment of the island and the protection of the crew, I would be alone with her alcoholism yet again. Mom and I had been in somewhat of an unrealistic bubble in the middle of nowhere, but once back in New York City she would be on the loose again. I would no longer easily know her whereabouts. The island and the crew and the tough schedule had provided me with a huge safety net, but now that this protective zone was receding, my heart began to grow heavy. Before long, I would be resuming my hypervigilance. Intervention and rehab had been a mere apparition. I was going back to square one in the battle to survive my mother's disease.

We got to the mainland and would have to wait for the 2:00 A.M. connecting flight. We would have dinner at the hotel plus a few hours of rest. Then we'd fly back to the United States and it would begin to feel like it had all been a dream.

The Blue Lagoon had a huge premiere a year later, in June 1980, at the famous Cinerama Dome in Los Angeles. It was my first time at this theatre and it was quite exciting. The building seemed immense and

I was blinded with light and by the sight of Chris's and my face covering the entire side of the building. There was excitement and anticipation in the air. My stepsister, Diana, came out to be with me for the press junket and kept me laughing the entire time. This was something that Mom had negotiated into my contract. This was unprecedented—getting the studio to pay for a companion for me during a junket. But it kept me contented, so they couldn't fight it. It was good for everyone.

Mom even had a friend flown in to the island to visit. I'm not sure if the studio paid for the ticket but she always negotiated multiple tickets so I could have a friend or Diana come to visit. Mom felt it important for me not to feel lonely or stressed by the press, who as we knew could be unkind. I needed a partner in crime. This was an unheard-of request, but I had no agents or publicists for the studio to pay for, so Mom could justify the expense. According to her, they were getting off easy. My mother and Diana were my entire entourage. Diana understood Mom's battle with booze and she also loved and laughed with my mom. She was on our side.

I was so happy to have Diana there. Press junkets are pure torture. You go to a hotel and whole floors are invaded and occupied by different press outlets. The actors and director trade off from room to room and do back-to-back interviews of about five to seven minutes each. You could do forty-two interviews before lunch. It's mind-numbing because of the repetition. I kept getting questions like "What was it like living on an island?" and "Were you and Chris Atkins really in love?" and "Did you do your own nudity?"

I could answer these questions in my sleep. In fact, Mom, Diana, and I had a running joke about how a journalist would not even have to ask one question and I could give them a complete interview. After surviving *Pretty Baby*'s press tour, I was a pro on nudity and romance and the rigor of filmmaking.

It got to the point that I started answering the questions before the journalist even finished the question. Finally my mom, who would watch my interviews, took me aside and reminded me to allow the interviewer to get the question out. We had a big laugh about that. On our lunch break in the hotel room, I posed as a journalist and Diana pretended to be me answering the questions. We thought it was hysterical. Chris played along, and he and Randal did their own version. We made an otherwise tedious necessity fun and silly.

We kept things interesting in other ways. Randal would quietly sing the words to the Robbie Dupree song "Steal Away" under his breath as we passed in the hallways on the way to the next "firing squad," as I nicknamed the press. We were all so bored and tired and all wished we could just run out the door and escape. Having the spurts of laughter and my stepsister and mother doing whatever they could to keep me laughing made it all more enjoyable and helped me maintain perspective. I was also excited because Mom promised that once I had finished my obligations, I could go shopping. Mom would let me loose in the store and Diana and I would spend all my per diem. The combination of this, good restaurants, and hanging out wearing our hotel robes was enough to sustain me.

All I kept thinking during these press days was that the journalists were all going to slaughter me in this movie. It just seemed to me that after *Pretty Baby*, it was decided that I was worthy of attack. Mom would not be able to shield me as entirely as she had from the negativity of *Pretty Baby*, but at least that had been a European director and an incredible cast.

This was a cast of two, and I carried most of the burden of ensuring its success. I suppose I was more equipped to handle it by then, but I was slightly apprehensive. I knew enough by this point to be concerned but realized there was nothing I could do.

The movie made a huge splash and was a box-office hit, ultimately the ninth-highest-grossing film of 1980. The studio was over the moon, and I was once again a commodity they coveted. But strangely,

I never paid much attention to how my movies did. In my mind, they were done, and I was thinking about my next job. If I had enjoyed making the movie, then it was a success in my eyes.

I'm also glad that I was unaware of the true power of ticket sales. I didn't pore over the reviews this time, either, and because I sort of couldn't be bothered, I remained somewhat protected from any negativity. There were mixed reviews for *The Blue Lagoon*, and Mom did not hide them from me as actively as she had with *Pretty Baby*. I also didn't really ask to read them. I simply wanted to move on. I had done the movie and it was over. A year had passed. I was attending a new school and had basically moved past the experience. Plus, I did not want to hear bad critiques; I knew they would attack me and I knew my feelings would get hurt. For whatever reason, I subconsciously knew that it was probably healthier for me to be somewhat separated from the reviews.

Thinking about it now, though, I am a bit conflicted about the fact that I did not read reviews. Perhaps if I had read the reviews, I may have chosen to steer my career differently. Perhaps I could have made better choices or might have given it all up entirely. I will never know.

Once the press junket was over and we were back in New York for good, Mom and I fell into our familiar pattern. We kept busy: I studied, she drank, we went to the movies, she drank, I navigated her moods, and she drank.

I had hoped that a fresh start and a successful film would make everything easier. But the more in demand I became, the more complicated everything got. My mother reacted to the press by defending herself to journalists like Barbara Walters or by choosing to give random interviews to the press. Normally you don't see the talent's manager on TV, but she was my mom and the world ate it up. She wanted to prove she was still protecting me and that she was guiding my career in the best way possible. She loved that she was known as Brooke Shields's mother. It gave her a deep and personal validation.

We were making it in the world. I think a part of Mom loved all of the attention because it was shared with me but was sadly often not articulate enough to get her point across the way she hoped.

She was trying to keep us talked-about and to make sure I was adored. She wanted to secure enough money to ensure us a substantial and comfortable future—something she never had as a kid. Mom wanted to make the best lives she could for us. Whatever choices my mother made, positive or negative, they were what they were. She believed she was acting in my best interest always. And the cathexis I experienced rendered me immobile. It was so acute that I never questioned her judgment. Mom and I were symbiotically enmeshed and it would be years before I was able to see us as separate people.

My codependence was easily perpetuated because it felt familiar and I believed my mother knew the right way about everything. I was never given the space or the opportunity to make my own choices. I simply followed what she said and tried not to rock the boat. My priority was keeping my mother alive and that meant never leaving her. I believe I was primarily trying to protect my mother from herself and keep her from her own demise. It was an enormous distraction. I didn't have the time to focus on reviews, the trajectory of my career, boyfriends, or much else. Dating seemed almost silly. Plus, boys rarely asked me out because I was famous, and even though I was mature for my age, I was hardly experienced. I really only concerned myself with my studies and with my mother's well-being. I believed my mother held the key to my security in the world and my ticket to the future.

The main problem, though—aside from alcohol—was that Mom had no system of operations. She had no long-term plan except to gain financial security and keep my name out there. Her unconventional and often maddening approach to managing me solidified her lack of popularity within the entertainment business. She did not, however, seem to care or feel the need to adjust or justify her behavior. She also showed no signs of intending to ever ask for professional help. According to her, the system worked, and I lovingly agreed.

The Blue Lagoon remains the most successful movie I have ever made and the film with which I am the most identified. I'm serious when I say that a week rarely goes by in which *somebody* doesn't mention this movie to me. Generations have passed, and now those who watched the movie as teenagers are playing it for their children. For many it was their introduction to sex. Today, sex is introduced in a much more provocative and graphic way. Comparatively, *The Blue Lagoon* is mild. I still probably won't let my girls watch it. Too weird.

Chapter Nine

The Brooke Doll

Soon after I shot *The Blue Lagoon*, Mom bought a huge Tudor-style house in Englewood, New Jersey, right over the George Washington Bridge. The week before we moved into the house it was broken into and robbed. We suspected the interest in the stolen items stemmed from my being a recognizable name and the attention our move had gotten within the town. But *The Blue Lagoon* had not even been released yet and I was hardly famous in comparison to what I would soon become. Whatever the reason, a bunch of kids, conveniently led by the daughter of a local policeman, broke into the huge house and were caught walking out with rugs and other items.

The next day, Mom put the house back on the market, and since school had already started, we had little time to look for and move into a new home. I began an uncommon reverse commute from our New York City apartment to my new high school campus. Mom still had our black Jeep Renegade, and I loved the ride in the mornings, going against commuter traffic as the sun was rising.

Mom kept up the search and eventually found another big Tudor-style home in a town called Haworth.

When we permanently left the apartment on Seventy-Third Street after almost fifteen years of living there, I wasn't sure whether I felt excited or apprehensive. It was probably a combination of both. I did love new starts and experiencing new lifestyles. But in the past, I had always been able to return to Manhattan. The drive to Haworth was only about forty-five minutes from the city, but it might as well have been a different country. I was not a Jersey girl. I was a native New Yorker through and through, and I felt my mom was the same. I knew that Mom always maintained her bond with New Jersey, but Newark was a far cry from the suburban town of Haworth and could not have been expected to quell her melancholy for her "homeland."

I began attending the Dwight-Englewood School in 1979. It was a shock to my system. Not only was I a new kid from Manhattan in a new high school in New Jersey, but I was also suddenly taking classes with kids who had actually seen some of my movies. This was really the first time I was around peers who were aware of my celebrity. They were old enough to see movies like *Tilt* or *Just You and Me, Kid* and were very conscious of my fame.

To their credit, they were never unkind. I am sure that the school somehow made them aware that they should treat me just like a regular kid. It was a bit disconcerting, I'm sure, having a celebrity in your ninth-grade math class, but the kids seemed to be respectful of my space. They did so almost to a fault, however, because I ended up feeling set apart and lonesome. They were not being standoffish as much as reserved and slightly intimidated. Most of these kids had gone to the same grade school together and had become a tight-knit group that would take time to penetrate. The transition for me was going to require some effort.

My first term was pretty miserable and I was overwhelmed. The workload was unlike anything I had ever experienced. I had never seen so much homework and I had zero experience in navigating such a tough class schedule. Just navigating the vast campus to get to my classes on my own created a challenge. My grades were not great,

I was living in isolated New Jersey, and I practically had no friends. I didn't mind the lack of friends, quite honestly, because I was fraught, awkward, and uncomfortable, and I wanted to hide. I dreaded getting out of the car each morning. Whenever I got the chance, I'd cry to my mother from the pay phone outside the science building. Mom kept reassuring me that it would all get better and that I had to just stick to it. She guaranteed me that I would soon make friends. I just had to keep holding my head up high.

My mom and I were getting along fine, and although I was concerned about her drinking, I was more concerned about her driving while drunk. We did not drive a lot in New York City, so it had never really been an issue, but now we were in need of a car for everything, and that created a new set of potential problems. For now, however, I had little time to dwell on her as much because I had to focus on getting my high school experience under control. How could I become integrated into this new school? How could I make friends?

Mom decided that I should invite my class to some party to help break the ice. There used to be a restaurant/club called Wednesdays in midtown that turned into a roller-skating rink one night a week. The owners offered to throw me a roller-skating Halloween party. All I had to do was take some photos and be seen enjoying the club. Mom told the owner that my entire class must be invited.

I sent out invitations and was terrified nobody would come. But as I was taking pictures for a few photographers, I saw a group of kids I recognized walk through the door. Soon the whole class was there and we were all dressed in Halloween costumes, rolling around to the music. It was so much fun and it turned out to be a perfect icebreaker. I worried at first that maybe it felt like bribery and that I was buying the friendships. But it ended up being the social event that would show my peers that although I had lived an unusual life, I was, in fact, just a regular kid.

The best part about the whole thing was that the kids did not expect me to keep having parties and inviting them. They saw it as a bit of a job for me because I had to take photos with people and do interviews, and they realized that the party was in a way more for them and was in no way me showing off. From that night on, kids started slowly including me more and inviting me to study together or have sleepovers. I began to make friends all across the board. My closest friends were Lisa, Missy, Diane, and Gigi. All five of us remain friends to this day.

I tried to include my friends in my life whenever I could at photo shoots or events. Mom always made sure at least one of them accompanied me. When I worked with famous photographers like Francesco Scavullo or Bruce Weber, Mom always asked them to take a group shot of my friends and me. They always obliged, and my friends now have some pictures of themselves taken by some of the giants in art photography.

Mom loved joining my two worlds together. This was something I have never forgotten and have always appreciated. I kept inviting friends to events and parties. The events were actually work for me, so having a friend from my real life share it eased the burden. I also lived vicariously through their obvious enjoyment of the experiences. It was never the whole class again, but my close group of friends would get put on the list at places like the Red Parrot, Xenon, and sometimes Studio 54. Studio 54 was always easier to go to with just my mom because of the way the VIP area was set up. (How about that for a sentence? Ah, I was just a normal kid!)

By the time *The Blue Lagoon* was released and I had been labeled "The '80s Look" by *Time* magazine, I was already completely accepted by my new friends and they were unfazed by it all. High school can be a rough time for kids. Being a famous kid was not without its unique burdens, but I have always been thankful that my mom consistently forced us all to be accepting of the differences and not let my celebrity create a barrier. It was not easy, but she would not have it any other way. The press never gave Mom any recognition for this unique approach at all.

It was strange, too, that on the one hand Mom fought for my integration with kids my own age, yet on the other, she craved for me to become singled out and put on a pedestal by the world. This was a true contradiction—and some could say hypocritical—but it was the Teri way. I believe I managed to better regard my more grounded personal life because it was there that I felt unconditionally accepted. My mother constantly reinforced the importance of my life outside of work.

But the pressure was mounting in our public lives. During this time period, especially after *The Blue Lagoon* was such a hit, my professional life grew exponentially. It was all getting bigger and busier in many ways. Fans were now becoming a constant part of my life.

When it came to fan mail, Mom was incredibly diligent. I signed every autograph and honored every photo request, and Mom began by mailing each one out personally. It was getting to be too much, though, and we decided we needed help. My godmother, Auntie Lila, was working with us, and we had formed a corporation and named it Brooke Shields and Co. The "Co." soon grew to an office with two other women as staff members. One lady dealt with business requests and mail and the other with schedules. Mom soon hired another woman, who handled accounting and financial transactions. We had a handyman to help with the house and the office maintenance. We had lawyers, a money manager, a cleaning lady three days a week, and a part-time driver named Dick. We even hired a student to read through and categorize the letters.

There were the photo requests, people asking for advice, posters to be signed, as well as letters from "The Crazies." These were fans that raised a certain level of concern. They were basically stalkers who we

handled differently than the honest fan who just wanted an autograph to add to a collection. These letters were separated out and sent
on to Gavin de Becker, a security expert we'd also hired, to be filed.
The individuals were placed on a watch list. Mom did not want me to
see these letters. Although I knew the people existed, I had no interest
in reading the contents of their correspondence because I would only
get scared for my life.

Once the piles of letters were made, I would sit for blocks of time
and hammer out all the signatures. Mom said that every correspondence meant another loyal fan. In press lines or at appearances I signed
every single fan's outstretched piece of paper or photo. She said they
were all individuals and I must not alienate them. I posed for every
paparazzo. I even signed the index cards from the "pros." The pros
are the ones who ask for a nonpersonalized autograph, which they
then sell. I was always the last to leave an event because Mom wanted
me to personally engage with every single person taking pictures or
asking for a poster to be signed. I admired her care for people's feelings, and because I also collected autographs myself, I understood
how it felt to get passed over or denied. However, it was exhausting,
and I do admit part of me wanted to avoid all of it.

Earlier on in my career, my mom and I had bought tickets to see
the Academy Awards. Actors, celebrities, and presenters in the orchestra are invited, but there are additional seats, up in the mezzanine, that are open to the public for purchase. Mom and I were in
California for some reason and, after years of watching the award
show together on TV, had decided it would be exciting to attend in
person.

We were seated way up high in the top balcony and I spotted Paul
Newman. I jumped out of my seat and ran all the way down to the
middle orchestra to ask Paul Newman for his autograph. He graciously declined, explaining that if he signed one for me, it would
start a chain reaction and he would then have to sign everybody else's

program. I was slightly hurt but remained what I thought was polite, and I said, "Oh, OK, then could you just wave up to my mom?"

He obliged and turned back up toward the balcony. He did a sweeping wave in the general direction of the mezzanine and had no idea whom he was addressing. It was very sweet but awkward, because when my mom saw to whom I was gesturing, she immediately ducked behind a seat. I think that she was actually embarrassed by the fact that I had asked him to wave to her, so she hid. She weirdly did not want to have the attention shifted to her. I thanked Mr. Newman and returned to the balcony.

Even though I remember being a bit sad he did not sign my book, I would fully appreciate the situation years later when I was forced to respond the same way to a fan. All it takes is one person at a restaurant or any crowded area and you could literally be signing autographs for an hour.

The funny part to the whole story was that years later, when I was invited to be a presenter at the Academy Awards, I still brought my autograph book. After the broadcast, the presenters and winners and Academy members were all seated on the stage to take a huge cast photo. I was in the middle, a bit to the right, and I spotted Paul Newman a few rows down. I passed my book and a pen down to him and asked for his autograph. I guess he knew that I'd be the only one in that crowd who would ask, and he kindly obliged. I was thrilled. I thanked him and chose not to try to remind him of my previous disappointment.

Mom made me so conscious of my fans that I began dreading being anywhere. There seemed to be no boundaries. I understood Mom's philosophy, but the sense of obligation and the fear of losing a fan's devotion were often too much for me to take. I could never say no.

Mom would not let me be disturbed when I ate, however, and would instead explain that I would take the photo or sign the autograph as soon as the meal was over. She explained to me that if they really wanted to, they would wait. She hated when people would say they were leaving—could I just sign it now?

She'd respond, "Well, I hope you enjoyed your meal, because she is not yet finished with hers. She will be happy to sign for you after she's done."

Sometimes the people would wait and sometimes they left disappointed. I felt tortured and unable to enjoy the meal knowing people were wishing I'd hurry, and when those impatient people left, I felt hurt that I wasn't worth the wait. Mom would joke that they were not my "biggest fans" after all. I know she was trying to make things easier, but the end result was that I could never relax.

Because of her hypervigilance toward my public, I felt as if the world owned me. It was the feeling that everybody wanted to take a piece.

I was offered *Endless Love*, and even though it was yet again another loss-of-innocence love story, the promise of working with Italian director Franco Zeffirelli made the project much more appealing. I had seen his film version of *Romeo and Juliet* and thought it was heartbreaking and beautiful. I had not worked with such an artist since Louis Malle. My mother and I both felt that this was going to be an important movie.

The story comes from a novel by Scott Spencer. Two teenagers, David and Jade, have an intensely romantic relationship as high school students. When Jade's grades suffer, her parents force the two of them to break up, resulting in David's breakdown, a criminal act, and much drama on both sides. The film shot in New York and on Long Island in the fall of 1980.

I am proud of my work in this film and attribute it all to Franco. He was tough, dramatic, and often insulting or drunk, but he expected your best and would not stop until he got it. He often made fun of my voice and sometimes made me cry by picking on me. But I felt he actually believed I had talent and could be better. In one scene without dialogue Franco wanted to see a certain expression on my face as I looked through a window at my scorned boyfriend. He wanted me to show love and longing and sadness, and so he told me to hum the theme song to *Romeo and Juliet* in my head while looking out. In doing this, I forgot about my face and did not try to project the emotion with an expression. I thought it was a brilliant trick and it helped me understand how much you can do by not trying too hard.

The actors in the film were all rather serious, accomplished actors with the exception of Martin Hewitt, who played David. Don Murray played my dad. I had seen him in *Bus Stop* with Marilyn Monroe. Shirley Knight played my mom and James Spader played my protective brother. They were all generous actors and I felt honestly supported. I'm not sure I took my job as seriously as they did, but I was very professional and learned from them about acting. Martin and I got along well and enjoyed working with one another.

We neither fell in love nor hated each other, and Franco did not force the issue. After experiencing such pressure during *The Blue Lagoon* to be in love, this opposite approach came as a relief. All we were required to do was *convince* people we were in love. This approach freed us both up to become actual friends. There were nude scenes, so just as on *The Blue Lagoon* I had a body double. Once again the heavier love scenes in the film were shot primarily between Martin and my double. This, too, helped keep our friendship intact.

Mom did not have to protect Martin in the same way that she felt she needed to protect Chris, but she made sure that Franco knew she was a person with whom to reckon, should a line be crossed.

I would like to add only one unfortunate truth: Both Chris Atkins and Martin Hewitt, my costar in *Endless Love*, hit career heights very quickly but would forever struggle as actors. Chris went on to develop a severe alcohol problem, and both of their careers took unexpected turns. It is harder, I believe, to become a "star" after your first movie, especially at an age when you are on the cusp of making one of your first monumental life choices. For instance, by the time the film was released, Chris had deferred college, put his sports-medicine degree on indefinite hold, and had bought a red Ferrari. Later, a manager screwed him out of most of his money.

Both these men have recovered and have matured into wonderful and kind people. Chris has never lost his sweetness and openness. I have yet to witness any underlying anger. Martin maintains a chip on his shoulder in my opinion but was always a sensitive young man and fine actor. For me, even though I achieved fame at a younger age, I was guarded by my mother and allowed to face celebrity in a surprisingly nurturing environment. Even if my talent may not have been protected, I somehow was. Mom's drinking was way more damaging to me than fame.

Her protection didn't stop with me. She insisted on trying to protect my costars whenever she could. She looked out for young Tom Cruise, who had been hand-chosen by Franco to play a bare-chested boy with a short but memorable scene shot in Central Park.

Years later Tom would recall how kind my mother had been to him during the shoot. We were sitting alone in my living room in LA, and Tom had come to personally apologize to me for attacking me on the *Today Show* for my use of antidepressants to treat postpartum depression. He said my mom had made it a point to look after him on the set of *Endless Love* and he'd "never forgotten it." Even though Tom only appeared in one scene, he said he was surprised by Mom's kindness toward him and always remembered it. Tom apologized to my mother as well, saying that he did not know why he chose to attack me "of all people." He added that he basically felt cornered and I was the "scapegoat."

Mom and Franco were both big, drinking, theatrical personalities who liked being dramatic and in control. He would tease her and give her a hard time about staying out of his way, and she would challenge him perpetually but never overtly interfere. They were like two proud peacocks splaying their colorful tails and puffing out their chests. Each of them owned part of the film; my mother possessed me, and Franco controlled all the rest. Both sides were needed for the film to be made. I believe she once again felt I was in good hands by working with a European filmmaker.

I clearly remember how mad and upset I was when, three months after wrapping this film, we were called back to reshoot the ending. It hadn't been emotional enough and Franco wanted more. The ending was kept the same, but Franco wanted a more powerful, more emotional breakdown by my character. In a conflicted, angst-ridden final scene, the two lovers heartbreakingly say good-bye. Franco wanted to show the buildup of pain, irreparable loss, and sadness that the arbitrary separation of these two lovers had generated.

Somehow, Franco got me to connect to the character and really cry. There was a famous story that the press picked up where he said he pinched my toe in order to get me to express ecstasy, but that was not true. It was actually in this scene that I remember him pinching me, and it was because he wanted me to connect with pain as well as sadness. It didn't hurt, but I got the message. It remains one of the best scenes I have ever done on film. I was raw and honest and tired and I was directed.

It was during my high school years that Mom decided she wanted to get her eyes done. She consulted with Dr. Sherrell Aston about an eye lift. Her top lids were drooping slightly, and her theory was that if you got such work done in your earlier years, it was less obvious. Your skin had more elasticity and therefore healed better. The doctor agreed but suggested that she also get a slight face-lift. Mom agreed but said that, so help her God, if she came out of surgery with her bottom lids looking pulled down she would "break every bone in his hands."

She made him swear he would not give her bug eyes and that her lids, when closed, would completely meet in a clean line. He assured her she could wear makeup in a week.

"Yeah, if you want to look like a friggin' *clown*," she said. "Forget makeup—just make sure my eyes close or I'll come after you!"

Even though she was joking (sort of), Mom was scared about her eyes being too taut and skeleton-like. She had seen some actress or news anchor whose bottom lids looked as if they were being pulled down by invisible strings with tiny lead weights at the ends. Mom was terrified of a similar result. She had always been savvy about plastic surgery—she could pick out a nose job from miles away and could often even name the doctor whose work it had been.

Well, anyway, she got the surgery. Afterward she developed some kind of infection that traveled down her neck and she had to stay in the hospital for a few extra days.

One of the horrible nurses tried to get Mom to give her a tip when her shift was over. The woman began rummaging through Mom's closet for her purse to get her money and to get her own tip. I guess Mom was getting scared and upset and obviously, because of medication, did not have her wits about her. She called me in New Jersey sounding upset and a bit panicked. The large Jamaican woman spoke little English but seemed to be raising her voice, trying to get my mother to understand that she had to leave and wanted a tip.

Mom put me on the phone with this crazy nurse and I threatened to get her fired if she did not leave my mother's room that instant. I called our part-time driver to take me into the city to settle everything. I had my license but did not feel comfortable driving into Manhattan. By the time I got there the woman was gone (angry and without a tip) and Mom was doped up and chatty but more relaxed. I made arrangements for a different nurse and remained near Mom while I completed my homework. I kept my schoolbooks with me at all times because I never knew when I might be called to work or find I had some spare time to study. Mom had a small drainage tube coming from an insertion in her neck and connected to a little plastic bag. It was meant to drain the fluid from the infection. Mom called it her "purse." Every now and then she would loudly say, "I should have given her this purse and told her to fuck off!" She was obviously uncomfortable and in pain, but I was sure glad she still had her humor.

However, I was trying to do my French homework, and she would not shut up about any of it. I could not really follow all her jabbering and really needed to get my work done. I patiently suggested she shut her eyes for a bit and take a nap. I would be right there by the window and would not leave without telling her. She quieted a bit and I began, once again, to study. At one point I glanced up at her and was shocked that even though she had stopped babbling, she was sneakily peeking out at me! I couldn't believe that she could not resist spying on me. Did she not trust me to stay?

I jumped up, went to her bed frustrated, and said, "Mom! I'm right here; I'm not leaving, close your eyes and rest!"

Well, she had actually been asleep, and after being startled awake, she growled, "They arrrrrre cloooosed!"

Oh boy, I thought. Her eyes were swollen and could not yet close all the way, and it looked as if she was squinting through them. I prayed for the doctor's sake for that to be the actual truth. I apologized for waking her, told her she was fine, and got her to settle again. But it was a laugh we had for years to come. It was always laughter that maintained our deep bond. It was the truth in our connection. The sound of Mom's sober laughter was like music and medicine to me.

While she was in the hospital recovering, it was one of the best times for me. My aunt Lila was living with us in the house in Haworth, so I was not alone, but this was the first time since Mom went to rehab that I could be calm knowing she was alive and not drinking. I could relax. I had peace of mind and a regular schedule.

It was around my sophomore year in high school that I was approached to do the infamous Calvin Klein commercials. Mom and I knew Richard Avedon and his creative team, and she was friends with Carl Rosen, who ran Calvin. We were going to do a series of commercials all playing on the word *Calvin* or on famous sayings or songs and their connection to the concept of genes and jeans. There was a great deal of excitement surrounding the whole campaign. No one had ever attempted this approach in advertising. It was also groundbreaking to have still photographers directing the actual TV commercials.

We were also going to be the first brand to advertise in movie theatres before the coming attractions. We filmed a minute-long uncut shot of me describing Darwin's survival-of-the-fittest law while undoing my hair and loosening my blouse. I memorized the minute-long definition of genes and the concept of natural selection. The funny thing is that the idea that the commercial would show in movie theatres was rejected because the agency said, "The day will never come when brands will be allowed to advertise in movie theatres." The spots were run only on TV instead. Today you can go to a showing of a movie twenty minutes after the scheduled time, because of how long the advertising spots are before the show.

For a different spot, I was supposed to laugh hysterically and try to get across some messaging. I was so nervous that I would sound fake and that I would not be able to actually crack up on camera. Crying felt easier than laughing to me and I was extremely stressed about it. The sound department gave me a set of earphones and they had prepared a bunch of jokes to tell me to get me to laugh.

The jokes were not really that funny and it wasn't working. But then, all of a sudden, I heard my stepsister Diana's voice in the ear-phones. She was recounting some of our favorite inside jokes. I couldn't believe my ears and was so happy she was there, and I got a case of the giggles. It was a "cut and print," and Mom was thanked for her innovative surprise.

We filmed many different spots for this campaign and they were all unique and fun and amazingly clever. They all had smart histor-ical, sociological, political, and biological references. The only one, however, that will forever haunt us, was one in which a colloquial phrase was grossly taken out of context.

Now, in hindsight, it is possible that somebody in the writers' room had an inkling that there might be different ways the statement could be interpreted, but I maintain that I was never aware of the double entendre. It would hurt me to think that the creative team was trying to exploit my innocence, and I uphold the belief that their in-tention was not as crude and juvenile as was the interpretation. I am, of course, speaking about the famous "Nothing comes between me and my Calvins" line.

I think there are a number of misunderstandings about this. First of all, the actual line involved a rhetorical question, not a statement about ejaculation. The line actually was: "Do you want to know what comes between me and my Calvins? Nothing."

The second misunderstanding is about the tone and meaning. In no way did I think I was saying something controversial or sexual. This was just another spot in which I was affirming how much I loved my blue jeans. I had used a similar expression often, and it had al-ways been meant as a declaration of my love for something: "Nothing comes between me and my mom." "Nothing comes between me and by favorite doll, Blabby."

It never occurred to me it could mean that I wasn't wearing under-wear. Or that the spelling of the word *come* was really meant to be *cum*. I swear I don't believe my mother read into it that way, either.

We just thought of it as another well-conceived commercial. We filmed a number of spots in all and didn't think about it again.

But when the spots began to air, they were incredibly popular and controversial. My mother and I had been away in Europe, where I was working for *Harper's Bazaar Italia* shooting the collection, and returned to an onslaught of media attention. The commercial was pulled from the air and I was ambushed by questions as to the "true meaning" of my words. It was ridiculous and insane. Mom was attacked for allowing me to verbalize such smut, and I was once again perceived as both a Lolita and an abused daughter.

We laughed it off at first, but the controversy continued. At times I felt compelled to try to explain, but this proved useless. The press wanted to hear what they wanted to hear. Just as they had after *Pretty Baby* and *The Blue Lagoon*, they wanted to assail my mother and me with criticism and judgment. This one incorrectly quoted line would usurp all positive attention surrounding this innovative, landmark ad campaign.

Nobody talked about how brilliantly the references to history, literature, music, religion, and science had played into advertising blue jeans. Nobody commented on how I had memorized a minute-long monologue and what a brilliant play on words "survival of the fittest" actually was. (Although I would go on to get an A on a pop quiz in school because I wrote out a very in-depth answer to the question "What are genes?" So I guess all wasn't lost.)

This proved to be yet another example of the press preferring a sordid story to a creative one. I was not immune to criticism, but I was getting familiar with a certain amount of controversy surrounding almost everything I did.

Mom capped it all off once again with her "Fuck 'em" attitude. "You know what you meant. Are you proud of the commercials?"

"Yes."

"So fuck 'em."

And that was usually Mom's attitude about these types of things. I don't know if she was actually hurt, angry, or regretful, but if she was, she'd never let me know.

I am not sure if my mom knew how conflicting the images of me she was projecting were. When I was young I was looked at as a provocative young woman, yet I became the virginal "America's sweetheart." I went from doing movies like *Pretty Baby* and *Endless Love* to working with George Burns and Bob Hope and having a doll made in my likeness.

The body of the doll actually had to be altered to honestly represent my flatter chest. Most dolls by the same company take their template body and just change the heads. My mom contractually made the factory create a new mold of the body with a smaller chest. The fifties' big pointy boobs did not represent a teenager. Mom insisted.

This was all very weird for me. Not only is it strange to have a doll made of you, but to then also have it be publicly known that the boobs had been shaved off did not make me any more comfortable in high school. To be called a beautiful doll was too outrageous for me to bear, but it was fun to help design her fashionable leggings and long sweaters, as well as her prom dress, which was a copy of a McCall's pattern I had modeled and Lisa and I both actually wore to our junior prom.

Mom even had the Brooke Shields Glamour Center (a head with hair you could style) sent back to the factory three times because the cleft in the chin was not right.

All the while, I was being photographed looking much older on the covers of major fashion magazines and doing ads like the controversial Calvin commercials. There were such polarized views of me concurrently being disseminated that it is no wonder I wasn't the only one confused.

During this time period I began to more frequently get invited to and attend parties at Manhattan clubs. Excursions to Studio 54 were always connected to some event. It might have been a Warhol party, a Calvin Klein launch, or a film premiere. I had been on the cover of *Interview* magazine and had become friendly with Andy. I would always go at the beginning of the night and the event. The paparazzi would line up outside on either side of the infamous red rope, and the crowds waited to be selected for entry.

My mother would get so mad at me because I never wanted to get out of the car and go in first. When we arrived at the club, I always cringed inside once I saw the mob. I'd wade through the throngs of people to reach the rope, which would suddenly be dramatically lifted, like a magician pulling off a cape to reveal the rabbit in the hat. I would apologize to those waiting as I was ushered ahead of them. The flashes blinding me helped mask the looks of rejection from the crowd.

Even though I loathed the feeling of waltzing right past everyone, once inside I could fully relax. Even today I can easily picture the long corridor that led into the club, with dark red carpet stretching the distance and red-painted walls. There was always a moment after the mayhem of the outside, when the doors closed behind you and you were temporarily free from photographers, fans, and disgruntled, rejected, and desperate people. When all you'd hear was the faint thump of the music and the promise of a good time. You'd get a feeling in your stomach, like right before a roller coaster takes its stomach-flipping descent.

I would quicken my pace a bit in anticipation of going through the main door. I was probably going to see famous people and I was going to hear all my favorite songs. Even though I was a celebrity myself at this time, I was always a bit starstruck by the people I'd see inside. There was always somebody famous to say hello to and take some photos with. Whether it was Calvin Klein, Diane von Furstenberg,

Bianca Jagger, Cornelia Guest, or Debbie Harry, Steve Rubell corralled them all and took very good care of us.

I must admit, I had no issue with special treatment once inside the club. Sitting inside the club was always easier than getting in because people were busy dancing and having fun and were not focused only on people coming in. On any given night it was dark enough to feel anonymous, and there was a roped-off VIP area I could use. There was always some group laughing and drinking on couches placed a bit higher than all the other seating areas. I was relieved to be seated there, not because I felt superior, but because I felt protected from drunk, intrusive, and usually stoned clubbers.

I would usually sit to take a few photos with people in this area and then it was all about the music for me. Mom rarely danced but stayed with our stuff and drank and chatted. Once it was time to dance, my heart would actually pound a bit faster and I'd look to my mom with an excited expression. She was happy. I would immediately ask my mom if I could go dance. All I wanted to do was dance, and I would dance with anybody who would dance with me. People hardly ever interrupted me when I was dancing.

I don't remember much of Mom at Studio 54 since I hardly ever sat with her for any length of time. The minute I'd get permission, I'd be gone. I would basically stay on the dance floor, dancing and sweating the entire time. I felt freedom and anonymity amid the throngs of dancers. I always found a good gay dancer to be my partner and I would not stop dancing until I heard two songs in a row that I did not like.

Mom never posed for any of the photos. I assume she knew either she'd be cut out or I'd run the risk of not making it to Page Six in the *Post* the next day if pictured only with her instead of being flanked by famous people.

I always loved it when Andy Warhol was there because he was incredibly sweet to me and I could always make him laugh. He often had his camera and would click from all different angles but never look in the viewfinder and through the lens. I never saw the photos after they were developed.

I would leave by 11:00 or 11:30 if a party was during the week or stay until midnight if it was on a weekend. I don't recall Mom making any drunk scenes while we were at Studio 54. For me it was a fun place to go, even if Mom was drinking, because I was distracted by dancing. I'd dance. I'd sweat. I'd go home. I don't remember signing autographs at the club, either. It was as if dancing created a force field around me.

I'm sure there was plenty of drug use going on around me, but I never noticed. Steve must have put some kind of word out to his employees or something, because even though people always asked me about the drugs during the 54 days, I never saw any. The infamous "little cloth bag of pills" was never in my eyeline. I was like a mascot or somebody's kid sister. I don't know if people were scared that my mother was there, or if they just tried to shield me from the darker side of nightclub life, but I was basically exempt. Mom never smoked or used drugs. Alcohol was her sole vice.

I don't believe it was all about age, either. We all saw how poor Tatum O'Neal and Drew Barrymore were not able to dodge the substance-abuse bullet. They both had eccentric mothers, but they didn't have the experience that I had of choosing to become the sole caretaker at such a young age. I was friendly with both these young ladies, but I never went out with them back then. We remain friends to this day.

For many years, I thought I avoided addiction because my mom was an addict. But I believe there were other factors at hand that contributed to my safety. Part of it was just who I was—the spirit they could all see. Part of it was my mom, and another part was people's desire to protect me. This last part may be a naïve assumption, but I can honestly say I never felt preyed upon or tempted.

This period in the eighties had a fast and furious pace. Although I wasn't personally experiencing a carefree life filled with promiscuous sex and rampant drug use, I was engaged in my own personal high-energy race. I was burning my candle from both ends, but instead of its being a negative thing, I was met with success. I was working extremely hard at school with four or five hours of homework per night, and I was either filming or modeling the other hours. I did not need a great deal of sleep and I drove myself harder than anybody else did. I believe it was during these years that I began to be a perfectionist. I saw how much I could get accomplished and how I could have two equally full lives. I felt motivated by it all. It worked for me.

During high school, my mom's drinking escalated. She did not try to hide it or curtail it. It was as if we were back to the time before rehab. It was simply a consistent factor in our lives and I still tried everything I could think of to get her to stop.

Sometimes after a particularly bad night, she might stop for a few days, but it never lasted. We fought a great deal about it, but it never seemed to have an impact. Even when Mom started an evening attempting to curtail her drinking, she'd end the night switching to vodka and getting angry. She never actually passed out and would never allow anybody else to drive us home. I never took over as the driver, strangely. I was insecure about my driving and believed her driving drunk was better than my driving sober.

I am not sure how she managed it, but Mom rarely lost her control in front of the press. My honesty about her rehabilitation was what alerted the public to her struggles. We both did press for various projects after her stay in rehab and spoke openly about her drinking. After publicly claiming that I had loved my mother so much that I had asked her to go to rehab, I felt that I could not now say she was drinking again. It felt like such a failure. The story was just too good to refute. I adored my mother and she adored me and this young daughter was mature enough to save her own mom from the jaws of alcohol and everything had turned out well. The truth was just too sad to admit. I felt terrible upholding what was now a lie. This dilemma would only get worse.

I buried myself in my schoolwork but we often had ugly outbursts that ended in tears. I remember once screaming at my mother during a particularly bad evening. It was the angriest I'd ever been. I remember wanting to say something—anything—to hurt her. I had a vague memory of the name of a boy. As if there was a baby before me, or some child named "baby somebody." The mentions I recalled were usually in conjunction with a reference to this boy in one of Auntie Lila's prayers. The word *angel* was often used. I never knew whom they were talking about and was too scared to come out and ask. Instead, I waited until I needed to pull out the big guns and I fired.

I once blurted, "Well, maybe if you had taken care of me the way you took care of Baby John, then I wouldn't be here, either, and I wouldn't have to live with your drinking!"

Well, she turned on a dime, and with instant, steely cold sobriety she glared at me.

"Don't you *ever* mention that name *ever* again."

I stopped cold and saw how deeply I had cut her. I felt empowered knowing what I held in my arsenal. But, like intervention, you don't get too many opportunities to use such tactics. I would never again use this partial information in anger, and I would only find out the truth when she was on her deathbed, and not by her tongue.

High school basically continued with bouts of her getting drunk and then stopping for a day. There was not one major moment or birthday celebration during which she could remain sober. I learned how to plan my joy. I would front-load my birthdays with breakfast activities or plan to be with her for only the beginning of an event. Then I would go off to be with friends and know that that would be the last I would see of my mother's real facial expressions.

She still managed to get up every morning and get me to school. She was never the kind of drunk who passed out at the dinner or party or who stayed in bed all day with a hangover. She slept little, drank a lot, and had found a way to continue through each day. Plane rides were the worst, however, because even if she'd start off the flight with soda, she would end highly inebriated and needing help off the plane. This was before *TMZ* waited at the airports for celebrities, and I could usually get her through baggage claim and into a waiting car without too much fuss.

She had her drinking down to a science and switched up her methods whenever she needed to do so. Sometimes it was red wine at dinner and an endless slide into a boozy, sad, wanting-to-sing-soprano drunkenness. Then there was the "I'm only drinking diet soda" (a.k.a. rum and Coke) at parties where people knew her issue. She had bartenders all over New Jersey who knew what it really meant when she ordered her Diet Coke.

Then there was her new favorite: vodka bottles hidden all over the house and garage. She hid bottles everywhere and sometimes even forgot where she had hidden them. I'd find empty bottles in cowboy boots, behind cereal boxes, in purses at the back of her closet, and wedged in between folded sweaters.

There were times when I thought I had gotten her into the car and out of the house drink-free. But just after the engine was started, she'd tsk and say she forgot something in the house. She would put the car in park and run inside to retrieve some item and make a quick pit stop for a slug of something. I'd demand to smell her breath and she'd either already have a mint at the ready or perform her go-to open-mouth, held-breath move.

She'd smirk as if it were all on her own terms. She claimed she could drink socially and I guess that was not a lie. She was like a girl who claims, with all honesty, that she did not "sleep with" a certain boy because, in fact, they had had sex all night. Mom could *absolutely* drink socially. She drank and was social. She could just as easily drink while out and then go home and finish off half a bottle of vodka while getting ready for bed.

I ran out of ways of asking her to quit. Tears didn't work, rage didn't work, pleas when sober didn't work, and letters didn't work. Other people tried and I prayed.

On the day of graduation I decided to finally get drunk myself. I was at my friend Diane Coleman's party and we were all in the pool. I wanted to show my friends that I could be "cool" and drink like they all did. I took the screw top off a bottle of Riunite and opened up the back of my throat. I poured as much as I could down my open gullet while standing in waist-deep, cool water and enjoyed the gasps and applause.

I then looked around and knew I was going to be sick. I called my mother from the guest bathroom on the house portable phone and asked her to come get me right then. I hung up, groaned, and called her right back. Why hadn't she come yet? It had been a long time. She chuckled and I knew she was actually sober. She said to stay calm and Mama would come and get me as soon as possible. I felt too sick to even be embarrassed and I went home. In the car I sat in the backseat and put my forehead on the headrest in front of me.

"Are you mad at me, Mom?"

And she actually came out with "No . . . I'm just disappointed."

I was unaware of the cliché and she was unaware that she was a hypocrite. Her rules didn't apply to her. Unlike me, obviously, she could handle drinking.

Part Three

I hope you will see that I can't ask you to change, but I hope you let me change. . . . It's like pruning a tree or rerooting plants so that they all keep growing.

—*Letter from Brooke to Teri*

Chapter Ten

Remember the Hula-Hoop

had always known that I wanted to go to a school like Princeton. I had a romantic view of what I thought a college experience would be like, and it included old architecture and ivy on the walls. There would be wise-looking professors and students carrying books. I pictured a big, old campus and autumn leaves. I didn't focus on my future education as much as I thought about the entire experience of college life.

My dad had gone to the University of Pennsylvania, where he rowed crew. But he never mentioned my going to an Ivy League college and did not keep tabs on my application plans. My mother had never gone to college at all, so she was entirely unfamiliar with the process. Both my parents were supportive but didn't press me to follow any particular path.

It was a given that I was going to go to college, but what I studied and where I went felt entirely up to me. When my parents divorced, they'd come up with the idea that my father would support my education until I graduated from college. I was earning my own living by this time and therefore was able to pay for myself, but my father insisted on holding up his end of the deal.

I had always assumed I would find a college not too far from home. Despite the fact that my mother's drinking was getting worse and worse, the idea of escape never entered my mind. I wanted to be near my home and near my mom, and I wanted to find a school that did not require a plane to get me back to visit. I was so attached to my mother that I did not want to leave her. I was also attached to saving her. Subconsciously I also wanted to remain near enough to rescue her if need be.

I thought I had as good a chance as anybody to go to a good school. I had brought my grade point average up rather steadily over my four difficult years at Dwight-Englewood, I was a cheerleader, and I had an impressive extracurricular résumé. My life experience was rather eclectic by this point and I was committed to various charitable organizations. I approached the admissions adviser at my school and informed him that I was thinking of going to a school like Princeton but was also looking at Vassar, Trinity, and Brown.

Right off the bat, he insinuated that I should probably just forget about Princeton, because although I was finishing with strong grades, I had not taken enough AP courses, my SATs were not high enough (I just broke 1000), and I didn't play sports. He reiterated how hard it was to get accepted to a school like Princeton and that I should concentrate on schools that were less selective. He was the college adviser, so I accepted and heeded his advice. I figured he must have known what he was talking about.

I began collecting applications and making arrangements to visit and interview at various schools. I put the Princeton application aside and kept the others to fill out once I had visited their campuses. I visited Trinity with a friend who was an undergrad, and John Kennedy Jr. gave me a tour of Brown. We spent the day together on campus, and I told him the sugar-cube story, carefully omitting the part about my marrying him. I had a huge crush on John and remembered nothing about the school.

Each university was special in different ways, but they all felt a bit far from home for my comfort. I decided I could be happy anywhere as long as I was getting a college degree and rashly decided that I would just apply to Vassar early-decision and be done with the trauma of it all. I went to see the campus and didn't feel at all as if it was the place for me. It neither had the old-school, ivy-covered charm nor fit the image I had in my mind, but by then my choices felt limited. I submitted the early-decision application and got word back almost immediately. Of course they would love to have me attend their university. The admissions team was lovely and I could tell they would help make me feel at home there. But the fact that they were so eager to have me at their school made me wary. I was put off a bit because it felt as if they needed me more than I needed them.

I didn't have to commit for a while, so I decided take some time to decide. In the meantime, I had forgotten that I had said yes to going to a Princeton football game with a friend of a friend who was a junior there. It was too late to cancel because he had tickets to the game and plans to show me the fun part of the school. We were going to hear the a capella singing group the Tigertones sing under one of Princeton's echoing arches in what was called an "arch sing." This was just a few days before applications were due, and I hadn't even looked at my Princeton application since my college adviser's discouraging words.

Well, I got onto the beautiful campus and I was awestruck. The architecture was stunning and the gargoyles atop the massive library seemed alive. There was actually ivy growing up the walls that had witnessed the education of Woodrow Wilson, F. Scott Fitzgerald, and Jimmy Stewart, just to name a few. The atmosphere made me giddy. The campus was exactly what I'd dreamt about all these years. Surrounded by academia, I could feel an excitement for knowledge. I met up with my friend, who introduced me around and gave me some insider's information on what it was really like to go to Princeton.

I thought about my adviser's advice, but I was slowly getting a different picture from these students. Maybe he was wrong about what Princeton wanted? Maybe he had just wanted to protect me from what he thought would be rejection based on my fame?

It was time for the game, and as I sat in the bleachers, my heart started to pound. I was so comfortable with these people, who were unassuming and seemingly unfazed by my professional persona. They were extraordinarily genuine and smart, but not affected. I felt at ease and accepted. I absolutely had to be a student at this university. The only way to ensure that I would not get in was to not apply. That was no longer an option.

Halftime arrived and I practically took off running. I explained that I hadn't yet even applied to Princeton and that the application was due in the mail by Monday. I needed to go home and get it done.

I went home and fished around on my rolltop desk for the folder with the orange and black shield and began feverishly filling out the pages. My mom was concerned that I hadn't had a good time, but when she realized what I was doing, she just let me complete my task. I was so focused on my mission that I did not notice whether she had been drinking.

I worked throughout the rest of the weekend and had the application completed and postmarked on Monday. I went into high school that day and told nobody except my adviser. I told him I loved the school and wanted to take my chances before saying yes to Vassar. I don't remember his reaction, but it must have involved one or two raised eyebrows.

I guess it was my mother who called the Princeton admissions board to set up an interview for me. Mom had never pushed me to go to college, but it was always presumed I would. She supported my decision to apply to Princeton and wanted me to be happy. We also never discussed purposely taking time off from my career. It was just assumed that I would attend college as I had attended high school and continue to work on my breaks.

Mom got me an interview and drove me out to the university on her own. I think she was more nervous than I was, but shockingly she did not drink that day. She sat in the waiting area while I went in for my interview, and she whispered, "Just be yourself, darling."

During the interview the dean of admissions asked me why I wanted to go to college and why Princeton. It was not a trick question but rather an attempt to address a curiosity shared by the press and the public. Why bother going to university when I already had a full-blown career?

I explained I had worked my whole life and needed to expand my mind and my personal experiences. I was very realistic about how unique my life had been but how much I craved education as well as a conventional scholastic experience. I don't think I was as articulate as this sounds, but he claimed I was disarmingly "down to earth, and surprisingly unaffected."

I explained that I realized my SATs were not stellar but that I had worked hard to improve my GPA and that I was very serious about attending university. Even though this Princeton admissions officer had alluded to the fact that their school really was looking at students as whole entities, rather than just walking SAT scores, I worried that he was just being kind. It was really a very informal interview that stressed the diversity of the university and the commitment to excellence. This last part sounded a gong in my head and I said a prayer in my brain. I made a quiet promise that if I was allowed into this school, I, too, would commit myself fully to the same "excellence." I went back home and to school to wait for the verdict.

The next few weeks I felt as if I was waiting for a crush to call. Mom and I kept passing the phone, which hung on the sidewall of the kitchen pantry, a tiny room that was under the stairs, where you had to sit on a small chair so as not to hit your head. We both would randomly lift up the receiver to see if we still had a dial tone.

These weeks were some of the most excruciating ones of my life. Vassar was getting anxious for a response and I had heard nothing from my real first choice. What made it even worse was that a friend—who had better SATs and was also a legacy—didn't get accepted. I felt terrible for her and believed that if she had gotten rejected then I obviously had no chance. By this time it was known around high school that I had decided to apply to Princeton.

Well, the days kept going by and everybody in the high school had heard about colleges except for me. Everyone who had applied to Princeton from my school had gotten rejected and I still had heard nothing. Something had to be wrong.

I moped, I cried, and I fretted. I still don't remember if Mom was drinking or not. She seemed pretty present for this drama. It always amazed me the moments she chose to show up and those when she could not. In this case she seemed shockingly cognizant of the importance of this situation. This was my future and consequently hers as well.

Finally, Mom secretly called the head of admissions and apologized, but said that every single child applying to colleges had heard about their fate except her daughter. Could he shed some light on what was happening?

She stopped him before he gave her the news and said that she did not want to be the first to know. To this day this remains one of the most important moments in my life. Mom was standing up for me in an important and unselfish way. She was being a mom. She took the determination she had had her whole life to help me, even though it meant that she would eventually have to let me go. She physically and emotionally stepped aside and let me have the big moment for myself. It impressed me that she was willing to sacrifice like this.

And it's interesting that I interpreted it as a sacrifice. Wasn't that a mom's job? Mom motioned me over to the phone and said the call was for me.

The admissions director explained what had happened. This was the last class he was to admit to Princeton because he was retiring, so he was taking everything very seriously. Somebody had leaked to the press that I had applied, and there had been an onslaught of press inquiries and controversy about my application. The school was faced with a complicated situation.

I was crushed and thought, *Oh God . . . they don't want to deal with me because I'm famous. Why did I apply to only one other school? I don't want to go to Vassar. But wait. . . . Hang on. . . . He's still talking. . . .*

He continued to say that he was currently on vacation and had left Princeton with two letters in his hands. (The admissions office had called him on his vacation because my mother had been polite but quite insistent.) To ensure that another leak did not occur, the director had had his secretary print up both a letter of acceptance and a letter of rejection and seal them tight. His plan was to take both on vacation and personally post the one he intended to send by himself. Only he would know which one he sent. This was the reason for the delay, and I would be getting my letter of acceptance in the mail in the next few days. I had just heard the word *letter*—then he started sounding like the adults in *Peanuts* cartoons. I struggled to ask, "Oh, so in a few days I'll find out whether I got in or not?"

He must have wanted to run to the mailbox and switch the letters. This student didn't even know what the word *acceptance* meant!

"Oh no, you got in, Miss Shields; it's just that the letter is on its way. I am sorry for the delay, but it was necessary for all of us."

"Thank you, sir. Thank you very much."

I hung up the phone and screamed. I hugged Mom, whose eyes were welling with tears, not because I had gotten into an Ivy League school, but because I was so happy about it. I phoned my dad to tell him the good news and I could hear the pride in his voice.

The next day at school I didn't want to tell anybody. I eventually had to, but I played it down. I knew people would think I had just gotten in because I was famous, but I knew that this fact was actually a deterrent for universities for a myriad of reasons. I also knew that I was the right fit for Princeton. I loved every aspect of what the university stood for. They believed in hard work, excellence, and joy. These were things I sought after daily. Princeton did want well-rounded students who showed consistent improvements over the four years of high school and who had many extracurricular activities and varied tastes. Turns out the interview also had a big impact on their decision. One thing I was extremely comfortable doing was being interviewed and being honest.

I had been accepted to Princeton University, the academic institution of my dreams. I glowed instead of gloated, and for the rest of the year, I had an overwhelming sensation that I was really going to be OK in the world.

I had no idea of the feelings I would have when I actually went away. But more on that in a minute. On graduation day from Dwight-Englewood my mother and father beamed with pride. I had done it. I had graduated from high school during one of the busiest times of my career. Alex Haley was the class speaker, thanks to my mother. Mom and I had befriended Alex Haley after he'd expressed his interest in charting my genealogy. He had invited my mother and me to a festival in Tennessee. And we had all truly bonded. I think my mother was actually a bit in love with him. He was a kind and gentle soul who really warmed to my mom. She made him laugh. Mom suggested that I ask him to speak at my graduation and he lovingly obliged.

Mom was able to stay sober during the ceremony but quickly began drinking at lunch. I remember being relieved that my father left before she got sloppy. I hated the thought of him ever thinking any less of my mom. The idea of Mom embarrassing herself in front of my father killed me, but for the most part, she kept it together, and at least for a moment we were a happy family.

Mom and I had taken a vacation every summer to one new place that I usually chose. In the past we had always had a lot of fun. My inspirations usually came out of a movie I had seen, and it was true that the reality often didn't match up with my fantasy. I once wanted to go to the isle in Scotland that had a magical red telephone booth. We went to the spot and realized the booth had been a prop, only placed there for the film.

Another time we went to a remote city in Italy to learn how to marbleize paper. I had seen some movie about a woman leaving her urban life to find her soul in a remote Italian village. Mom and I thought marbleizing paper—like the paper we had seen at specialty stationery stores—would be fun. We arrived at the beautiful villa to learn about paints and oils, only to find out that the class was actually in bookbinding.

The summer before college, we went to the Greek island where the movie *Summer Lovers* had been shot. But of course, it looked nothing like the film in real life. You'd think that we, of all people, would have been able to foresee the fantasy aspect of moviemaking. But I guess we both wanted things to always be like they were in the movies.

In the past it hadn't mattered to me, because we always had fun, and kept busy, and laughed like hell at our insistent naïveté. Mom and I loved to travel and shop at local places and meet people and eat interesting foods. But in this place, and at this age, it was different. Thankfully, it was only a week.

I had no idea what I was feeling. I was sad and mopey and bored. I had never actually felt boredom before. Mom remarked that nothing was wrong with me. I was just restless and bored and not used to re-laxing. But that wasn't it. I was on the most romantic trip of my life, and I was holed up with my mother. I should have been on a trip with my girlfriends or on some type of adventure before the grind of college. This did not feel right. This place would have been perfect for a honeymoon, or a recluse, not a mother and daughter.

We finally returned home and the day came for me to go to my orien-tation week. The car was loaded with clothes and things I thought I might need to make my dorm room cozy, just like a home away from home. The drive was only an hour and a bit. Our driver, Dick, took the wheel, and Mom and I sat in the back and talked about how much fun it was all going to be.

Dick was a man my mother had hired as a handyman-driver a few years earlier. He often drove me to work appointments in the city and always to events so we would not have to hire a limo. We had a safe black Mercedes that he maintained, and he acted as somewhat of a caretaker for our home in Haworth. He also served as a huge safety net for my mother and was the main reason she wasn't either dead or arrested. It wouldn't be possible to count the number of times she was drunk in the backseat and we had to maneuver her to the house. To a certain extent he alleviated a great deal of my stress with regard to her safety. He also was the perfect addition to the enabling plan. She smartly eliminated the risk of being pulled over and I could be under the assumption that she was being responsible.

For many people, the threat of an impending car accident was enough to tell the person you loved that you wanted them to quit. That factor was eliminated from my arsenal and I just accepted Dick as a safety net for all of us. This was probably just another subconscious way for Mom to justify that her drinking did not have any adverse effects on our life. I was fed, clothed, housed, and would not have to be driven by a drunk driver. This by no means meant that she would never drive drunk. It just meant she was limiting the opportunities to do so.

Dick drove and when we hit the tree-lined road leading into the town, I felt nervous but excited. I looked up at the canopy of green and flickers of sunlight leaking through and I thought it was truly one of the calmest sights I had ever seen. The path opened at the end and you could see the majesty of ivy-clad buildings waiting to fill young minds.

I got my dorm-room assignment and went to drop my stuff off. The dorm consisted of three rooms. There were two bedrooms with a bunk bed and two dressers. The common living room had a couch and a big armchair. We would need to get more furniture. For now I brought clothes, linens, and electronics. I opened my room and was the third to arrive. The first two girls were a premed student from Texas and another student who was studying politics or medicine. They both chose their rooms. Both chose bottom bunks. I was next and chose the room closest to the front door. We all politely chatted and I began to get a sick feeling in my stomach. This was slowly becoming real. This was not a summer location where I could pretend to live an entirely new life. This was it. I was here, with these people, and we were going to actually live with each other, for the entire school year. It was actually happening.

What I had not factored into this new adjustment was the moment of my mother's departure. I hadn't really accepted the reality of her leaving me, especially with these strangers.

Princeton is divided into what they call "colleges." I was assigned to Mathey College, which contained Blair Arch. Blair was where I had heard the singing group perform. The architecture was all beautiful and the grounds richly green. I walked Mom to the entrance to the Matthey College archway and went with her to the car. I kissed both cheeks and hugged her good-bye. I planned on going home on the weekends, so I knew I would see her Friday. Mom was not crying and remained upbeat. This idea of going away to college was an entirely foreign concept for her, and my not living with her was borderline alien for both of us. I had spent vacations with my father and his family, and there was time during rehab when we were separated, but Mom and I had never honestly lived apart from one another. Remember, she was the one who nightly slept with me strapped to her chest.

I watched the black Mercedes getting smaller and smaller, and exhaled. Within an hour and a half I was on the phone with her, sobbing and asking her to come back and take me home. Our dorm phone's cord stretched just enough to make it to the floor of the entrance to my room. The other girls had all gone to the dining hall to check out dinner. They probably thought I was a snob or anorexic because I said I wasn't hungry.

I had waited till they were out of earshot and, like a husband sneaking a call to his mistress, quickly dialed my mother. She was just coming in the door when I explained to her that I had made a terrible mistake and wanted to come home immediately. I wasn't kidding.

"Oh, honey . . . you'll be fine. I promise. Try to get involved and go have some dinner, settle your things, and let's talk in the morning."

Sniff, sniff. "OK."

I never realized what a safety net my mother provided for me. And I use the term *safety net* fully aware of the irony. Even though in many ways I primarily took care of her, she was still there. Just knowing she was near was enough. It had gotten to the point that I almost didn't care that she was drunk, as long as she was near and alive. She still held the proverbial lifeline that I guess I had never intended on having cut.

For years, people attacked my mother for holding me down and for not allowing me my freedom. The press painted me as frustrated and bound. But the truth was, I didn't want freedom. Being bound was just fine. It was all I'd ever known, and it felt safe. I was not trying to escape.

It wasn't as if I wanted to return to the comforts and routines of a tranquil home life or a mom who baked and cleaned for me and held me softly underwing. I wanted to return to my mommy. I may have felt lonely when she drank, but a window of sobriety was never far away, and at least we were together.

I realized that this new situation—this whim I had to go to college—was not going to work for me. This pit in my gut was just not going away until everything returned to *normal*. Fine, I'd give it a fair amount of time to make it look as if I really gave it the old "college try" (the language seemed perfect for this scenario), and then this silliness could stop. The regular pattern of my life could peacefully resume.

I am shocked that it never occurred to me that I might feel home-sick. I had dealt with scarier, more adult situations and had powered through much more dramatic scenes in life. I had suffered but sur-vived. I had seen more, and was more adult, than any of these fresh young ones. I was mature. Or so I thought.

As the weeks went on, I realized how sheltered and immature I was in many ways. I wasn't mature enough to deal with passing the boys' dorms on the way to a bathroom consisting of communal sinks and multistalled showers. Everybody had these square garden buckets filled with their stuff and shower slippers and terry cloth robes. But it was all totally foreign to me. It wasn't as if I expected the Ritz or wanted an en suite toilet, but I had never even gone to sleepaway camp. A raft trip with a movie crew down the Colorado River did not constitute roughing it. To be fair, neither did this, but somehow I felt more uncomfortable and exposed here.

I managed to learn to deal with the living and showering arrange-ments, but I couldn't shake the sadness. My classes were great and I started to find a bit of a routine, but my life mostly revolved around studying and planning on seeing my mom. I did not extend myself much farther than the library and my dorm room.

The room itself began to be a war zone as well. My roommates would stay up incredibly late every night. It seemed that I was the only one who wasn't a vampire and who wasn't afraid to roam outside while it was daylight. I also decided to rent a small refrigerator, only to repeatedly find experiments growing inside and peanut butter–covered knives with stuck-on M&M's plastered on the top of the minifridge. This was not what I was used to, that's for sure.

In the beginning I had a very tough time finding a niche. The stu-dents were all being respectful about giving me my space, just like my first months of high school, but it meant I felt even more solitary.

I thought nobody wanted to bother being my friend because I came with enough baggage to fill a cart. I believe the students thought they were doing the right thing. I don't think they realized that I did not want space or respect. I was terrified of space, and because I had never really had respect, I did not even know how to regard it as freedom. It felt irresponsible and unproductive. It was unfamiliar to me and grossly uncomfortable.

The paparazzi tried to sneak onto campus, dressed like what they thought college students looked like, and follow me around. The students were great and they alerted the school and me if anyone saw anybody suspicious. One photographer hid in a vent to photograph me walking to a class; another attempted to bribe a Mathey College freshman to take a camera into the showers and snap me in the nude. They would have been in for a surprise if they tried, because I had taken to showering in a one-piece bathing suit! My roommates asked whether I was on the swim team and I just said yes. I was pretty sure they were not fans of water sports and the secret would be safe.

Not one student took the bribes for information, and I established a rapport with campus security. I gave them my class schedule so they could be cognizant of my whereabouts without being obtrusive. I felt protected by the student body the most. It was not just about my safety, but also about my integrity, my freedom, and my personal growth. I was delighted. Who would have imagined that there were people out there who didn't wish to profit off of me?

But I didn't stop missing my mother. I fixed my class schedule so that I was most free on Fridays to go home and see my mother. I didn't think I wanted to give up going to Princeton and forfeit an education because I was "Mom-sick," but why was everybody else so seemingly settled in and happy?

Every night I would call Mom and fight back the tears. Her voice made me ache because I thought the feelings I had would last forever. Leaving Mom was something I had prepared to do when I threatened to live with my dad, but that was temporary. This felt different. I missed my house, my home, and the good parts of my mother.

For the first term, I spent most of my time in the library or driving back to Haworth. I would have Mom drive out every Wednesday to take me to dinner. We would either go have Indian food or go to a healthy diner in a club car that served things like veggie burgers. I was still a vegetarian at this time from a stint I had working at the San Diego Zoo during my senior year in high school. Many times I would actually cry during dinner. The only other time I had ever cried like this was when it was over a boy. It felt like a similar heartbreak, only not romantic. I was being forced to understand the feeling of being on my own. I was worried about my mother being alone and not properly looked after, but I was also just missing my house and my mommy.

I would always cry as she drove away. I'd bury my feelings until after my one Friday class (or sometimes as early as late Thursday night). Then I'd have Dick drive me straight home. Mom and I would go to the movies and eat Japanese food. I'd happily study in the car or at my rolltop desk. Sunday night, at about *60 Minutes* time, I started to feel heavyhearted once again. I resisted going to sleep, because I knew when I awoke Monday morning I would have to leave her and go away again.

Being away from Mom made me idealize her and her alcoholic behavior. I had learned how to navigate her drinking and to deal with every element of it, but the feeling of being released into a totally foreign way of life (and only possessing resources that worked in rare and unique circumstances) made me buckle emotionally. During this first term I was so antisocial and lonesome that I would have taken drunk, nasty Mom with all her insults over being without her.

I grappled with the idea of going home and commuting. I could get my courses done and still be home with Mom. Everything could go back to the way it was. One night at dinner I told Mom that it was time to quit. I couldn't do it emotionally. My studies were great, but I did not need or want the life part of college. I did not fit in.

Mom was calmer than I had ever known her to be, and her drinking at that time had curbed (temporarily) for some reason. She insisted that she knew me and that I knew me, too, and that if I quit the whole experience, I would never, ever forgive myself. High school had been a tough adjustment, and look how wonderfully that turned out. I had had a great high school experience and my best friend in the whole world, Lisa, I had met in ninth grade. I needed to give it my all this time as well, and just keep moving ahead.

She somehow kept encouraging me, even though I know it must have cut her up inside to know she was ensuring that I stay away. I realize that nothing would have made her happier than to have me back under the same roof.

She said, "Remember the Hula-Hoop, my darling."

"OK, Mom, I'll try."

And I did. But trying was tiring, and I felt a little bit like a failure and an ingrate. I tried out for dance companies and singing groups and did not get accepted. I had zero experience with anything musical but thought I could figure it out. It was also getting a bit more annoying with people trying to infiltrate the campus to get a glimpse of me. I kept my head down and went to class and the library, and I studied as if my life depended on it. And it did.

Then exam time came, and although I had never experienced something so intense, I was very prepared. No surprise, since I had spent none of my time socializing and all of it in the library.

Then a crazy thing happened. I took an early-level pysch course and the exam was a multiple-choice one. My grade would not be debatable. There were three hundred kids in the course and out of all of them, only four got A's. I was one of them.

I saw each student checking the grades posted on the bulletin board. The students would each look at their grade and then slide down to look at my name. I thought this was understandable, but it was still enraging. But this time I didn't mind, because they'd see my A.

Maybe the professors were not playing favorites or giving me any kind of break. Maybe I had actually studied my ass off to get through it.

After the class realized I'd earned such a good grade, people started to approach me more. Some kids asked me if I wanted to study with them, and others asked me to share my notes from class. I would have rewritten every page of notes if asked because I was so excited that people knew I was a serious student and not there expecting any special treatment. It was an academic icebreaker, and I took it.

As the year went on, the scholastic aspect was picking up and my social life was smoothing out a bit. I was making friends and decided to join a theatre group called the Triangle Club. I was no longer crying and Mom no longer had to visit me every Wednesday. I still enjoyed going home on the weekends because my roommate situation had not improved and our dorm was depressing. I was hardly in my room and could not wait to get out. But I was making friends and I had a better living situation planned for the next year.

I'd made it through the year. But at what cost? Mom very selflessly convinced me to stay at school instead of leave and go back home. Mom undoubtedly missed me, and her life lacked any focus.

At this point her drinking had become worse than ever. I couldn't do another intervention because she was too savvy. Addicts can see one coming miles away. In my opinion you get only one real impactful shot. I could no longer claim I would go live with my father, because I was already separated from her and she was, seemingly, in support of this separation. Mom still felt she did not have a problem with alcohol and claimed she could keep her drinking habits under control.

I was gone, but she knew it needed to happen, no matter the personal cost to her. She missed me unbearably because the day I left for school, our dynamic basically changed forever. Of course this would be traumatic for both of us.

But this was the first time that my mom put her pain and her deep fears aside to do the best thing for my future and me. She didn't want to live alone, or with anybody except me. This was the ultimate sacrifice for her and the first time she actually chose to physically let go. I will forever be grateful she would not let me quit.

"You're not a quitter, my darling."

Nobody would ever have guessed that Mom would have the strength to sacrifice herself for my benefit. She was always fighting for me and protecting me, but I was attached to her at the hip. Up until now, I hadn't wanted emancipation. But here I was, with the perfect opportunity to cut loose and rebel, and I was fighting it with all my might. We both profoundly knew that a shift was occurring, and neither one of us wanted to fully commit. It meant a breach of some kind. One we both never thought we'd see, but one we silently knew was inevitable. Yet without the change, we might not survive. (It would be just like *Grey Gardens*.) I would become Little Edie to her Big Edie, and although we would be tied to each other, our relationship would fester and love would turn to hate.

I wanted my mommy but I trusted that the outcome would most likely be better for me. Mom let me go and she did so as her ultimate sacrifice. I believe that this was a beginning to her end in many ways. In her mind, she was losing me. Now she had no impetus to not drink. I suppressed the guilt that I was leaving her. Sometimes when drunk she would glare at me, call me an ingrate, and coldly claim that she knew I would eventually leave her all alone.

I suspect she held the conviction that everybody she ever loved would leave her. Her father and her first fiancé—and a baby, I believed—and my father all disappeared from her life in one way or another. Why would I be any different? To her it was a self-fulfilling prophecy.

Chapter Eleven

America's Sweetheart

During the years I was at Princeton, even though I worked very little, the press remained interested in everything from my class schedule to my romantic life. Ever since *Pretty Baby* I'd been the subject of all sorts of speculation—much of it unfair—and I don't think my mom reacted to the press in a systematic way, especially in regard to my sexuality and potential romantic relationships. Did she try to actively change my image from *Pretty Baby* and Calvin Klein model to an America's sweetheart saving her virginity until her wedding night? I don't think so.

The most poignant part of all was how disassociated I was with my own body. As a model, I was primarily a cover girl. I was labeled "The '80s Look" by *Time* magazine. People said I had the most beautiful face in the world.

Well, that seemed ridiculous to me. It didn't register as true. "Most beautiful" was an arbitrary concept and I was afraid to buy into it. Because I shot cover after cover and never did runway, I simply avoided ever really thinking about my body and consequently my sexuality. I was a face first and I knew how to work that face according to the demand. I'd be shooting a cover for *Vogue*, and underneath the table

I'd be wearing jeans and Top-Siders. I thought about my persona as existing only from the neck up. It was as if I was disconnected from my body from the neck down. So when I became the most celebrated virgin of our time it became even easier to not think about my body.

All my life, I'd been terrified of physical contact with boys. Perhaps it was because of the closeness and easy affection I shared with my mother; I didn't feel a void or a need for affection from boys.

I believe my mom wanted me to stay a virgin for as long as possible. I think she wanted to keep me her baby. I have to be honest: I'm a mother myself now, and I get it. I look at my girls and want them to be my delicious babies forever. I want to create designer chastity belts! The thought of them losing their virginity makes me cringe. Even the thought of them not letting me kiss them on their little rosebud lips makes me cry. I also hope and pray that their first experience is about love and trust and that they are not at all traumatized but feel free and safe.

When my mother did talk to me about sex growing up, it was brief and she didn't have to play the bad guy. She was raising me Catholic and it was the church that preached the sanctity of virginity and waiting till marriage. She was just the messenger. I also was so genuinely naïve and was kept so protected by my mother—Rapunzel in the tower—that intimacy with anybody seemed out of the question. I just didn't want to deal with any of it.

On top of all of that, my mom said I had a responsibility to my fans, who often wrote letters to me about pressure from boys and asking how I dealt with it. I would get hundreds of letters a month and most of them asked for autographs and advice.

Villard Books approached my mom and me and presented us the idea of my writing a book. Unlike *The Brooke Book*, which my mother had put together with a friend, the plan was that I'd take an active part in writing this second one. I had almost finished my first semester at Princeton and had become much more confident in my writing than I had been in high school. I was excited by the chance to tell the truth in my own words. The price was evidently right and Mom was happy with the contract.

The book was supposed to be an honest account of being a young woman during her first year of being away from home and going away to college. I was, of course, a famous young woman attending Princeton University, which was far from typical, but the book would integrate several universal themes.

I had taken many psychology courses by this time and felt I had a lot to say. I delved into the first chapter with excitement and clear self-awareness. The chapter was a heartfelt account of how scared and alone I felt my first semester away from my mom. I wrote about how strange it was being the only recognizable person on campus. It was humorous and vulnerable and focused on the complexities of trying to grow up.

My mom read it and was proud. I even showed my writing to a professor and he said he was impressed by the writing and my candor. He thought it would be a good book for young people. I handed in the first chapter and an introduction and awaited editorial notes.

To my dismay, the editor read it, trashed the whole chapter, and hired a ghostwriter. They said something about it being faster and easier for me . . . blah blah blah. My mom thought that because of my heavy workload at school, it might actually be more convenient for me to meet with the ghostwriter and have the questions and conversations recorded, rather than having me pen the whole book. I remember thinking that if they were not interested in publishing the book I wanted to write, then I'd just have to give up on the tone I was trying to create. I had committed to the book, so I did not have much choice other than to just follow along with the new plan. It didn't occur to us to scrap the whole thing, because it was a job. We had a contract and it was money in the bank.

According to my mom, it would keep my name out there while I was at school and on hiatus from Hollywood. I am sure she had never thought to include an out clause in the contract should we be disappointed with content. Mom would have been satisfied with anything because it was all about me. I never read the contract and I doubt Mom read the fine print. I had no agent to help draw up or review anything. That was the way most of our deals were handled. We only thought about if the job would be interesting, pay well, and keep me in people's minds. It was a bonus if it fit into my school schedule. And that was about it.

I began by meeting with the ghostwriter on the weekends. Mom always left us alone to do the taped sessions. She said it was important that it was in my words.

When I started seeing the pages the ghostwriter was producing, I was appalled. All the deeper feelings and observations I made about this period of my life were overlooked. I hated the questions she was asking and kept trying to steer it all to a deeper level. The result, sadly, was a very silly book with short sentences about important things like the versatility of leg warmers. I gave up. I had bigger things with which to concern myself, such as surviving away from my mom and getting a degree.

Mom seemed unfazed by the vapid direction the book was taking and seemed to have no problem with its content. She hired the amazing Robert Risko to do illustrations and went about helping the publisher gather permissions from various photographers who would be featured in the book. I could tell she was happy to have a project and one that revolved around her finest creation: me. She liked being busy and necessary. She also seemed thrilled with the wholesome image that was being created by the book, which portrayed me as a hardworking, responsible, chaste America's sweetheart. I don't think my mom ever wanted to face the deeper side of all of it. Photos of me in leg warmers and a unitard, taking readers through a series of leg lifts and jumping jacks or describing packing the perfect weekend wardrobe, did not bother my mother one bit. She was satisfied with creating and upholding the sweet, untouchable, yet "normal" teenager image on the pages of a book ironically titled *On Your Own*.

One chapter of the book was dedicated to the idea of peer pressure and the subject of my virginity. I had agreed to divulge this truth because of a responsibility I felt to my female fans; I wanted to be a good role model. I admitted to being a virgin and expressed my plan to save myself for marriage.

I felt no shame in admitting that I was still a virgin at age nineteen. I had previously spoken out about the evils of drugs and smoking. Talking about the value of waiting until marriage to lose one's virginity didn't seem like a big deal. I also did not think it was going to cause such controversy. But I cringe now at the thought of my being so open, because there really was nothing off-limits with regard to my personal life. Looking back, I think it was actually sad that there was so much access to my life for press (and consequently the public). I mean, one of my orthodontist appointments was filmed! I guess it was all in attempts to paint me as a regular kid.

I did want to help however I could, though, and when you read the outpouring of admiration and respect from kids who wrote to me, it was easy to want to uphold my image in their eyes. I basically wanted to tell my young women fans that they need not fall prey to peer pressures regarding anything including their sexuality. My mom said it was important to include this in the book so my fans wouldn't feel alone. If Brooke Shields was a virgin, maybe it was OK for them to be as well.

Mom always impressed on me to lead by example. It became a torch I would happily carry. Mom had not lived her life that way, and I believe she used her sexuality slightly desperately and as an attempt to feel loved and accepted. The hypocrisy of it all would not become evident till decades later.

Here was my mother, an alcoholic who had lost a baby that she had conceived out of wedlock and had become an unmarried pregnant person a second time. Yet Mom was telling me to uphold the virtues of virginity and abstinence from all vices. I have recently wondered if it was all an attempt on my mom's part to counteract the overly sexual image with which I had been associated in my younger years. Was Mom now trying to dictate how the public viewed me? I believed my mom wanted me to be universally adored and untouchable. It is hard enough just dealing with being a teenager, let alone bearing the burden of the fate of young women everywhere.

In addition, because Mom and I had been so enmeshed, I wasn't able to have any romantic feelings without making her somehow a part of them. I told her everything and was constantly seeking her approval. There was little room for anybody else.

Looking as far back as my first "official" kiss, back in seventh grade at New Lincoln, my memories of it are not only that it was disturbing, but also that the first person I told was my mother. It was with a boy named Chris Serbagi at a friend's party. He asked me to go to a back room, and when I got there, he had set up the couch with pillows and had drawn the shades. He told me to lie down and he proceeded to slobber all over my face. (Maybe I should have made Keith Carradine my first official kiss after all!) I was so grossed out and sad that this was the first kiss, which I had so eagerly anticipated. Not only was it not romantic or spontaneous as I had hoped it would be; it was tonguey and gross, too. We got busted and sent home by the mom of the house.

The next day, my mom was driving me to school in our black Jeep, as she often did, and her response after I recounted the horror was only to ask if I planned on doing it again. I told my mom "No!" and that was the end of it. It would have been nice if Mom had explained to me what a first kiss could be like and how I could still have one with the right person. Instead, I then shut myself off to all boy kisses in general.

Basically my "relationships" had always been orchestrated by my mother in one way or another. She directed my romantic life sometimes subtly and sometimes not. She didn't focus on romance (never mind love), but instead wanted to associate me with names that connoted fame, money, and power. These were the relationships she supported, also because they were less attainable.

She loved that I had briefly dated John Travolta, Jimmy McNichol, Leif Garrett, Scott Baio, and John Kennedy. They were all on *Teen Beat* magazines and stars in their own right. She trusted I'd keep my vow of chastity and like the attention paid to me in these couplings. She genuinely loved Michael Jackson and said I was good for him as a supportive and honest friend.

My fame, my mother's choice to support certain romantic relationships more than others, and my increasingly complicated feelings about my virginity led to an enduring insecurity about my sexuality. The book's release the summer between my freshman and sophomore year didn't help. My virginity was the only thing anyone could talk about. In my opinion many things were wrong with the book, but the tour was fun. Mom and I went with Gavin and made the most out of every city we visited.

I had recently gone on *The Tonight Show* to promote *On Your Own* and Johnny had asked me with whom I would want to be stranded on a desert island. (Such an original question!) I said I had a crush on George Michael. Mom had decorated a denim shirt of mine with "WHAM" in glitter paint and Bedazzles. She glued pins and little pictures of George and surprised me with it to wear to his concert. I almost wore it on Carson.

As luck would have it, while in Chicago on the book tour, we discovered we were staying at the same boutique hotel as George. Mom

was enamored of the fact that he was famous, and she loved his voice. Mom had contacted George's publicist to say that I was staying in the same place and hoped to meet him if possible. He said he would love to take me to dinner but because of our being bothered by the press we should probably just arrange dinner at the hotel. I nearly fell on my face.

George decided to get food delivered to the private dining room on the rooftop. I arrived at the meal in colored jeans and a blouse. The table was beautifully set and all the foods I liked had been ordered. George said he had read some place that I liked to be healthy so he picked accordingly. There were flowers and candles and we talked nonstop. He complimented me on my blouse. When dinner was over, George walked me to my hotel room and said he wanted to see me again. He left without even trying to kiss me. I was so touched by what a real gentleman he was. (I wanted to yell, "Wait, please don't 'go go'!")

Back in my hotel bedroom Gavin and my mom had put CAUTION: POLICE LINE. DO NOT CROSS tape all over my bed. There were signs that said THIS MEANS YOU, GEORGE! I guess this was payback for my sign-hanging stunt down the hallway for Mom after her date with Woody Allen.

George and I managed to go on a few more dates in New York City that involved shopping or meals. He held my hand and even bought me a mauve cashmere sweater from Charivari on the Upper West Side. I thought he was a remarkable, respectful, and patient gentleman who was obviously aware of my hesitance regarding sex. Mom was thrilled. She said he had good taste and was sweetly old-fashioned. Nobody had ever been willing to move so slowly. It must be love.

On the night before I was to go back to Princeton for my sophomore year, George invited me to a party for Grace Jones. When we arrived at the club, Boy George ran up to us and started screaming about how he had heard the rumor but was happy to see us actually together. Before the evening got too late, my boyfriend George "carelessly" whispered into my ear, "Why don't we get out of here?"

We got into the limo and headed back to my home in New Jersey. As we were nearing the house, George put up the partition and turned to me. I thought, *Oh my God—I'm going to get to have my first time with George Michael in the back of the limo!* Forget Catholicism and the book. Forget my mother. God would understand! I gazed at George with puckered lips. He looked deep into my eyes and said, "I think we need to take a break. I need to concentrate on my career." WHAM!

I was devastated. Mom tried to comfort me and promised that I was going to be OK. She obviously didn't see him as a threat at any step of the way. Mom encouraged friendships with people like George Michael, Michael Jackson, and John Travolta, because I believe she was impressed by their genuinely sweet natures as well as their level of fame. These were the types of more gentle male friends who loved my mom and did not pose a threat to her.

I went back to my new place just off campus and cried myself to sleep for weeks. But my sophomore year went by and I finally got over George. I began dating, doing theatre, studying even harder, and was adjusting extremely well. I knew Mom was drinking, but I did not have to see it, and as long as I spoke to her before going to bed, I knew she was safe and fine.

During my junior year I met and fell madly in love with my first real love. I met Dean Cain, who was a football player at Princeton. He was a year behind me and we were instantly crazy about each other. I saw all his football games and he saw all my dance and theatre performances. We were a golden couple and everybody loved us together. I loved his family. His dad was a director and his mom was also somewhat of a blond bombshell who loved to laugh and hang out with the kids. She was an ex-model and always wore the current beach-babe fashion.

We got along wonderfully and she made me feel extremely accepted and like one of her children. He had a slightly older brother and an adorable little sister and they all lived in Malibu. Dean's parents were very California liberal and I was always a bit shocked whenever they had Dean and me stay in the same bedroom when I came to visit them, sometimes even giving us the best room in the house. This was such a contrast to how my mother always insisted Dean stay in a guest room. His family took me in as one of theirs and I fit in.

Dean's mom was always also a bit larger than life and a bit dramatic. She was never inappropriate but just loved to have a good time. Even though his dad was working hard and was very present, Dean was like the little man of the house from the time he was a baby. Maybe Dean just simply knew how to handle beautiful, flamboyant women who needed attention. But he was always very patient with my mom. Mom loved Dean at the start but began negating our relationship the longer it went on. She started to act disdainful and she would often blurt out or whisper under her breath, "Oh, it's just physical with you two!" I tried to overlook her comments because I really was in love and of course it was *not* physical. I was too bound to my virginity and to her!

Being with Dean was the best thing that could have happened to me. It made such sense for us in so many ways. We shared the same sense of humor. He understood Hollywood from a personal perspective but was not yet an actor. He was not intimidated by my success or my fame, and he was a great dancer and fit in anywhere I took him. Everybody loved Dean and he was incredibly and painfully patient with me regarding sex. But it felt as if Mom was always lording over us, and I was self-conscious because the world assumed we were sleeping together. In truth, though, I was even more scared and shy with him because I was so in love. I had this fear that if I slept with him, I would want to run away.

Even when Mom wasn't around, I felt as if she was watching. We were in love and so incredibly attracted to one another in every way, that it would make sense that we were having sex. We were always holding hands and trying to find ways to be alone and kiss. But, poor guy, I made him wait and wait, and my mom kept track. She knew we were not sleeping together because she could pretty much guarantee that (like my first French kiss) I would tell her if we were. Still, I think Mom was actually threatened for the first time. But even though I really felt scared about sex and paranoid I was being watched by Mom and the world, Dean remained loving and patient.

We were almost the couple who got married after being college sweethearts. We did everything together and were well-known on campus. He was the first man (and the only one for a very long time) who really knew me and loved me. He even knew me better than my

mother did because we had deep personal talks and he asked questions. He was witness to my struggles with my mom and he respected how much I loved her. I was honestly, truly, and purely in love. It made me the happiest person I had been in forever. And he loved me even more. He would have married me right out of college. He said he knew that I was it. He didn't need to keep looking. But he was a year behind me, and when I graduated, I was scared about our next year apart.

Even though being with Dean felt so right, I couldn't completely give myself to him—in any way—without my mother's approval. Her approval opened my world for me. I remember calling her to ask if I could drive up to Sierra Summit with Dean to go ski after I had graduated. She granted me permission and therefore I felt liberated.

First of all, I was twenty-one and still calling home for permission! But the second point, and the bigger one, is that I would have gone even if she had said no. But my enjoyment would have been dampened. I would have felt distanced from the ability to be free and have fun. But in this case, since Mom said I could go and have fun, I was liberated and free to enjoy myself.

It is fascinating how my mom's laugh could make me smile on the inside or how her being joyous could ease my mind and relax my hesitance immediately. And not just in person. Even from afar, I needed her to be accepting and condoning to let myself feel the same way.

When I was twenty-two, I finally lost my virginity. Dean and I had been together for what seemed like a lifetime. He was incredibly tolerant and admittedly long-suffering. I confess that I wish I had not made him wait as long as he did—for his sake and mine. I did not need him to prove anything to me, but I was still so bound and guilt-ridden by my mother. In retrospect, it was not fair to any of us, and all of this is still a regret of mine. Dean's and my relationship was exactly the kind that any parent would hope for. It was based on love and respect and should have been allowed the freedom to unfold.

Mom was unjustly judgmental of our romantic relationship and she feared it on a deeper level. I don't know if she would ever admit to it but this threat went beyond Catholicism. I believe she wanted me to stay hers alone. She believed in an absolute hold she had on me. And she prayed that I would never ever want to breach that bond in any way. And growing up, and having sex, would mean that I was leaving her. If I loved (and gave of myself to) another, I was no longer in her control. To her, losing control meant I did not love her.

When it finally happened, we were in Sun Valley, Idaho. Dean and

I were in a bedroom upstairs and my mother was downstairs, drunk. In a strange way, it was her being drunk that freed me up. If she had not been drinking, I would have found it more difficult to follow through. But even though I knew she was totally out of it, the potential threat that she would hear us or walk in and shame me was crippling to me. Her drunkenness emboldened me, but it wasn't an act of rebellion as much as it was one of my own temporary autonomy.

The whole experience was beautiful. It was what you would wish for your daughter. It should have been what I had wished for myself, but in an instant, guilt slapped me in the face. Instead of giving in to what was a loving, and emotionally safe, relationship, and escaping into the most intimate and deserved moment, I began to cry deeply and silently. I didn't regret sharing this with Dean and felt so secure with him. But I deeply regretted being preoccupied and fearful and not allowing myself to enjoy how much we loved one another and how long we had been together.

I got so overwhelmed that I jumped out of my bed, which was a handmade pale-wood bed made from local trees and faced a window and a fireplace. It was very high and I actually kind of tumbled off it and started running. Out the window the moon and the stars burned so bright that you could practically read a book, but I saw none of the beauty. Instead I ran from the room and down a long hall as if I were being chased. I have no idea where I was going but it was probably to go sleep in another bed so my mother wouldn't find out.

I was buck naked, streaking down a hallway and running as if I had just stolen someone's wallet. What a sight! Dean leapt up and ran after me with the comforter in his arms. He threw it around me, grabbed me around my shoulders, and stopped me from running. He hugged me tight and quietly asked me where I was going. He then said the most amazing thing. He said, "Hey, stop running. Why are you running? Where are you going? I am not going anywhere. I am not going to leave you."

I was the one running and he was the one trying to take the responsibility. I was worried that once I slept with him I would become too vulnerable and would no longer own myself. I was afraid I was leaving my mother. As long as I kept that part of me untapped, I could remain emotionally closed. Being that exposed would destroy my escape route. I had always seen myself as alone, but with Mom. This meant I was possibly not alone. This meant I was attached to Dean and I feared that responsibility.

Even though I knew I had taken such a big step in committing to stay at Princeton, I remained entangled with my mother and our life. I didn't know where I began and where my mother ended, and that meant I didn't know how to fit Dean in.

I wish I had been more in touch with my own feelings about all of it, but I had my mother's voice in my head, the public's voice all around me in the press, and the shame of Catholicism in my heart. It wasn't so much about being a good Catholic as it was a promise I had made. I couldn't become a liar. And because the whole world knew I was a virgin, the whole world would know when I was not.

What should have been the beginning of a wonderful phase in my relationship with Dean turned out to be the beginning of the end. I regret the way I handled it. Without school and without virginity, I really was floating in a strange limbo. I suddenly did not know who or how to be around him. It all generated from a twisted sense of self. Dean never put pressure on me for anything, and he respected me in every way. I panicked. I was much better at arm's-length relationships. I was better with an exit-route strategy. I could not handle loving somebody more than my mom.

My fears had much more to do with my mother than they did with religion or public opinion. I knew Mom felt that if she protected my virginity, I could still remain her baby. She probably didn't have the confidence to not be threatened by someone I loved.

The moment I slept with Dean was the moment I left my mother. I chose him. I felt this and I am sure she did as well. I couldn't handle having made this symbolic decision. There really is no such thing as choosing between a parent and a love—but there kind of is. In a moment this intimate, you are choosing your partner over anybody else. It is a rite of passage, and this molting is terrifying and uncomfortable. It needs desire and commitment. I had buried my desire and I had misdirected my commitment.

Yes, Mom would always be my mother, and yes, it was natural and right. But this was a severing of a cord that had become brittle. I would exert efforts at trying to reattach said cord for many years to come.

I feel sad for these two young lovers. I feel sad for myself, and for him, and for us. I wish I had had the strength to revel in our relationship more, even from the very start. I gave it what I could, but I remained tethered. The leap was too much for me to handle.

Going to college was, in a way, an ending to the first major era of my career, and it was a closure to the first and longest chapter of my mom's and my relationship.

Chapter Twelve

I Wish I Only Knew You in the Mornings, Mama

E ven before my relationship with Dean became intimate—and before the life-changing trip to our mountain home—Mom remained in the swing of excessive drinking. By the beginning of my senior year she had progressively increased the amount she was drinking and began to mix the vodka, wine, and the rum and Diet Cokes. I was home less, and when I was, I was buried in homework and my thesis work. That and having fun with my now best friends as well as Dean. I loved him.

I begged her to stop. I'd say things such as "Can you at least try not getting drunk on the day of graduation?"

"I promise."

She had gotten so used to lying to me and to believing her own lies that the pattern just kept being repeated. I gave her one last request not to drink at my graduation. I should have specified *all day and also at the party*.

She managed to not drink before the actual ceremony. She was sober as I was walking up to the podium to accept my diploma: "cum laude, for French literature."

The honors were a nice surprise and might have been higher if I had gotten an A instead of an A-minus on part of my junior paper. Anyway, I walked up and hoped Mom was proud. I knew my dad was. I believe he just felt I earned and deserved it because of all my hard work. Dad left after lunch.

By the end of the day Mom had managed to smuggle alcohol in and either surreptitiously or openly drink it—I can't remember which. At the big graduation dinner Mom wanted to dance and I wanted to be as far away from her as I could be. I left her with Lila and my gay "godparents," Hank and Richard, who were my mom's friends from way back. They were the ones with the Fire Island house and the poodle who exposed the fact my mother wasn't wearing any underwear. At the dinner she had not done anything majorly embarrassing, but when she was drunk she cursed more and flirted more. I wanted out.

After I left the dinner, I went to Dean's room and found him drunk after having just been punched in the lip. He had actually demanded a friend of his punch him. I have no idea why. I instantly felt as if I were surrounded by immaturity. I took my leave from him, too. I actually remember thinking at that moment that I was alone in a different way. I felt sad and disappointed in both my mom and Dean. Both of them felt out of my reach, and even though Dean did not have a problem with alcohol, alcohol had interfered with my enjoyment of this special day. But I forgave Dean.

College, which had been the focus of my life for four years, was over. I was about to start on a very scary, very uncharted path, and I would somehow have to navigate it.

After college, I basically moved more permanently into our townhouse on Sixty-Second Street. Up until then Haworth and Princeton had been where I lived. We had had the townhouse for a few years but only stayed there when necessary. But I wanted to live back in the city full-time, and I wanted to live alone. Mom stayed in New Jersey but would come and go as she wanted. But even though I liked living alone in the townhouse, I was constantly worried about my mother, just as I had been when I was at school. If we had lived in New York City only, I might have been less worried about Mom's drinking, because driving would have been less of an issue. Every time the phone rang later at night I was sure it was going to be the police. It was so strange because I did not want to be near her. But being away from her and not being able to monitor her was even more torturous. Dick, the driver, was only part-time by then because my work had diminished, and Mom always assumed she was OK to drive.

I did not have a movie lined up—or anything else professionally for that matter—but I was not yet concerned. I was enjoying being a graduate from Princeton University and I already had my vocation. Little did I know that it was all about to go horribly awry.

At this point in my career I did not have the luxury of not working and not earning. We had so much overhead. We had an office staff of five women, a handyman, a cleaning lady, and a part-time driver. We had four homes with mortgages and bills seemingly everywhere. We needed to make money, and much of the endorsements from the past—the doll, the hair dryers, the book, even the Brooke Jeans line—had all gone away. Great, I had a clean slate. What a luxury. Despite the financial pressures, I decided I had a degree and time and therefore would hone my craft.

I wanted to focus on myself as an artist. I started taking acting and dancing classes two and three times a day. I was still under the assumption that the jobs were going to keep flowing in. I was just going to be better in them because I was actually working on my acting ability. I was in an intense acting class that lasted for weeks and was six to eight hours long, including various exercises and scene work and two to four hours of meditation. We would spend the meditation portion lying on our back looking for a green light. People were crying all over the place and I felt incredibly alone. Basically this class was brainwashing and was incredibly unproductive for somebody like me. I needed to learn how to act, not how to get in touch with my "shadow side" while seeing the "green light" in my "mind's eye." It was a disaster because I became so stripped of any defenses during these exhausting, torturous techniques that I was mugged for the first time in my life. I had also basically stopped eating food, existing on fumes.

Mom and Lisa, my best friend from high school, drove into the city together one day and kidnapped me back from this pseudo-actor's religion. Lisa had graduated from Villanova and was working for a bank. She was still living at home and her house was not far from ours. Mom and Lisa talked often but mostly hung out only with each other when I was around. They usually drank together on movie sets or when I was nearby but working.

The two of them took me to a diner and ordered me frozen yogurt with fruit and granola and said they just missed me. By the end of the meal I confessed to hating the class and realizing it was not where I wanted to be. Mom and Lisa said that I was starting to act weird and they were worried. Even though Mom did not show any signs of giving up drinking when aligned with my best friend, Lisa, she was able to help me become grounded again.

Mom and I were trying to scrounge up jobs for me to do. I assumed that when I graduated, my career would pick up where it had left off. I did not realize that it hadn't left off anywhere because I was really neither an actress nor a model. I had become a celebrity and an advertising icon. But these days I was an ad icon without any ads. Back when I worked for Calvin, he had not renewed my contract for a second year because the jeans were being too identified with me and less with the brand. I got dropped. I had gained twenty pounds in college, and the deal Mom and I had—she'd stop drinking and I'd stop snacking—she broke in a day. I wasn't getting any jobs but shitty commercials, mostly out of the country.

We decided a movie was needed.

I had filmed *Brenda Starr* the summer between my junior and senior year at Princeton with the intention of its being released around the time I graduated. The movie was way ahead of its time and was brilliantly conceived. The movie had been my mother's idea. *Brenda Starr* had always been her favorite cartoon and she had been saying for years that she wanted me to play her in a film one day. She had optioned the rights at one point but was never able to set the project up. Our option ran out and Mom did not put more of our money into holding on to it. Finally, Mom found the original cartoonist, Dale Messick, and even got Delia Ephron to write the first draft, and Mom found some independent company to fund it.

The problem was it didn't have a studio behind it, and although the concept and the actors and the costumes and makeup and hair were incredible, the backers were questionable, and it got into terrible legal quicksand. The movie, although made before all the other cartoon and superhero movies, would not be released for three years, after a glut of blockbusters. It was doomed, but such a great idea. Mom had ideas like this and often seemed ahead of her time. She unfortunately was never able to parlay these trailblazing ideas into reality. She never had a team or the big guns behind her. We were the scrappy insurgent group that would get slaughtered trying to defend our small territory.

Anyway, the plan of having a movie released after graduation was foiled and I would soon begin to realize in what dire straits my career lay.

Every day I would ask my mom, "Am I going to get a movie? Am I going to get to act again?"

"Of course, just be patient."

I kept asking, and I kept believing her words, but I was stagnating and I didn't know where to turn.

Something had to change. Mom and I knew a few people who worked with an ICM agent named Sam Cohn, and she set up a meeting to sit down with him. He was a big agent and had clients like Meryl Streep and Louis Malle. I remember hearing him say that he would only take me on if I ceased being a celebrity and committed to being an actress. That sounded wonderful to me. He wanted to represent me, but only if my mother stepped down.

Well, there was zero chance of my mother stepping down from anywhere and she was very angry that anyone would even ask. Mom still had my utter support and I believed she would do whatever she thought best for my career. She refused and she made me walk away. I actually do feel that this was a pity because at the time it was a real opportunity that I was denied.

It's funny—I had forgotten all about this but was reminded of it recently by Lila, who said she begged my mother to reconsider. Mom got angry with her for trying to divide the two of us and for entrusting my career and my well-being to a total stranger.

Looking back at this now, I get a pang of regret. I start thinking about the what-ifs of it all and feel anger and sadness. For so many years I did not feel valid as an actress. Having been deprived of the opportunity to become a respected actress pains me.

But, thinking about it, I also see it as comforting—proof that I had actually always been seen as a valid talent. The endorsement from a big agent was very important and yet my mother denied me it. And I blindly believed in her, even at this older age.

I believe that if I had had an agent even earlier, there might have been more continuity in my work and a stronger focus on quality rather than popularity. But then maybe I would have never left the business to attend college. Maybe I would have done my coveted period movies and then never been heard from again. Maybe I would have never earned enough to be able to live as comfortably as I do. The piece I had to take away, even if it did not result in anything, was that an esteemed person in the film industry had faith in me as a talent. He had incredible taste and an impressive roster of clients and he wanted to add me to it. This I would take with me forever. But at the time, it was not enough to cause me to find the strength to "abandon" my mom. My instincts were secondary. I allowed her to make the decisions for me because I needed it and thought it was right. She had convinced me that nobody would have my best interests at heart as she did.

I had no idea that going away from the Hollywood game for years while getting an education would have such a negative effect. I also didn't realize that I had never really been in the Hollywood game. There wasn't even any footing to regain. Nobody knew what I was, myself included. Mom did not even think to ask me and didn't seem to care herself. We needed to make a living and keep our houses, and as long as I was well-known, I could earn. It did not matter how. We had no contacts with whom to reassociate. The connections my mom had were mostly with people of questionable integrity and talent. We thought the power of my face was enough. She had no idea that we had no groundwork on which to build. It was worse than starting from zero. It was like starting from negative ten.

I had no power at the box office. I was not the skinny, exotic woman-child I had once been. I had been marketed as a commodity that was obtainable to do whatever song and dance asked of me. I'd sell deodorant, dolls, hair dryers, shampoo, makeup, stockings, and socks—just about anything anybody asked. The last film of any quality I had acted in was *Endless Love* and that was already six years past. I hung out with people like Michael Jackson and Wayne Newton, my manager was practically pickled and useless, and I had no agency representation. Things were not looking promising for a career worthy of much respect. We were floundering.

All I knew at this point was that none of the choices we were making felt good. I thought they were bricks being laid. What I should have seen was that the bricks needed to be solid and not made out of sand. "Work begets work" has always been part of my mom's mantra and it had worked until now. But it should have been obvious to us all that shitty work begets shitty work and I was becoming trapped in a career path from which I might never recover.

The next few years featured creepy producers and shitty directors on independent films where my name procured the finances. They were bad movies without studio support and real low-rent talent at the helm. It was an extremely confusing and difficult time for me regarding my identity and my persona. Nothing was aligning.

I have no idea what Mom was doing to propel me toward anything except keeping my name out there. It still did not occur to her that we could use professional help. She did not want to share a percentage of the profits and resented giving 15 percent away to a person who did not get me the job in the first place. What I did not realize was that the jobs that she did get me were not the jobs I wanted anyway. It did not occur to my mom that there could have been a defined path if I wanted to be an actress. A path that included outside expertise and professional agents. I assume Mom contacted some old business connections, but what I remember from this time is *waiting*. I was trying to be patient by dancing and getting back in shape and by seeing films and by doing various less intense acting workshops.

Still, my patience was not paying off, and the Hula-Hoop had no need to be "remembered."

I got some horrible weight-loss campaign for a company in Japan in 1993. I needed to lose the stubborn twenty pounds that I had gained in college and had kept on for six years. I thought it would be a great way to get in shape and make money. Japan was still a world that wanted me.

Mom and I had been to Japan many times and we always had a good time. We'd travel with Gavin or someone from his team and we laughed our way through tatami-mat sleeping, geisha shows, and raku throwing pots. We pretended to eat the raw things we all secretly gathered in our napkins, and poured our whiskies into CEO's glasses. Gavin and I hardly drank alcohol, and getting the bosses drunk helped make the evenings shorter. I am sure Mom would have welcomed the pour, but neither Gavin nor I would let that happen. We made friends and money and I got to see another country. Diana, Lisa, and various buddies came with me on those trips.

This trip was different. It was not the heyday of my eighties experience, and the company I was representing was ambiguous and would later go bankrupt from fraud. The flight to Japan was long and while I was sleeping, my mother was drinking. She would usually start a trip off not even drinking in the lounge. But then we'd board and she'd plug into the steady drip of red wine in those dumb little doll-size glasses. She probably justified every new pour by exclaiming how small the glasses were.

While on the plane she must have struck up a conversation with two businessmen who worked for Nescafé. They no doubt recognized me. Every human being on the face of the earth seemed to be able to recognize me by this point despite the fact I wasn't really working.

We landed in Tokyo and went to the hotel to make that horrible decision whether to sleep for a while to combat jet lag. We had checked into our hotel suite and I had put on a hotel robe, when the doorbell rang. Mom had invited the two businessmen to meet me in our hotel room. I had not formally met them on the plane because I was asleep and Mom did not want to disturb me. She did not want to disturb me on the plane, but in the hotel, in a robe, jet-lagged and disheveled, it was perfectly good business. I yelled that I did not want to come out, only to see that the two men were already in the sitting area.

I gave in and in a few moments I was out there shaking hands and bowing and talking about how much I loved their country.

"Oh yes, I drink coffee but I especially enjoy the Japanese teahouses that we've seen in Kyoto. Oh yes, I actually prefer Nescafé. . . . How did you know? Are you saying I could use some right now, you silly you?"

I excused myself and tore the mask off in my adjoining room.

Wow, I must be in bad shape career-wise. That was gross. But this, too, shall pass. Just wait it out, Brooke.

Still, I did it. I got the Nescafé-businessman gig and was flown to Paris to shoot the commercial. How could it be that despite the fact I'd acted in quality films like *Pretty Baby* and *Endless Love* and box-office hits like *The Blue Lagoon*—and also had a degree from an Ivy League school—I would still find myself in France doing a Nescafé commercial that would be dubbed in Japanese?

While in France, Mom would disappear to have meetings in the lobby of the gorgeous hotel and would return just as dinners were starting or interviews conducted. We were there four days and I think she must have been inebriated the entire time. Again, she was basically safe because she was not driving and was more contained by her inability to speak French. I could forge ahead and complete the current job. It felt good to be working again and the shooting environment was similar to that in the States. The project was not something I was proud to endorse and something about it felt very wrong and a bit pathetic.

I wrapped the commercial and packed my bags. I warned my mother that we needed to pack up and be ready for the flight the next day. I went to bed and got up for early coffee in the glass-paned atrium restaurant. I had a book to read and kept my eye on the time. As we got closer to departure time, Mom still had not shown up. I knew she had come home but she was gone again. I had not slept a lot so she must have slept even less. I returned to her room and found out that, sure enough, she had not packed and didn't seem ready to get back to America. She had been out the whole night drinking and must have returned only for a short time.

I began getting the place packed up to go. When she finally stumbled in, I just stormed around the room throwing her stuff in bags and mumbling about how much I hated her. I had to get back to America. Staying another day was not an option. I had a bridal shower

I was throwing with a friend for Lisa and had to get back to New York by that afternoon.

I stomped and screamed and accused her of being a loser and made big claims about what a fuck-up my mother was. How fucking pathetic she was and what an idiot I was to think that she could ever pull herself together. How I was never going to get any acting jobs but be relegated to selling fucking instant coffee! Not even real brewed coffee, but *instant*. I was throwing her stuff in bags and she just watched. I always either moped or stomped and slammed doors and raised my voice when Mom drank, but there was a panic in my gut this time. I had to get out of this hotel and France and away from her, and I could not handle another moment of any of it. I did not want her to be the reason our travel plans got screwed up.

She refused to listen but instead left the room, having not lifted a finger to prep for the trip. I yelled after her, "Be downstairs when the car gets here!"

Slam.

I finished getting everything thrown together and called a bellman to help get the bags into the car. I waited in the car in absolute embarrassment and disgust. I was disgusted at her. I was disgusted with myself for being so helpless and bound to this dynamic. When was I going to learn? Mom showed up at the last minute and I was seething inside at how pitiable my life was. We fought and her words were imbued with vitriol. I was an ingrate, she said, and why couldn't I be as talented an actress elsewhere as I was during the act of fury I was displaying? She said I had a fat ass and I did not appreciate anything.

She had been drinking all morning, either at the hotel bar or at some place nearby. When she had left the room earlier, she must have gone to get a few last-minute nips before the flight. The last few must have hit her while she was on the drive to the airport, and she actually passed out in the car. I can count on one hand the times Mom had ever passed out. She never even took naps. I watched her as the car stopped and the door was opened. She was still not awake. I made a weak attempt to stir her but realized I did not want her to awake at that moment. I got my bags and stormed off to check in. I purposely took her passport with me because I had gotten it from the room safe with the jewelry. I planned on leaving France with it in hand but did not have the guts to keep her ability to exit the country. At the very last second, I ran back to the car where she was still slumped over, and I threw the passport inside the slightly opened window.

"Mademoiselle, what should I do wif yur muzzer?"

"Je ne sais pas. . . . C'est comme tu veux. Merci." *I do not know. It is as you wish. Thank you.*

I boarded the Concorde flight to JFK airport. I sobbed the entire flight. The actress Amy Irving was on the same flight and asked if she could help. Ironically her mother, Priscilla Pointer, had been one of the acting coaches hired for me on *Just You and Me, Kid*. I told Amy that I had just left my mom passed out in a car at departures. She gave me a warm smile. Once again I had the feelings of survival and sadness mixed with a tad of freedom of not having to be on the trip with Mom.

We landed, and while in baggage claim, my new video camera was stolen right from under my nose. Mom managed to show up the next day at 11:00 A.M. at the shower as if nothing had happened. She breezed through the party with grandeur and a wrapped Hermès scarf and began the red wine all over again.

I should have held on to her passport.

Something had to shift. I could only think of shifting my mother's behavior, not my life. If I could just get her to stop drinking, my career would pick up again.

Lila and I researched treatment facilities together once again.

Auntie Lila had moved away from Teri and from working at our company a few years prior and was now residing in her hometown of Tucson, Arizona. We both knew that it was bad with Mom, and even though I had much less leverage than the first time, we needed to try something. She'd never again fall for meeting us at a location with her bags secretly packed.

I put a call into Betty Ford herself. I explained my situation and she promised that if I could get my mother to go to the Betty Ford Center, she would have a bed ready for me. I would just have to get Mom to commit to going back into treatment. Lila knew an intervention specialist who flew in to places all over the country to help with interventions. We asked him to join Mom, Lila, and me in Haworth, New Jersey.

Mom saw us "interventing" a mile away. She sat on our long, low, floral-upholstered couch and dug in. She said she would *never* again go to treatment and was insulted and disgusted by us all. She was angry and adamantly refused to go. She attacked me for trying to control her, and even when I was being soft, and loving, and saying this was necessary and good for us both, she just shook her head.

"If I want to stop, I'll stop."

I told her about Betty Ford and she blurted out something about not being an addict or in bad enough shape for a place like the Betty Ford clinic. She claimed she did not have a drinking problem. Well, she was right there! My mother never had a problem with her drinking. It was the rest of us who did. I even think she meant this double entendre herself. Another one of her little word manipulations.

"Fuck you. Fuck you both, Lila." She looked at the intervention specialist and said, "I don't give a shit who you are, but I want you out of my house."

"Your daughter asked me to come, Teri, to help her," he responded.

"Well, great, help her and get the fuck out of my life."

"But, Mom . . ."

"I began in this world alone, and I'll end in this world alone. I don't need you, *Brooke*, to tell me how to live."

"But I really love you, Mom, and—"

"Yeah, and Peter really loved Jesus. Where did it get him?"

She had this cocky expression on her face as if she had just won. She would often say to me while I was growing up that one day I "would deny [her] like Peter." She sat there triumphant, seemingly pleased with the proof that I had denied her just like the apostle Peter did to Jesus when the pressure was on. It was crazy when she chose to pull out the religion card and how hypocritical she remained.

This attempt at an intervention was an abject failure. Money down the drain and a lost hot-commodity bed rejected. I called Mrs. Ford and apologized. I thanked her for the special treatment but said that my mom wouldn't be coming to the center. She told me that Mom would never get help until she wanted it for herself. I explained that it did not seem as if anything like that was ever going to happen. Mrs. Ford recommended that I never give up hope.

To this day, the ACOA kid in me thinks that if only Betty Ford's had been available the first time, maybe it would all somehow have been different.

I walked away in defeat and without any plan. I continued to live in New York City and go to events if asked. Mom proceeded as if nothing had ever transpired, but every now and then would throw the attempt up in my face to reinforce how I had failed and how she would never be outsmarted. She was a true addict.

I shot some interesting photos for *Paper* magazine and was kind of getting into the creative groups via the magazine. I did readings and performance pieces for fun makeup artists and was asked by the likes of Russell Simmons to join him on a panel to discuss what was in and what was out in our culture these days. I was hoping that maybe through my fabulous community of gay artistic friends I would find a niche and get back on top of things again.

It was during this time that I began to date Liam Neeson. He was a tall Irish actor and a drunk who was thirteen years my senior. He wooed me with his brogue, his poetry, and his shitty choice of cheap pinot grigio wine. I rebelled with him and poured myself into his rhythm. I would take dance classes all morning and then meet up with him at the bar at the Ritz-Carlton Hotel on Central Park South. We'd drink and talk to Norman, the bartender, and discuss literature and acting. We would daydream about our future. Norman was, and is, a living legend who looked out for me.

During those days, I existed on cheese and crackers and wine and the relationship. I was going to grow up and the Irish drinking actor was the perfect solution. I was so impressed with going out with a real movie star and I was so familiar with what it was like to live with an alcoholic who lived in dreamworlds. Liam and my mom were perfect for me. And, of course she took to him the way she did to all other tall, manly, gruff drunks. She flirted and welcomed him home. It did not get as creepy as it could have, since Liam hungered after any female attention, but none of it was healthy or real. I was struck by how it was somehow familiar. It was such a cliché and I could not see it.

We got serious enough after only three months, and I thought that this would get me away from my mother and earn me the respect I wanted so desperately. He was a real actor, and if he chose me, then I would be exposed to a higher caliber of the entertainment industry. I could finally be serious. He asked me to marry him but without a ring. I told Mom and she worried she would not be invited. That was her immediate response. Nothing about me, but about where she fit in instead. "Watch: When you get married, you probably won't even invite me!"

I told her I would always invite her for the rest of my life whether I wanted to or not. I added that even when she did show up for me, she was never really there anyway because she would be drunk. She brushed it off and said, "We'll see. . . ."

Who knows what she meant by that, but I pretended I was engaged. We spent a Christmas together and Mom suggested that I give Liam a copy of my brilliant book that had been crafted while I was at Princeton. She actually thought it was a clever idea just like her arranging for a Brooke doll to be delivered to John Travolta's hotel on his birthday. I inscribed the book with some mush about my days being in focus since he came into my life. The blurred handwriting was because of the steady flow of wine. I could not fight my mother's drinking, so why not throw responsibility away and join the booze brigade?

Everybody was staying slightly buzzed all day long and we were one big happy family. Until I went to Italy for some job.

Liam had to fly to LA that night to check on a basement flood in his home. I told him to phone me when he arrived.

"Oh, it'll be late, darlin'."

"Well, I won't fall asleep until I know you are safe. And you did ask me to marry you, so you can tell me the plane was safe."

I never heard from him again.

When I got home I crawled back to Mommy. I was too weak and sad and scared and heartbroken. My mama would let me cry and tell me it would pass. We were living in this old Tudor-style house that was too big for two people and beginning to get run-down, and we had no future plans. The Grey Gardens tenure had actually begun. I was obviously incapable of living in the big world alone.

This time Mom did not try to talk me out of it. She happily let me get right back into some of the old routines. Who was the more pathetic one now? We were holding on to multiple properties and fostering dogs in attempts to find them homes. Strangely, people adopted them because they had been in my custody and because people are *crazy.* So maybe we differed from Little and Big Edie, in some ways, but the writing was on the wall for us to transform seemingly into a mother and daughter living alone in a festering relationship of enmeshment and fear. I cried a lot and tried to start every day anew.

I wish I only knew you in the mornings, Mama. . . .

It felt like I was back to the beginning. Even though I had gotten an education and I had done a great deal of work on myself to separate from her, I had been defeated yet again. I was right back in the thicket.

Mom at the age when she'd sneak into the "movin' pictures."

Preteen Mom with her beloved sister, Louise.

Mom the majorette. One of the only times she followed the rules.

Mom while she was working at
Krueger Brewing Company.

Mom and her legs getting pinned.

Mom and Sal out on the town.

The "gams" that Mom was proud of.

Mom with some adoring sailors.

Mom out with one of her many attractive suitors.

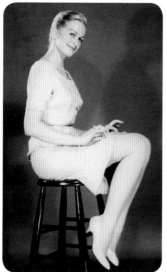

Mom making sure we notice her favorite asset.

One of the only photos I have of Mom pregnant and wearing a wedding ring.
Look how my dad is lovingly gazing at her.

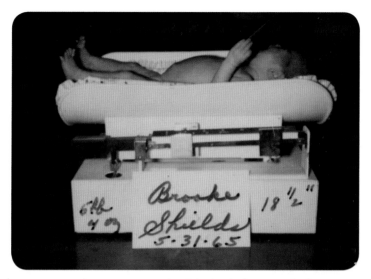

I was two months premature and weighed only five pounds, four ounces.

Mommy kissing her baby. I loved blowing raspberries.

Mom walking me into the beach club. Notice my diaper-only-clad body and hot dog with no bun.

Dad taking me on the same path. Notice the neat outfit and no hot dog. Dad was a smoker.

Chic Mom and me on the street where I met Greta Garbo.

Daddy and me at his Fifty-Second Street apartment. My baggy cloth diaper was Dad's doing.

Mom and me on
Southampton Beach.

One of my favorite pictures of me with my dad. I loved
to make him laugh by doing imitations.

"Hold still, Brookie."

Matching camel coats in front of my favorite store, Woolworth's.

The Kennedy look-alikes, Frank and Didi Shields.

Mom and true love Antonio Rius in Brazil. I did not like sharing my mommy.

Mom's birthday at our Seventy-Third Street apartment.

Teri Terrific shows off her bone structure on a flight to New Orleans.

I struck this pose every time I said trick or treat.

Mom with Chris Atkins in front of our bure on the Turtle Island location of *The Blue Lagoon*. Mom wore only blue jeans.

Mary Ellen Mark

Our friend Mary Ellen Mark took this pic of Mom and me for *Life* magazine. I am in all Calvin Klein attire.

Mom's famous laugh with best friend and collaborator John Holland on *The Brooke Book*.

Mom and me in 1996.

Us at a barbecue. Mom holding her ever-present inhaler.

On my wedding day to Chris.

Lara Porzak

Happy Mom and Dad at the lunch I missed before my wedding.

Lara Porzak

Lara Porzak

Mom's beautiful smile on the veranda during the rehearsal for the ceremony.

Surprise dinner party for Mom's seventieth birthday at our California house.

Mom being silly on Thanksgiving with a doomed turkey.

Mom, Lila, and me in our favorite New York City photo booth on the Upper East Side.

My favorite picture of Rowan kissing her mama. She peed on me a second later.

Two of my favorite baby dolls, Rowan and Blabby.

Easter—Toots and Rowan.

Chris, Rowan, and myself in our backyard, Grier in the oven.

Lara Porzak

Elizabeth Messina

Grier eating my face and me loving every minute of it.

My real-life doll.

Ladies who lunch.

Delicious kisses from my Gdawg.

Mom with her two dogs, Blabby and Donut. See if you can find both. . . .

Me and my ladies.

Winter in Southampton.

Part Four

She says things like how she hates me and then in the next breath like a crazy person says, "I love you more than life."

—Brooke's diary

Chapter Thirteen

We Met by Fax

I survived my heartache from my whirlwind three months with the Irishman and a few more random crushes after that, but it was the last time I ran home to Mommy. I slowly and steadily eased back into living by myself in the city and did a lot of soul-searching.

I had gone to California to meet some filmmakers who were looking for an actress who would want to go live in South Africa for three months and film a movie about raising orphaned leopard cubs in the wild. The movie would be called *Running Wild*. I jumped at the offer. Going to live in a camp in the middle of the bush was just what I needed. Mom and I both traveled there, but after I got settled, Mom went back to America. Her asthma was bad and the dust and wildlife were doing a lot of damage. She was not well and was better off at home.

The movie was very mediocre but the experience was incredible. I lived in a tent on stilts in the jungle and never needed to wear a watch. The experience was somewhat reminiscent of filming *The Blue Lagoon* because we were so isolated and were dictated primarily by the environment. But this time I was without my mother. We raised two leopard cubs and filmed them all the time. We were on a reserve park in the Eastern Transvaal and only left once in three months. I had

very little downtime but I spent all of it writing letters and walking these letters to our makeshift offices, which had various information-transmitting devices.

A friend of mine from Los Angeles (Lyndie G, Kenny G's wife) had been gently pushing me to meet her friend Andre Agassi. I was in no place to be in a relationship and had kept putting it off. While living in South Africa, I began thinking a lot about my life and what I wanted it to look like. I knew I needed to separate professionally from my mother so as to gain a sense of autonomy and career perspective. I also wanted to find a relationship with somebody not threatened by my celebrity and secure in his own profession. I still did not feel totally ready for a boyfriend or husband but I wanted to enjoy my solitude in this camp and settle my mind and my heart. I was always open to friendships and was enjoying those friends I had recently acquired on the film.

Lyndie wrote to me and gave me Andre's fax number, and said I should fax him, the only reliable and fast way to be in touch from the set. With thousands of miles between us, we began to communicate via long rambling faxes about life and God and the strange burden of fame and overpowering parents. Andre's father was, in my opinion, far worse than my mom ever was. He was the one who pushed his children to be professional tennis players and would throw away Andre's trophies if they were anything less than first place. My mom kept my Hula-Hoop trophy for twenty years. His dad had managed his career until Andre broke free and hired a manager. Andre and I both understood what it felt like to be famous and to have strong parents who controlled much of our lives.

We were similar in so many ways. Even though he was from Vegas and I was from Manhattan, we both still felt like little kids who had dealt with adult pressures and been given a great deal of responsibility at a young age. We both had begun very young and had been defined by others before developing our own sense of self-awareness. We had grown up in extraordinary circumstances and were desperate to find our place in the world. We were mirrors of one another, and we knew, somewhere deep inside, that we needed each other.

Every day on *Running Wild* I would wake very early before my call time and I would write my letter. Sometimes I had to finish it on the bumpy Jeep ride out to a far-off location and then give it to the cook to take to the office at base camp. I'd wait for Andre's faxes to come in and save them to read by myself at my favorite spot near the river. The people in the office would radio the set if a fax came in and everybody eagerly anticipated how happy I seemed when I got one. Let's just say I was pretty darn happy those three months.

It was like we were living in a different time. This was our carrier-pigeon romance. We poured ourselves into our faxes; they were like diaries in which we were able to explore who we were and who we wanted to be. We got to daydream and hope and cry and believe we could be deeply happy. My mom was nowhere near any of it and this freed my mind and my heart.

Both Andre and I were at a turning point in our lives when we met. He had just had wrist surgery and was not sure he would ever play tennis again, and I was desperately seeking to reclaim my floundering career. And we were falling in love by fax.

When the film wrapped and I went back to the United States, we began to talk on the phone and arranged to meet the next time I was in LA.

Back in New Jersey, Mom seemed to have settled into a drinking pattern consisting of binge drinking followed by a few days seemingly on the wagon before digging in again. Other times she'd maintain a low but constant hum of drunkenness throughout every day. What was different was that I was not living inside it and enveloped by it. I was preoccupied by it always, but the periodic distances—whether created by my being away on location or just by living in Manhattan and away from the dark Tudor house in Haworth—helped me stay afloat. Mom seemed to be happy about this kid Andre who was very famous and who, according to her, "obviously had a father worse than even me. Maybe you'll feel lucky, Brooke."

Mom and I flew out to LA to film some final city scenes for the movie, and stayed at a little bungalow we had bought a few years after Princeton. Andre came over to take me to dinner. He met Mom while wearing faded light jeans with serious holes in them, Nikes, and a T-shirt. His hair was vintage Andre hair, mostly blond with some brown bits and longer than even mine was at the time. I had no idea that he was wearing taped-on extensions but I would discover it much later, when he would tell me in an emotional and embarrassed admission. He looked like a rock star, complete with Oakley sunglasses and a cool sports car.

As he was walking away to get the door, Mom pointed to a specific hole in his jeans over his top left butt cheek. The hole had frayed and it was obvious he was either not wearing any underwear or wearing a thong. (I would later learn that it was a thong). Mom secretly pointed to it and seemed to motion to me to touch it. Without even considering that this might have been rude and possibly premature, I put my index finger right on the skin peeking out through the material. He jumped and I said I just couldn't help it. Who the hell knows what he thought of that intro? What type of a mother tells her daughter to do that? And what type of a daughter obeys without considering the possible consequences? But later on he would comment on the fact that after spending some more time with me, he realized he was with a "real woman." If he thought I was a "real woman," I can only imagine the level of immaturity he had been used to in dating. The truth was that I was far from being a self-actualized woman. But compared to the way he felt and to those other famous people he had met, I guess it could seem like I had my life together.

His perception should have sent up a red flag, but alas, I was on a path I would not want to or be able to get off of for five years.

After the scene I had to shoot was completed, Andre flew me out to Las Vegas in his very own plane, where he'd grown up and still lived. I spent a very chaste first weekend with him in his gated community house on a golf course. All the houses looked alike and there was a Stepford-wives sensibility to the community. It was quiet and clean and surreal. This whole existence represented the antithesis of every aesthetic I had ever known and loved in New York City. It felt alien and wonderfully homogenized.

We drank champagne and talked endlessly about the similarities between our upbringings and about the crush of fame. We had both reached stardom at very young ages and had demonstrative parents. We were both highly publicized figures and were struggling with the demands of being in the public eye as well as dealing with the pressure of trying to grow up under the scrutiny of the press. We understood one another. We complained about how deeply dissatisfied we both were with our careers. His was from a lack of love for it and mine from a seemingly unrequited love from it. The air in Vegas at the beginning of fall was still and the temperature perfect. The sky was like a pastel watercolor and Andre exuded respect.

I expected nothing from him, and in this environment I felt safe. And for some reason, I was not considering my mom's feelings in any of it. He was a very gentle soul and seemingly calm and devoid of unnecessary drama. I actually felt more settled than I had in years. I thought we were becoming special to each other in a very unique way. It was not clouded by passion or fear but fueled by respect and fresh perspective. It felt like a safe respite from a life that had been beating me down. I felt like I'd finally found a relationship in which I felt totally understood. Even though we were actually just kids, we both possessed a level of self-awareness. We were somehow grounded and individually intent on self-improvement. Andre and I wanted to thrive, not just survive.

I also had a foot surgery planned and was not sure I would ever be able to dance the same again. After years of being in excruciating pain, I decided to get both bunions on my feet removed. The surgery was the next week and I knew that I'd be out of commission for a least three months. I hoped we would keep in touch but had no expectations. I did not anticipate more than the probable reversion back to the fax machine, but I was in for the shock of my life.

Andre knew when my surgery was and asked if I minded his coming to New York to visit. I had nothing to lose and said yes. It was the first time I had ever had major surgery and was actually a bit nervous. It was elective but so necessary to alleviate the chronic pain.

Mom was supposed to take me but got drunk the night before and I couldn't count on her. She got angry when she realized that Andre was going to visit. I can't remember if he brought me to surgery, but I do remember transferring my need to be taken care of onto Andre almost immediately when I realized Mom was drunk. It was a perfect position for both of us. I needed to be cared for and he needed to caretake. He did it sublimely.

After the operation, he and his trainer and close friend Gil Reyes loaded me up in the back of an SUV for the drive back to New Jersey. Once home they carried me and got me settled into my hospital bed that had been set up in the first-floor sunroom. It would be easier and quieter there than in New York City. I was groggy and exhausted and in no pain . . . yet. I could tell that Mom was deeply unsettled that Andre was around and that his main focus was caring for me. I knew she was thrown but I honestly was too exhausted and drugged up to address any of it. Nobody had ever shown me such interest and seeming commitment, and I am sure she felt threatened. I could tell she liked him because she didn't whisper behind his back to me but I could tell this was all getting a bit too close for her comfort. She seemed awkward and uncomfortable. Mom tried to regain control and kept insisting that Andre sleep in the guest room, but he kept refusing, saying that he would rather stay near me. He put the sofa cushions on the floor by my bed and he refused to leave. Mom was getting visibly angry and did not like anybody not doing as she said.

"Oh, you're that kind," she scoffed, and went into the kitchen.

I went in and out of sleep all through the night. If I shifted and a foot fell of its elevated position, Andre would jump up to right it. This vigilant attention left me in a daze. Nobody had ever taken care of me like this. Honestly it felt too good to be true but I did not fight it. I guess it was his version of strapping me to his chest and it felt good. The irony was that Mom chalked it up to control issues on Andre's part, and the competition for my loyalty began. I knew Mom would ultimately have been capable of tending to me, but I also knew she would be drinking throughout. I also had Lisa a few streets away. I was extremely vulnerable and scared and the pain was mounting.

At one point, Lisa came to visit and I found myself trying to make light of the fact that she and my mother were in the kitchen getting drunk on Zima while I lay incapacitated and defenseless. Andre was appalled. I was broken and he was going to fix me. More writing on the wall that I should have seen, but the solid support felt intoxicating and I signed up with every ounce of my soul.

For the first time in my life, somebody stood up for what was best for me without any regard for, or disrespect of, my mother. Other boyfriends in the past either tried to ally me against my mother or were so threatened by her that they shrunk a bit around her. Those who thought they were going to be the ones to stand up to my mother and defend me were in over their heads, while the other, more intimidated ones lost my respect. There never seemed to be a loving happy medium. I couldn't strike it myself and needed somebody to help balance me.

With Andre I instantly felt a vicarious thrill. To me it seemed that he was never rude but simply forthright and steadfast. I could learn from him in how he dealt with things. He seemed straightforward and loving yet honest. There was no fight. He had come to support me and that was what he was going to do. It was a pretty funny sight—Tennis Boy from Vegas sleeping on the floor on three square floral chintz pillows lined up vertically next to a hospital bed holding a girl whose both feet were broken and held together by pins, while her mother and best friend were getting hammered on shitty malt liquor in the nearby kitchen. Oh, the glamour. Andre and I actually had such a laugh that I never wanted him to leave my side. I was going to be safe. I was no longer alone.

In a few days Andre had to return home. But he had made his mark on my heart and I planned to visit him as soon as I could.

I healed rather quickly, as did Andre from a wrist surgery, and he began a first comeback in tennis. I started spending as much time with him as I could, which usually meant I would follow him around the country to watch him play tennis. I did my rehabilitation alongside him in his training sessions and we both soul-searched and trained our bodies and our minds. It was an evolution and a security I had never experienced.

I had the space to expand my thinking about my life and about my career. Andre supported my every dream and helped me see how I could make them actualities. I was away from my mother and living a totally new and different existence. I talked to Andre at length about my mother and her drinking and my stalled career. I bared my insecurities to him and put my absolute, unfettered trust in him to guide me through. He said things like "I want your dreams to become my reality."

"What!"

"I wish you could see yourself the way I see you. You would really love what you see."

Oh, good Lord Jesus, where had this guy materialized from? He was too good to be real. And he would do incredibly thoughtful things like getting the LA house tented for termites when he heard we had a problem. He gave me books by Marianne Williamson and C. S. Lewis to read and thought *Men Are from Mars, Women Are from Venus* was a great way for the sexes to grow together. I did not question a thing he suggested. I just wanted to keep breathing in the fresh air of contentment.

I bared my heart about wanting to be an actress and feeling like a joke and a failure. I was out of shape and rejected and I didn't know how to turn my career around. He said that if I was serious about being an actress, I should be out in Los Angeles and I should get an agent. In order to do so I'd have to scale down propertywise and consolidate my finances. I'd have to sell and buy myself time to forge a new path and not be forced to take jobs just for the cash. And, most important, I'd have to leave my mother as my manager and establish myself financially and professionally separate from her and the debts. That last part I had come to know but hearing somebody else say it hit me like a Mack truck. I knew it was true, but the reality terrified me. It would kill her.

Andre said he would help, and I could use his office and lawyers to ease the transition. His manager and best friend since childhood,

Perry Rogers, was controlling his life at this point. Perry had basically facilitated Andre's breakaway from his own father. I figured that since he had guided Andre through a similar disengagement, he must have all the answers. Plus, Agassi Enterprises was a huge operation with many on its payroll. There were trainers, doctors, massage therapists, secretaries, pilots, assistants, lawyers, ex-girlfriends, all being subsidized in one way or another. I was property-rich but had both an entangled relationship with a drunk business partner and a depleted cash flow. I was in no position to say no to the possibility of reclaiming my future. I felt empowered and scared but knew I needed to cause a huge shift in my life.

Andre helped me believe in myself and in my talent and in the possibility of future success. There were concrete steps that could and should be taken, and both Andre and Perry presented me with a game plan. I had never before understood any of the financial aspects of my life. Mom handled it all with an accountant and I never paid attention. These two guys, who were five years my junior, tried to educate me on what needed to happen financially and professionally, which aided personal growth as well. Andre was never as emotionally connected to his father as I was to my mom. I deeply loved my mom, whereas he remained ambivalent toward his dad and all he stood for. My emotional separation was going to be tougher for me than his was but the goal was the same. Andre suggested I investigate the possibility of obtaining an agent from an important agency in LA.

I went alone out to visit my mother in Haworth to tell her that I had thought a great deal about it and I had decided that I wanted to go out on my own as an actress and that if I failed, I wanted to fail on my own. I planned on trying to go back to William Morris and working once again with my old agent. I wanted to try my hand at a career my way and with a vetted professional team.

I explained to Mom that I felt we were becoming polarized as people because of her drinking and expressed my dissatisfaction with the way my career was going. I said I wanted to try to salvage the mother-daughter part of our lives. I told her the only way I thought that could happen would be for me to separate from her professionally. It was all too confused and becoming toxic. I added that I really wished she would quit drinking for once in her life.

"Don't you worry about my drinking. Have you talked to a lawyer?"

"No. I wanted to talk to you first."

It was true that I had not told our lawyers yet. I wanted to keep to my word about this being a personal decision and I wanted to show her respect by coming to her in person, and first. I was a bit hurt that she thought I had already contacted an actual lawyer but felt clean knowing I had not. The idea had not come from Perry or Andre— they were just helping with practical elements.

"Well then, do whatcha gotta do."

There was a hint of her thinking it bullshit that I wanted to save our personal relationship. I saw her smirk as if I were just using it as the excuse. She was a mix of hungover and still drinking, ingesting enough every time she left the room to have her senses dulled but her edges nicely sharpened. Most people soften their edges with alcohol. My mom's protruded and hardened with booze. I started to feel a sense of panic rising in my gut, and the moment she drove off to rehab, I felt guilty and I wanted to try to make it better for her. I did not realize that I could never have gotten her approval for something that was going to destroy the very foundation of all she thought she had built. But I wanted her approval nonetheless. I wanted to help give her security in this moment, so I stupidly threw in that I'd just split everything we had together in half and she would be fine. It was never going to be that easy. I had no idea how difficult it would all be financially and legally.

I left the house feeling vaguely concerned that it had all gone far too smoothly to be true. As it had been with rehab, I knew this was just the calm before the storm.

I had made sure I had been clear and unapologetic. I knew I could not want her approval on something that would devastate her. But I told her I loved her and wanted to repair our relationship and that without the pressure of the career we could start anew. But I think we both knew that this was only part of my plan, and maybe Mom sensed what she thought was the falseness of my approach.

I knew this is something I had to do. I desperately wanted a better relationship with her but was finally convinced that it was never going to happen as long as she was still drinking. The career part was true in the sense that I did want to learn independently from her. But I also knew I would have an agency at the ready. I did not want to eviscerate her, or undermine all she had done. I had a goal and I was not dishonest. I just tried not to be cruel in my delivery. I had to say I wanted to try on my own versus saying I was unhappy with the job she was doing. Both were true and I was leaving no matter what, so why not remain kind and generous in spirit? She was the one who would be left alone. I was not.

But even though she'd seemed calm about it, she wasn't buying any of it. I knew it. I got out of the house before I would want to backpedal and apologize and ask her to tell me it was all OK with her and that I was making the right decision, and that I would end up getting work, right? And that maybe she was correct and I should just stay with her and we would figure it out?

Can you say ACOA?

I then called the William Morris Agency. I was humble and honest and said I had come to a place in my life where I needed a fresh start. I was separating from my manager-mother. Would I be able to sit and discuss the possibility of rejoining the agency?

I was given a bit of a scorned response that I played right into. I might not have known the business of entertainment, but I did know the business of people. Wasn't it all a game anyway? If my mother taught me anything, it was that it was all a game.

Bargaining and posturing was how the business was run, right? The only problem was that Mom would not bargain and she didn't consider her bravado false. But I'd learned from her mistakes as well. I had to find a way to make it their idea to represent me. I had to defer and slightly smooth their ego. After all, they had been scorned. I was sweet and humble, and even though I really was sincere, I played all the right cards on this call. After the agent seriously said his perfunctory "I'll have to run it by my colleagues to see if there is interest" line, I once again had representation.

I think Mom believed it was just a bluff and that I was being manipulated and brainwashed by the Agassi team. I don't think she believed I would follow through on any of it. She would come to hate Perry with such venom in her veins that she would never accept him. She reveled in the fact that even Andre eventually fired Perry. Mom would never come to believe that this was a good move for any of us.

I explained the split to the lawyers Mom and I had been using for years, but I also informed them I would be using another team to handle the logistics. I couldn't afford the legal fees but Andre said he would help detangle the mess and help me get back on my feet. I took the charity for the first time in my entire life. I had no idea that once reality hit her, my mother would dig in her heels legally for quite some time and emotionally until her death.

I was offered a role replacing Rosie O'Donnell in the Broadway revival of *Grease* as the Pink Ladies leader, Rizzo. Andre and Perry and my "new" agent all thought it was an amazing idea and hoped that the quickest way to Hollywood was via old Broadway.

I was to go on tour for three weeks as a sort of break-in/rehearsal period with *Grease* so I could get used to the grueling schedule of doing eight shows a week and performing live in front of thousands of people. Right before I left I did something that I will never fully forgive myself for, but which was ultimately the only chance I had at survival. Soon there would be no turning back.

I had visited my mother right before leaving for the *Grease* tour. I had personally told the three employees at Brooke Shields and Co. Incorporated in Norwood, New Jersey, that some changes were being made and they would all be taken care of, but that I was scaling down and that after Friday they would not need to go into the office. I asked for their respect in not talking to my mom so as to give her time. I did not tell anybody of the other part of my plan. My mother went to the office on a pleasant Friday morning as if it was business as usual. She had gotten into the routine of going to the office practically every day, and this Friday was no different from any others. I had told her good-bye and left for tour in Cincinnati to be put into the company. I was busy and avoided phoning home for fear I would break down from nerves and guilt.

Perry had told me that the only way to have a clean break in a complicated relationship like ours was to be drastic. I had to take a stance and make everybody know I was serious. He was used to dealing with big corporations and a very discordant relationship like the one between Andre and his father. But Perry was insensitive to the layers of hurt that his tactics incited. He ruled by fear and by very false bravado and he loved reducing people in business so as to win.

He and Andre had convinced me that as with interventions or corporate takeovers, damage inevitably had to occur. But this was not supposed to be a hostile takeover. It was supposed to be a sensitive, but firm, declaration of my independence. Easier said than done.

I was relieved to trust Andre and his trusted friend and follow along, by proxy, with their plan and their team of bad cops. I always felt better as good cop anyway. Mom left the office on a Friday at about 6:00 P.M. The office was four floors completely filled with all my almost thirty years' worth of archives, film, TV and photo files, memorabilia, scripts, office equipment, collected antiques, and furniture. When Mom arrived back at the office on Monday morning, she put her key in the keyhole and opened the door to find a completely gutted space. Cowardly or not, over the weekend, while I was in an entirely other city, Perry had organized movers and trucks to come empty the space. It was devoid of all signs that any of us had ever been there. Everything—all the legal files, film reels, photos, wardrobe, art, and even my mom's personal desk and furniture—was loaded onto huge moving trucks and en route to Las Vegas.

Mom would never forgive me for what I had sanctioned. But I needed to go cold turkey. I would never have had the strength to do anything other than close my eyes and rip off the scab. The bleeding would not stop for decades.

I buried my head in the tour and avoided her attempts to call me. I stopped the credit cards and began the legal transactions to establish a new corporation, which would be based in Vegas. I got in touch with my mother and said that I would send her money on a monthly basis and that as soon as I returned from tour we should sit down to discuss how to divide all the various assets. I told her that doing what I did was the only way I knew how to do it, that I was sorry to do it to her but knew she would never have made the actual break possible, and that because of her drinking I could not trust her or her judgment. I did what I had to do. She kept reiterating that she knew Perry was the one who put me up to it and that I was being brainwashed. I refuted her claims and said that although Agassi Enterprises had assisted me, it was generated solely by me. She just kept spewing hate toward Perry. She did not blame Andre but kept her rage directed at his manager, Perry. This gutting of the office was the beginning of a deeper, more painful end. We never fully recovered.

Mom started telling anybody who would listen that her daughter had divorced her. She asked Lisa to come over to the house to start to go through my personal things. What she planned on doing with whatever she found I have no idea. Lisa refused, saying she did not feel comfortable doing so. She had recently moved our safe from upstairs in the house into the garage for some reason. Mom did things like that all the time. She hid precious things all over the place out of some kind of paranoia and then usually forgot where they were. She accused me of probably stealing all the jewelry as well. I told her I had not touched the jewelry. But I admit this sent up a warning signal to me. Much later on I finally did orchestrate a sneak into the garage to empty the safe of its contents.

After the office incident, I knew Mom would never willingly give me the jewelry we had bought together over the years. It had all been purchased with the money we both had earned, and even the stuff she had gotten before I was born was all left to me in her will. So, technically, my going into the garage with a girlfriend when I knew she was out was not stealing. My goal was not to keep everything for myself, but it was to prevent her from doing something potentially irresponsible, such as giving all the jewelry to a troubled young woman she had just met at the movie theatre or selling it to a guy she knew who knew a guy whose cousin was from Newark. I placed it all in a safe-deposit box until things settled down.

When I had my debut on Broadway three weeks later, I invited my mother to opening night. She was my mother. I was opening on Broadway for the first time in my life. I knew she would be proud and I was keeping to my word of wanting a mother-daughter relationship. I was not pretending. I wanted my mommy to "look at me, look at me. . . . Mom, watch. . . . Watch this."

She came to the dressing room a bit early, and in her hands she held my trophy from the Hula-Hoop contest twenty years prior. It was filled with fragrant lily of the valley—my birth flower and her favorite scent.

"You did it, kid."

"I love you, Mama."

Mom did not seem happy in life but she did seem a bit less angry. She was still hurt and I still felt bad for the way I handled it, but there was no going back. I really believed it had been the only way. I did hope that without her being my manager, our relationship would improve. I always seemed to forget that little, ever-present thing called addiction and still naïvely felt that this change would help. It would really only help me. I admit I did not expect her to change her views entirely and all of a sudden, but I was sure that once I felt more secure professionally, I would be more tolerant and compassionate. I would have more patience because I could not blame her for my career, and maybe she would affect me less. Neither one of us felt the need to apologize for anything. We all just had to wait and see.

Mom enjoyed the show and I got a standing ovation and a Theatre Guild award for outstanding newcomer on Broadway. The fastest way to Hollywood was via Broadway. Things were picking up for me professionally, and Andre and I were inseparable.

But as for my mother . . . she seemed to be aimless.

Chapter Fourteen

MIA

T
hings were going well careerwise in late 1995. After my six-
month run on Broadway I was offered a guest spot on the Super
Bowl episode of the show *Friends*.

Andre visited the soundstage to watch me shoot my *Friends* scene.
In the scene I played a crazed fan who begins licking Joey's fingers
and throwing my head back with maniacal laughter.

As we were shooting the second pass of the same scene I saw
movement out of the corner of my eye. Andre had stormed off the set.
At cut I ran outside to find him and had to yell to him from the
doorway so as not to get wet from the suddenly pouring sky. He said
I made him look like a fool by licking Joey's fingers, and he got in his
car and drove all the way back to Vegas.

Upon arrival he systematically smashed and destroyed every
single trophy he had won, including Wimbledon and the US Open,
never mind all the others.

It took me three years to have them all replaced. I always believed
his kids would one day want them. I hadn't thought of their being my

kids at that point, but it was just a shame to waste the legacy. He probably threw them away, too, because I had them made.

But the *Friends* episode was ultimately a success, at least, and thanks to that one guest spot, I got the show *Suddenly Susan*, which ran for four seasons.

Suddenly Susan was the best thing that had happened in my career since being cast by Louis Malle in *Pretty Baby*. This was my real emancipation from my mother as a manager. This was all on my terms and with the help of an actual professional team. I was amazed at the support I had now. There were agents who said no for me. There were lawyers who negotiated better deals for me. I had never experienced the way the business should be run. I felt like I was getting away with something. I loved being able to say no and I loved being on a series on TV. I was in my element and I felt alive.

I wanted my mom to know I still wanted her to share the joy with me, but I also wanted the recognition for getting and carrying the show on my own. I never got to speak to her about it, but it was enough to know she thought I was funny. The bond that we always shared through comedy was shepherding me through what would be the next big phase in my career. I suspect that Mom felt a bit responsible for the possibility of this new turn because she always said I got my humor from her. I don't think it was selfishness on her part as much as pride for having nurtured and shared my sense of humor. It had amounted to something she could emotionally take part in. We were both still trying to define our relationship in the wake of the initial separation.

The actual separation of the business took years to complete because Mom would not agree to any way I offered to divide the properties and the various assets. She was becoming more sad and irrational and feared settling anything. I tried to tell her that she should sell off the Haworth and Sun Valley houses as well as the ranch in Montana and scale down.

She would agree to meet to discuss the issues, but then get drunk and either not show or leave in anger. I tried bringing in a mediator, but she refused to speak during our planned and paid-for meeting. It became a bizarre and frustrating situation that showed no signs of ever improving. I was so frustrated and exhausted by all of it and could not understand how I still managed to find myself on a hamster's wheel, getting nowhere with her. Meanwhile, Mom was drowning in sorrow and pickling her cortex more and more each day.

In many ways—both good and bad—I had basically allowed myself to be overtaken by Andre and his enterprise. It was such a relief to breathe for a change. He decided everything and planned everything and took care of everything. He was such a hero to so many that I could do my favorite thing; I would walk in slightly behind him into events or stadiums and enjoyed not having to be the center of attention for the first time in my life.

Our first few years together were amazing. I had never felt more taken care of and loved unconditionally in my entire life.

Once I was working again, I was incredibly happy. I loved performing in *Grease*, and Andre saw the show twenty-seven times. He loved it. He and Gil would stand in the back of the house and mime the dances, and the cast would send them secret messages from the stage. We were happy. Andre's game had begun yet another climb and he was feeling good about his road. He had begun slower and with qualifiers so as to regain his footing. I, too, was starting my career fresh and via a path that was undeniably the most difficult for me. We were an extremely famous couple and for the first time got to really share the burden. Because we were not in the same industry—and obviously not in competition—we could hold hands and jump into what we thought was real life together.

We were like little kids. We ate candy and huddled together like golden monkeys, with wide eyes and a giggle at the rest of the world. I always remembered what he said when we first met: "I want your dreams to be my realities." And it was happening.

Andre was loving and generous with my mother. He bought her a safer car and invited her whenever he could. He struck a very healthy balance, treating her with acceptance. He knew the sadness she caused me, but he also knew I loved her. He had the distance I would never have but would covet. He was a "reformed born-again Christian" who could name the origin of any quote from the Bible.

Mom hated Perry but could not reject Andre. I could tell from early on that she liked him. There was something about the essence of Vegas and his lack of formal education that rendered her less intimidated and less desperate. She also knew he was genuinely sweet and loyal and admired how he had built himself up in the world. I think she knew he helped me stay connected to her and saw herself being taken care of as well. Mom never really believed that I would completely abandon her. Now with Andre, she felt she would be protected somehow. I thought we'd all reached a happy place, and hopefully, it would last forever.

But, of course, there will be the inevitable bump in the road. One night while on hiatus from *Suddenly Susan*, I was in New York City and got a call from the emergency room at St. Vincent's Hospital. They had my mother there. She had taken a bad fall or had some kind of altercation that left her with an enormous hematoma on the side of her head. I rushed downtown and was terrified of what I'd find. She was so relieved to see me—weepy and oblivious to the fact that she looked like the Elephant Man.

As I was walking the corridor outside her bed's little pulled curtain, I looked up to see *Suddenly Susan* being aired on the TV up in the corner of the ward. There was a homeless man who had been beaten up and was off in his own area. He recognized me and said he wanted to give me a gift. I told him it was not necessary but that he should just take better care of himself. He insisted and he handed me a cardboard box with a turtle inside. He smiled a bloody smile and presented me with this gift as if he was one of the wise men following the North Star.

I thanked him and excused myself to check on my mother, who was starting to feel the pain of her bulbous, mushy, swelling mass of blood. I showed her the turtle and realized that it was in fact dead and stank up the whole area. The smell of the dead turtle and the sight of my mother's beaten-up head mixed with the one-liners being wittily emitted by my character on TV made me feel like puking all over the linoleum floor.

I excused myself to find the doctor and was relieved when he told me they wanted to keep Mom overnight for observation. I kissed my mom's good side and said I had to go home. She panicked, but I told her she should sleep. I waved bye to my homeless buddy and thanked him again for the turtle, promising to take good care of it. I waited until I got outside and out of view before I threw the box of dead turtle in a Dumpster. I walked a while and didn't even know how to feel.

Still, I told myself that things were going to keep getting better. I was doing comedy and I had found my home. My mom adored *Suddenly Susan* and watched it religiously. Even my dad, who never saw any of my movies (or if he did never told me), watched the show and loved it. Comedy was in my veins and it unified us all.

Suddenly Susan changed my life in another way. It gave me David Strickland. The day I met David, I knew I had met the brother I had never had. I really felt like his sister. I basically didn't need anybody as long as David was in my life. We were all at the first table read of the show, and right before beginning to read the script we were mingling around and chatting. I can't explain it properly, but we each simultaneously made a comment under our breath and it was the same comment. I heard him and he heard me and we both began to laugh. We were obviously on the same wavelength. I was four years older than he was and we even looked like we could be related. He understood me completely. He was the first person, since college, with whom I felt utterly myself. Even more than I did with Andre or Dean, to tell the truth, because it felt like blood.

David played Todd Stities, the music reviewer at the show's magazine, *The Gate*. He became my best friend. By this point Lisa and I had become temporarily estranged because of Andre. Andre believed I needed to rid myself of any friend of mine who would choose to drink with my mother while I worked or was recuperating from surgery. Andre was very rigid and judgmental that way. All it would take was one meeting or one story and he could completely cut someone off from his life. I obeyed his wishes. Without Lisa in my life, there was a huge void. David overflowed it. It was love at first sight and a love not many would ever understand.

We loved each other on a level devoid of the complexity of a romantic relationship. People could not define it and we couldn't care less. We confided in one another about the deepest, darkest secrets we held and about our love lives and relationships. We gave each other sound and honest advice. We were connected and I hated being without him.

It was also meaningful that David was a recovering addict and he understood my mother deeply. He helped me and I helped him. David had been battling addiction practically his entire life. He had been diagnosed as bipolar at a later age and was struggling to live a balanced life. A fight he would never win.

Like most addicts, he was gorgeously and attractively intense. I was drawn to him like a moth to the flame. The difference, however, was that compared to my mother, this relationship was relatively stable and drama-free. He was actually feeling more contented and grounded by working on this show and by being with me, so much so that we all were able to take a bit of a breath. He was actively trying to lead a grounded and sober life. For the first time in my life I wasn't acting as the codependent. I consciously refused to fall into the same trap that I had with my mother. I insisted I not be that person in his life. And because we were never romantic, it was easier to enforce this healthier connection. During our short life together he was mostly clean. Mom, of course, adored David. I always wondered if she saw in him her lost baby boy. But we never spoke of it.

David and I worked together, worked out together, and had meals together. We helped each other in every way we could think of, and we laughed harder than I had ever laughed in my life. Not since Gavin had I found a partner to laugh at life with in this way. David and I understood how the other felt and thought. He knew me and I knew him with a depth that felt healthy.

Andre was not jealous of David. David understood Andre. Between David and Andre I was satisfied. My life and my circle was small but happy. David filled in the emotional and intellectual gaps and it all seemed to be a rather well-balanced, not overly dramatic life. We had the most connected and enjoyable platonic relationship any two people of the opposite sex could have. I was working, I had found a home in comedy, and life was great.

Andre and I got engaged and the wedding was stunning. I had wanted David to be my maid of honor but decided against it at the last minute. I chose to have a female bridal party only.

We had the ceremony in a boiling-hot, tiny chapel and had the reception where most of us were staying, the gorgeous Tuscan villa in Big Sur, California. While taking some photos before the actual wedding, Mom poked her head into the hallway from her room. I saw the look. I knew she would not do anything disruptive during the ceremony but it momentarily crushed me. I moved back to the opulent fantasy wedding and was determined to find the joy in the day. My dad cried in our photo together. I never got one with my mom. The wedding and reception went off without a problem, but I avoided Mom most of the night. I took photos with her table, then just danced. I'm sure she continued drinking but caused no scenes that I was aware of. That would come later.

The next day promised to be a fun and very relaxed event. We had a big western BBQ, and Mom arrived like the belle of the ball. She looked happy and radiant and entered with a grand air of fabulousness.

We were all departing. She was to take a ride down the coast with friends on their way to LA while Andre and I dropped off some relatives in LA and Vegas by plane before spending a mini honeymoon at a friend's house somewhere in Florida. I had hugged Mom good-bye in the driveway of the beautiful hotel nestled in the midst of beautiful Big Sur and said we'd talk later that day when we arrived in Florida.

I remember being in the back-bedroom cabin of the equally beautiful private plane that we were using to fly out of Carmel and suddenly being overcome with fear and sadness. Gavin came into the cabin and I looked him in the eye, unable to speak. I could not form a sentence. I kept shaking my head as if I had duct tape across my mouth.

It hit me all of a sudden—I knew I had made a mistake. I did not want to be married. I wanted to have the wedding because I wanted everyone I loved to be together. I loved Andre but was not sure I wanted to live the life we had been living. I wanted to be a bride, but I should not have been married yet.

When we landed in Vegas, I called to tell Mom we were safe, but she was nowhere to be found. I tried her friends but they said she never showed up to go on the drive. Mom had disappeared. She never left with her friends—they had waited and then departed without her. She was MIA for four days in Big Sur.

Mom being missing added to my anxiety about all of this being a terrible mistake. I felt stuck and hoped it was just because I felt like marriage meant leaving my mother more profoundly. Truthfully, however, I believed my professional life was finally opening up and I was entering a new phase and I wasn't ready to settle down. I had been so afraid that Andre would leave me if we didn't get married. I feared that if I had not said yes to his proposal he would have cut me off emotionally and it would have been over. I needed more time with him and I did love him, and I wanted the idea of being his wife.

My life and career were just beginning and I had wanted to know that I could have been OK alone before saying yes to marriage. I suddenly felt terrified and my mom was nowhere to be found. Gavin told me it would be fine and that it was just scary because it was new.

We finally arrived in Florida and walked into a house belonging to a business associate of Andre's. The place was a dilapidated seventies ranch house on the Intracoastal that had not been used in years. Yes, we would not be bothered, but that was because nobody would want to be anywhere near the place. There was really nothing to do and it was not relaxing or in any way honeymoon oriented. It felt run-down and I got even more depressed. I could not find my mother and I felt really lost instead of settled.

Mom finally resurfaced. I was told she had wandered around Big Sur drunk and alone. Apparently she believed either nobody would care or that it would serve them right to be worried—she could do anything she fucking well pleased. She was Teri Shields and she was born into this world alone and would leave it alone. She answered to no one.

The hopelessness and loneliness of the addict will never cease to amaze me. She hated being alone yet perpetually isolated herself in the alcohol. She ended up back home in New Jersey, and the cycle of my trying to keep tabs on her resumed yet again. Maybe I, too, was addicted.

Life on the show continued, and for the next two years Andre and I saw very little of one another. I was working so hard on the show and he was really working hard playing at various tennis tournaments. He alienated me when he lost and was on to the next tournament after he won. We did not experience much of our lives together and I had no idea we were really drifting apart. I then began to experience the other side to being an athlete's girlfriend and now wife: the side that gets shunned after a loss. Somehow I was made to feel it was my fault. I'd get the silent treatment or a projection of disdain that cut to my core. Sometimes he would not even look at me or speak to me when he lost but instead became even more isolated. In the past he had been more open, but he was changing drastically. It felt hateful at times, but I waited it out. Navigating someone else's moods was a task I knew all too well. This would be a piece of cake. I almost liked it, quite honestly. It was familiar and the hint of martyrdom was not a bad fit.

Overall, the marriage was just existing, but if it felt somehow not what it was supposed to be, it was easy to avoid dealing with it. I maintain that it was not due to a lack of love as much as it was a lack of life. David gave me advice. When I told him I thought I needed a relationship that had more mutual interests and desire for intellectual discourse and shared references, he said he worried I would regret my decision to move on. I wasn't saying I was some highbrow scholar whose intellect was being hindered or stunted. I was saying that it was becoming evident that Andre and I had less and less to talk about. Without an immediate trauma through which we needed to navigate, we floundered a bit. We had love, but it did not seem like that was enough. I always thought love was enough. But the truth was we were growing past one another. And I'm not sure if we individually enjoyed how the other liked to live.

I mentioned it to Mom on the phone one night and she made some snide comment about Perry. I said I was not married to Perry.

"Really? Are you sure about that, my dear?"

Wow. Every now and then, Mom came out with a zinger like this that made you realize how much she really did intuit. She was often not productive or helpful with her knowledge, but she had it in her arsenal, perpetually at the ready, just when it was needed.

It was at about this time that I adopted an older female pit bull. She had had litters of puppies and was older and slower and needing a home. Andre had said, "If you go get a dog, you are getting a dog for yourself only. Not for me."

Well, I'll show him, I thought.

David said I should focus on this dog. He grew up with dogs and would help. He said I had him and the dog and the show and my health, and my mother was relatively safe so life was not bad. He was right. What more did I need?

One day I took the dog into the gym on the Warner Bros. lot to meet my favorite staff members and she wandered away. I dropped the leash and knew she'd be fine. Soon a man brought her back to me, asking if she was mine. I was flustered and began explaining that she was, indeed, mine, because my husband had not wanted a dog but I had adopted her anyway. I must have said "my husband" twenty times. He must have been like, "I get it, you're married. I'm not hitting on you. I just thought the dog was lost."

I ran back to my dressing room and called my single girlfriend from college and told her I had met a guy she should go out with. "What's his name?"

"I have no idea."

I never got his name, but later learned it when he and David and I would work out in the gym together. He was a writer and had an amazing sense of humor. We all became friends. I didn't think anything more of it at the time—I was totally cut off from my feelings. I was not technically lonely, but I was not happy, either.

Andre and I were supposed to take my upcoming hiatus and go on a yacht trip that Andre had won at a charity auction. I dreaded going and thought it would be a mistake. He came to LA to take me out for sushi, and I said I didn't think the boat trip was a good idea because we would be pretending and we needed to figure some stuff out.

He said I would go with him to Vegas, then, and he could train. I did not want to go to Vegas, either. I would stay in LA. He looked at me and asked me if I thought we would ever want to go on vacation together again. My throat closed and the tears came out in hot, thick sheets of salty, blurry despair. I could not talk and needed to leave at once. As I left, I saw Liam Neeson sitting at one of the tables. I could not have cared less.

Andre and I drove home in silence and then he asked if I was happy. I told him no.

He did not say another word to me. He pulled in the driveway and disappeared upstairs. It was quiet and I began to panic. Suddenly I felt I was with my mother when she'd disappear and go guzzle from some hidden bottle of vodka or sneak out into the garage and take the car quietly out to drive to a bar. Sure enough, it was happening. He was leaving without a word.

Panic rising, I ran outside. His old convertible car was loaded and he was getting in the car to drive away. I begged him to talk to me. I explained that this was when a couple was supposed to fight, and scream, and sleep in separate beds, and cry and get back up and talk all night and get closer. Plus, it was starting to rain torrentially.

"Please don't do this. Don't drive away. Where are you going?"

"Home."

He drove off and I began to weep. The rain kept coming down and I was actually getting nervous for him. I knew the roads would be bad and this all felt so wrong. I would be lying if I said that I really wanted him to turn around and come back to make it all right, but I did not want to not try. I would never forgive myself if I did not try.

I called his cell repeatedly and he never picked up. I used to do the same thing with my mother, except we didn't have cell phones, so I would instead call her friends and restaurants and bars looking for her. I had slipped right back into all my old codependent habits.

Finally, Andre phoned from Barstow and said that the rain was so bad he had to stop. I half wanted him to come back, and I was also just so relieved he was not in an accident and had pulled over to spend the night.

I took an Ambien and went to bed. The next morning Andre called me and said he had something to tell me. My heart sank. I was instantly so scared, and I could feel my chest start to compress as if a vise was being tightened. I sat down in the window on a little window seat–like area in the kitchen.

He said he was about to tell me something he had never wanted to tell me because he had feared I would leave him. Then why tell me now? I thought. What was it? What had he been hiding? Had he had a child with his ex-girlfriend or somebody more recent for that matter? Was he sick? Was he having a long affair? Was he gay? All sorts of ideas flooded my brain.

I never could have guessed what he would say. He explained to me that for the whole first part of our relationship he had been addicted to crystal meth. I was shocked but immediately got hurt and insulted that he had not come to me at the time. I was the codependent queen! That was how I related to the world. I was the one who supported him unconditionally when he told me he was basically bald and had been wearing hairpieces most of his adult life. I took all of his innermost fears and had tried to quell them. Why should this have been any different? I would have been his biggest advocate and supporter in both the addiction and in his recovery.

"Why didn't you tell me?"

"I knew how difficult it was with your mother. I was afraid you would leave me."

I was really not sure what he wanted me to do with this information. None of this was about giving or getting forgiveness, so I was unclear as to the tactic involved in suddenly disclosing such information. What was I supposed to do? He was already forgiven because I had never known about it, and he attested to quitting cold turkey before our marriage. He added that he was entirely clean and had been so for quite some time. He had managed to evade the USTA and pull some kind of a Lance Armstrong so he was able to stop and get drug tested and come out clear without the embarrassment.

I really couldn't have cared less about how it all affected his game or his reputation. I was trying to go back and remember the mood swings and chart the outbursts.

I feared our life together was not based in absolute truth. But it had felt that way early on, before the drugs. He had had his core confidants and his secrets, and then he had us as something different. I was relieved he was not gay and very relieved he had not fathered any kids I did not know about, but I questioned a lot. I also did not really care that he had had an addiction. Who cared if he had had an addiction? Many people have addictions, and he seemed to have gotten his life together by this point. He swore he quit before we were married but I don't think his book (the ironically titled *Open*) supports these details.

The way I remember it, I said I needed to think. He pleaded with me and said he would finally go to therapy and even resume couples therapy. We had gone briefly before getting married and were both so scared to be wed that we sought out this help.

I told him that we should both take a moment to collect our thoughts and suggested we talk in a week. I was going to have that hiatus and I would go to New York City, where I could go to therapy and get perspective. I called David and told him everything. He was going to be back east as well.

I called my mother to tell her that I was coming to New York instead of going on the boat trip. I did not have the energy to tell her that we were having problems. I was afraid of her response. I needed to have my own uninfluenced perspective.

I remember calling Andre during the next week and saying that we could not just throw away five years without somehow trying. I said we should try to get help and see what needed to be repaired. I'm sure I wasn't being completely honest with myself about wanting it to work, but I knew I would feel terrible to walk away after he said he would get therapy and he pleaded with me to try. I wanted to be sure I wasn't making a mistake. David had planted that seed and I needed to give it my best try in order to know.

"Why bother?" Andre said, interrupting me. "I don't see the need to delay the inevitable."

Was this what my mom had done to my dad?

Part of me was shocked and hurt that he didn't want to try, and part of me felt he was the more truthful of the two of us. I never discussed any of this with my mother. By this point I did not feel like I could go to her to get healthy advice regarding my relationships. I felt like my stomach had just been violently punched. I got so sad and knew I could never go back.

I went back to work and tried not to think about it and just be happy with the life we had had.

One night before a Monday table read I went out with some friends. I returned home to many messages from David's mother. I had gotten used to getting these calls and then helping locate him somewhere in Los Angeles. David had had a few slips since we met and had periodically gone on a tear or two. Because of my history and our closeness, as well as my connections to the world of security and addiction, I was very familiar with situations like this and I usually became involved. I would enlist Gavin, and David always ended up showing up some place. In every case I would be up all night sick with worry, and then he would eventually show up and be fine (or not so fine) but alive.

Tonight was the first time I did not jump on board the rescue mission. I knew I would see him the next day. We had had an event we were supposed to be going to, but because of my pending divorce, I did not feel like going out in public. The night before, David called and had suggested I join him and his soon-to-be fiancée. I had been helping David decide what type of engagement ring to get for his girlfriend.

I explained that I was not in the mood because of the recent developments in my marriage and that I did not wish to be a third wheel. I was sure his girlfriend would have preferred to be his date alone. I begged him instead to come over to my house that night for dessert, but he said his girlfriend was asleep because she had an early call the next day. I told him to stop by on the way home. That was the last I ever spoke to him.

David hung himself in a Las Vegas motel sometime between when I last spoke to him and when I awoke the next day.

The next morning when the show's producers told me the news, something in me shut down, and I was never the same after that. I called my mom and sobbed to her. All she could do was say she was praying for him. My life was over as I knew it. I was ripped into two and no longer cared about Andre or my mother or the dog or my show or my career or any of it. I did not want to waste my time on anybody or anything I did not want in my life. I was finished being anywhere I did not want to be.

Nobody knew about the divorce (which took eight days to execute and nine minutes to file and be finished) just yet, and Andre and I went to the memorial as a couple. I was the only one not included in the memorial. His ex-girlfriend and his current girlfriend and his best male friend all had a part to play. I was not a party to any of it. I actually understood how I didn't fit in, but felt desperately sad in any case. I sat next to Andre, who generously paid for all the floral arrangements, and felt like I wasn't even there.

My one consolation would come later at David's family's get-together. His dad said that his life changed when he met me and he was happy for the first time in a long while.

"He looked at you like his sister."

Not long after David died, my stepsister, Diana, called me and told me that Dad had been diagnosed with stage-four prostate cancer. He would end up dying within two years of that phone call.

As if this wasn't enough, I had also been informed that I had had an irregular pap result and had a cervical dysplasia that was precancerous. I would have to have most of my cervix removed if

I was to survive. I recalled a hurtful comment that Andre blurted out in anger: "Be thankful we never had kids because I would not have made this easy for you." He was referring to the divorce and the fact that if we had had children, there would have been a much bigger fight. But what if I had missed the opportunity to have children at all?

Too many things were hitting all at once and I wondered if this level of fear and sadness I was experiencing was enough to make a person just cease to exist. It was like my mother had written: "Does one start to slip from life this way, then suddenly it's over?" I had hit a real low, and for the first time in my life, my mother had not been the catalyst.

Chapter Fifteen

Toots

I did not want to continue on with *Suddenly Susan*. Without David it was a different show. The studio tried to revamp it to make it feel fresh. But the problem was that it hadn't been that broken and didn't need to be drastically fixed. It was never as good as it could be because of the focus of the writing, but people loved it and it could have endured if the cast had remained.

We did a farewell tribute to David in which my character goes all over the city trying to find his character, Todd. Along the way I learn how he impacted various people's lives and what a unique person he was. It was a fitting and beautiful tribute, but it did not bring David back. I would have done the show forever if David had been alive. But for various reasons the show was cancelled, and although I strongly missed doing a sitcom, I wasn't sorry. I was relieved to be away from everything that continuously reminded me of David.

I called Andre after I got the word that our divorce had all been filed and done with. I was driving in the Jeep that had been a gift from him and I called to ask, "So do I just take off my ring?"

"I guess so."

"OK, then."

I went to a bar where a friend from college was waitressing and I drank whatever they served me. I played with my thin platinum band in the booth and was very sad but felt like I was simply where I was. I called my mother to tell her it was over and she commented on it being fast. I could tell it was more important to be rid of Perry than it was sad for me to actually be divorced. Somehow I never thought I'd be. I had seen myself alone, even with a child, or married. But never divorced.

I could not admit it, but I was actually already falling in love with the guy I'd met when I was walking my pit bull. We had stayed in touch from working out with David in the Warner Bros. gym. He had eventually met the girlfriend with whom I was trying to set him up. Thankfully, they had not hit it off. I had kept him at a safe distance but believe subconsciously I'd wanted him close by. Nobody had yet known I was getting a divorce, and I needed time. I was dealing with too much with losing David, actually being divorced, and with my dad's diagnosis that I feared any relationship. Chris stayed around but had his own very busy life. He finally said that it was pretty clear he wanted to be more than friends but would rather be my friend than not have me in his life at all. But I had to tell him whether it would ever be possible. I told him yes but asked for his patience.

He did not pressure me but after a respectful amount of time finally said, "I'll wait, but I won't wait forever."

I leaned on him for support regarding my diagnosis and my dad's. I finally admitted that we were dating and I was falling in love. Andre had moved on, too, with my blessing. I helped Andre get dressed for his first date with Steffi Graf. He called me from a hotel room where she was waiting in the lobby. I was happy to oblige.

I told Mom I had met someone and I had wanted her to meet him. He was Irish and from New York and was a writer. I was planning to go to New York City to have my surgery to hopefully clear up the dysplasia and rid me of probable cervical precancer.

Mom was supposed to take me to the hospital the morning of, but I could tell she was not going to be able to make it. She was still drinking, and even though she probably could have rallied, I didn't want to be around her. I couldn't deal with her drinking and with going under the knife at the same time. This seemed to be a pattern. But she was always around to attend to me when I was sick. Maybe surgery and death terrified her. Justifying again, am I?

I suddenly broke up with Chris a week before the operation out of fear that I had not given myself a real chance to be free. I thought that the feelings I had for him had to be false rebound emotions. But I called him every day during this breakup.

He finally said, "You know you broke up with me, right? Technically you can't call me every day if we are broken up."

"Oh, yeah, right. . . . Well, bye, then, I guess."

I admit I made one last call before the impending surgery. I was actually scared and just wanted to hear his voice.

I called his cell and he sounded different so I asked where he was. He was in Vermont visiting his writing partner for a few days. I told him I just wanted to call him before my surgery and he asked if anybody was going to take me to the hospital. I said no, which was true, but my mom was going to pick me up. He volunteered to drive in to take me and meet my mom. It seemed like a lot, but I said yes before I could change my mind.

He came in to take me to the hospital and he met my mom for the first time. I went under and the two of them went for a walk and a bite to eat at some diner. While on the walk, Mom handed Chris an envelope and asked him to keep it safe for her. She needed to mail it and would do so after the meal. It was a hot summer day and Chris kept the envelope in his breast pocket for hours. After the meal, she took it back from him. He asked her what it was and she replied that it was her dog's stool sample—her Maltese had had diarrhea. She thought it was hysterical. He knew instantly what he was getting himself into.

The operation ended up being much more invasive than they had anticipated. They practically had to remove my entire cervix. I recovered in Vermont with Chris and his friends, and I finally admitted once and for all that he was my boyfriend.

Mom seemed to like Chris. His parents were from New York and were from the same era and background. Chris's family consisted mainly of firemen, cops, and nurses. They were the kind of people Mom had known growing up and always felt akin to.

On a trip to Ireland over the millennium a year after we started dating Chris gave me a promise ring. I nearly passed out when he showed me the box while we were overlooking Dingle Bay on the last sunset of 1999. He saw the look of terror and pressure on my face and quickly said it was only a promise ring. I had no desire to even think about getting married again.

A year later, when he was finally prepared to propose, ring in hand, he got the shock of his life. The man who sold him the ring had his sister secretly photograph Chris leaving the store after the purchase. I had no idea he had bought the ring, and when he opened the paper that morning he turned sickly pale.

I saw the photo, slammed the paper shut, and said, "Oh God, I am so sorry, Chris. . . . Whatever you were going to do, don't."

"What?!"

"I mean do it, but reclaim the time and do it at another time."

"Oh, OK, wow. . . . How could he . . . How could they . . . ?"

I felt terrible that because I was famous, his first time proposing was ruined. I felt terrible because unfeeling people and the press once again chose to rob me of the beauty of my personal experiences for their own profit.

I told Mom about the whole thing and she said, "That's a shame, honey, but you can make it your own again."

I wonder if she was secretly a tad bit relieved that the press still paid attention.

I put it out of "our" minds, but when Chris finally did surprise me a few months later by proposing to me in Mexico, I said "Yes!" and then had the jeweler's name buffed out of the ring.

And a year after he gave me the promise ring, I was saying, "I do."

Before we got married, the in-laws were all sitting at a diner in LA and the mothers began talking about what they wanted to be called by their grandchildren. My mother-in-law claimed "Cha Cha" and my mother coined herself "Toots." God forbid they be called Nana or Grandma or Granny. . . .

I loved the idea of having children with Chris. Despite my fears about my cervix, I was encouraged by my doctor and told it should all be fine. Chris and I wanted to start as soon as we could.

My father was going through chemo at the time, so we decided that instead of New York City we would get married where he lived, in Palm Beach, Florida. Dad's close friend Terry Kramer had a stunningly beautiful home on the water and graciously offered to have us hold the wedding there. I humbly accepted but on one condition: that we hold the reception in a tent outside. As much as I really wanted to be seated inside, surrounded by the priceless paintings and incredibly precious art and furniture, I didn't trust any of our relatives not to do something somehow damaging. This home housed original Picassos both from his Blue Period and his later works. Many masters were on the walls, and real Fabergé eggs were scattered like confetti. I pictured my mother feeling up a server or kissing a portrait with fire engine–red lipstick, or one of Chris's old friends stealing the Cuban cigars or somehow pocketing an egg or silver monogrammed matchbox.

My mother had gotten another DUI a few months before the wedding and was placed in mandatory rehab. Her license was suspended and she went under psychiatric treatment. I was called when she was first arrested and put in the hospital for observation. They said she was confused and they would keep her overnight. I tried to have them keep her in for a few days but she insisted on leaving. She could not drive and had to take a taxi home.

The courts decided that she should go to a mandatory alcohol treatment facility. I was relieved and thrilled and thought the timing was perfect. She would be out just in time to get her life together and be at the wedding sober. She would even make the shower.

My girlfriend Sherie from Broadway threw me a shower. I did not want to have a typical shower because we needed nothing, but I did want to celebrate and also give Chris's friends and family a chance to do so as well. We had a crafty type of shower, where we all put together mosaic tiles to be put some place in our home. Mom and my mother-in-law and sister-in-law all seemed to be getting along beautifully. Mom did not drink the mimosas and acted fine, but I could tell she was a bit vulnerable. She was just not able to relax. She was awkward and restrained and I felt bad because I could tell she was struggling. I

must admit, though, I was much less on my guard believing she would not drink that day and was subsequently seemingly able to relax a bit and basically enjoy the festivities.

I had a romantic idea—maybe I could invite Mom's old love, Antonio Rius from Rio, to be her date to the wedding. I'd found his number and called him years before, only to find out he'd had a stroke and didn't want her to see him in such poor (and disfigured) health. I encouraged her to try him again, though. But it still wasn't meant to be, sadly—when she finally called, he was thrilled to hear her voice. He was doing better, but had married his nurse only two months earlier. Another chance at happiness lost.

"But I waited. . . ."

The wedding date arrived. The hostess was incredibly generous and housed the whole family. My mom and Lila were in one room and Chris and I in another.

Dad and Didi threw the rehearsal dinner, and Cristiana organized the after-party. It went off without drama—it was actually rather peaceful in Dad's home. Mom did not drink that night and it was looking like it was all calm on the Teri front.

We had not hired a wedding planner, which in hindsight was a huge mistake. To save on costs and keep it simple we had decided to do it all ourselves. With the money saved we splurged on hiring Tuck and Patti to perform. The planning was relatively easy and I had assistants to help, but once in Florida I realized I really needed extra support. I had to organize the entire event myself. I could not rely on my mother for a myriad of reasons and the pressure was too much for any of my in-laws. We needed a person other than the bride or groom to take charge. I had two assistants helping, and Gavin's guys were taking care of security, but nobody had been designated as the captain of the ship. The problem was that without a point person, the mothers began to get involved. The day before the wedding, during the rehearsal portion of the day, I was being pulled in all directions. There was no one to tell me where to go and yet people also needed instruction. I instantly wished I had had a logistics director. It became obvious that I was getting a bit harried.

At one point my mother-in-law and Mom were wandering around aimlessly, trying to be helpful. My mother-in-law evidently said to my mother, "Can I help you, Teri?"

Mom responded with "No, thank you. . . ." And as she turned away, Mom added, "You fucking cunt."

Oh, dear God. Chris heard it but I did not. My assistant told me what had transpired and I knew alcohol had finally reared its ugly head. Chris and I both prayed his mother had not heard. She was gracious and never mentioned a thing, but it was a horror show. Then, not too long after that, Cha Cha took it upon herself to order my assistant Patty to come to my rescue. Everybody was on high stress alert and acting out. Patty had been my assistant for eleven years and always knew when I did and when I did not need anything. She was insulted. She did have it all under control but admittedly was getting a bit flustered by the tension and mounting confusion. I make it a rule never to order my assistants to do anything. I apologized to my longtime and excruciatingly (for her, I'm sure) loyal employee, explaining that tensions were high and these strong mothers were simply needing to be needed.

On the day of the wedding our hostess held a lovely lunch for the houseguests. Didi stayed at their house to deal with the rehearsal-dinner aftermath, and I went to get a massage with my sisters. Mom stayed at the house for lunch and was evidently charming and on point. She and my dad laughed together and were very sweet with each other. Mom was gracious and not inappropriate and seemingly very in her own skin. She did not drink any of the delicious wine that flows like water at this stunning home. I will always regret not witnessing my mother and this meal.

Later that day, I was getting ready and putting on my big princess wedding dress. I was getting the veil adjusted and my father awkwardly came up to the room and said he had to ask me a quick question. He pulled out a letter from a buddy of his who freelanced for *People* magazine. The guy was begging my father to just be able to be invited to the BBQ the following day so he could cover it for the magazine.

I looked at my father and, pointing to myself, said, "Dad . . . *wedding dress . . . bride*! Can we not discuss this right now, please?"

"I'm just saying, he's a nice guy and he's a buddy of mine from—"

"I am sure he is, Dad, but I am not going to discuss this with you right now, seconds before I am going to actually walk down the aisle."

"OK."

"Don't worry, Dad, I get it. We will figure something out. But please let's just focus on this first."

I was standing in the doorway, surrounded by beautiful marble pillars and shiny steps, and I was about to walk out and down the path to my waiting groom. Mom would be walked down the aisle by my brother-in-law, and my stepsister, Diana, was my maid of honor. Her girls were flower girls and my other sister Marina was going to do a reading. Our youngest sister, Olympia, was serving as the oldest ring bearer ever and helped the flower girls down the aisle.

I was helping my dad navigate his Rollei camera, which did not fit in his pocket, and I could tell he was nervous. It was the second time he'd walk me down an aisle, but we all knew this was different. Chris had actually flown to Florida to ask him for my hand and that impressed my father more than ever.

It was about time for me to start walking. I looked at my mom and said, "Well, Mom, this is it. I am about to go get married. Tell me something."

She motioned for me to come closer, and I did. I leaned in and she sloppily whispered into my ear, "No *People* magazine cover."

I reacted so suddenly and actually shoved her away. I pulled back in a daze and stared at her. I saw the look. The lips were dry and the liner had begun to bleed slightly into her wrinkles. She had obviously been drinking from some stash or had made some arrangement with the staff. She was on her way.

She cocked an eyebrow and pursed her lips into a smirk and said, "What?! I'm just saying. No *People* magazine cover."

She wanted to be the one who perpetually controlled my image. It was all she knew. She could not give me advice, support, or words of wisdom. She did not have any. She knew nothing but how to try to dictate my public persona. The shove was on the wedding video but I had it erased.

I felt so terribly sad for her at that moment. I got it. She had no idea how to just be my mom and was lonelier than hell. She felt she was losing me all over again.

I grabbed Dad's camera as he fumbled to try to fit it in his pocket and I hurriedly put it on a table. I wanted him to watch, not to take photos during the ceremony. I wanted him to be present. I looked at him and at my mother and I thought it was all crazy. I panned past my father, who was adjusting his jacket, and then to my mom, who looked like a little orphaned kid, and then I looked out to the lawn by the water to where Chris stood in his white suit, his hands clasped in front and his neck craned to see me. I thought, *Crazy to my right. Crazy to my left. Not crazy ahead. Finally, not crazy. Just walk toward your future, Brooke. You get to leave the crazy and go to this man you love.*

During the reception, people started making toasts. There were a few comedians in attendance and I swear I saw them working on their speeches *during* the actual ceremony. Comedians are like that. Each one wanted to be the funniest.

They were all great. Once I got over the fact that I did not think any of them had paid attention to their best friend's vows, I laughed harder than anybody. Dad got up to make a toast. He was always

tremendous at making toasts and was warm and funny and even got a bit teary. He held out his glass and you could hear a pin drop. I knew he would not drink its contents because he had given up drinking a while earlier.

My eye was immediately drawn to his beautiful hand with his gold bracelet and crest ring, and I suddenly saw my father through a child's eyes. He held his pinky slightly extended, not from affectation but from necessity. His hands were just too big to fit the stem. He explained how impressed he had been that Chris had asked for his permission and he was comforted that I had found a man who made me so relaxed and happy. It was a beautiful moment.

But the next thing I knew, the owner of this stunning estate, who was also named Terry (only spelled differently) and was also quite a larger-than-life character, was suddenly guiding my now drunk mother up toward the mike. They were both Leos and loved to be in control. They were quite a team. She must have thought it safer to accompany my mom in case something went awry. My heart sank. *Oh, Mama, please don't do this. You are better than this.* She could never speak in public unless drinking. She actually could do very little without the numbness of liquor. She was so insecure about how she spoke and sounded that she lost her train of thought and would go vulgar so the shock value distracted everybody and counteracted everything. If she was sober when toasting, she would just say, "I love you with all my heart." And then be done.

Hostess Terry explained she thought it would be funny for the two powerful Terrys to make a toast together. She said something first and then it was Mom's turn. I started to feel like I was in the middle of a car accident right before impact. I heard nothing and my vision narrowed to a pinpoint. All I saw were my mother's red lips moving. She bizarrely made the toast about her and I began to clap the second I regained my hearing and felt the first pause between her (slurred)

words. Mom brought attention to this vaudeville hook, this gong-show gong she said I was wielding, and blurted out some remark regarding my being rude as usual.

"Sure, look at her trying to get rid of the old lady. It's OK, I'm almost done."

I just wanted it over so she would not embarrass herself. I was not angry, but I was humiliated for her. I was so pained to see Mom doing this in front of my father and Didi. She did end with something sweet but I knew she had just perpetuated her already less-than-stellar reputation. For the first time in my life I suddenly felt strangely jealous of my stepmother, because unlike my mother, she easily commanded more respect. Why hadn't Mom allowed her last impression from lunch to be her new image? Thank God Mom did not mention my father's wife, who remained reticent and graceful as usual.

Chris was ultimately OK with it all because his friends were funny and my dad laughed his booming laugh, which resonated throughout the tent. The comedians all mentioned that they were in a gazillion-dollar estate and they had all been led to a tent in order to bypass the house entirely. That was my plan, and even though I missed being surrounded by the fantasy of luxury, I would breathe easier because of my decision.

In the end, however, Chris's friend did steal the Cuban cigars and I would get a call late that night from the police regarding my in-famous drunk mother.

Chris and I had met up with some friends after all the festivities and were enjoying the warm weather and the water when I got a call that the police had been called to the house because my mom was be-ing disorderly. I don't know who called them, but clearly she needed some kind of help. The medics asked her a series of questions. Of course she knew the answer to each one. She could access names, dates, numbers, and so on. So fuck all of you, she was fine!

Terry Kramer had seemingly no intention of pressing charges. Be-cause Mom had been on private property, there was nothing anyone could do. Chris and I were told that Mom had gone to her room and things had calmed down. I was absolutely mortified and grossed out and had lost all respect in a way I had never experienced before. I did not care how sad or sick she was. It was outrageous and selfish and unfair for her to do this to our generous hostess, and on her only daughter's wedding day. Mom was burying herself, and all hopes I held of the Teri Terrific from lunch becoming her new and improved image were dashed.

Chris and I left for Bali on our honeymoon. I did not look back until I had to. I have no memory of how she got home but knew she would figure it out. I remembered Paris and Big Sur and her disappearing into the dark and wandering on a highway in the middle of nowhere while on a book tour in some city. And I remembered her inevitable reappearances when you thought it impossible. She would do what she wanted and get back to where she was headed when she was good and ready. Her wake or those caught up in it never concerned her. She was her own riptide.

Mom made alienating herself from people her personal art form. She did it so consistently and so often with those she loved that she found herself decidedly alone and isolated with the booze. She could hurt people like no other. I believe it was because her capacity to love was immeasurable. She knew how to hook into people and register with them deeply, but if it got too close or she felt an ounce of vulnerability, she would lash out. I was the only one who kept returning for both the love and the lashes. She was, as always, my mom.

Chris and I wanted to start a family as soon as possible, but it would not be as easy as we had hoped. We had *not* been actively trying to get pregnant, but for the past two years we had discussed being fine even if I were to become a pregnant bride (and thus need to alter my wedding dress). It had not happened as of yet and we assumed it was because of our busy schedules and stress. We had not really factored in my cervix because surgery had been successful, and the threat of cancer had been our main focus.

Upon consulting with a doctor, we learned that because so much of my cervix had been removed, it was proving almost impossible for me to become pregnant naturally. We immediately started the process of IVF. It was a crazy experience with hormones and drugs and shots. But after the first successful transfer of my fertilized eggs, I became pregnant. We were so thrilled, we told all our friends and relatives. Mom sounded teary on the phone and offered up a name for the baby. She assumed it would be a girl and we should name her Willow. We thought it was too soon to pick names. Not because of losing the baby, but because we needed to do my favorite thing and make lists!

Within three months, I was writhing in our bedroom, enduring an insanely surreal and painful miscarriage. By the time the night was over I had banned Chris from coming near me, only allowing our new dog, Darla, to sleep at my feet. I was exhausted and angry.

I was again different after that night. I lost innocence and a belief that everything would turn out OK. Like most children, when I was a little kid I had an incredibly naïve belief that all things would be positive and work out the way I wanted. I believed perpetually that my mother would one day stop drinking and be healthy and happy because she was sober. I held on tightly to that hope. I even believed that if I had babies Mom would become a sweet, happy, fun-loving little old grandmother.

I always knew I wanted to be a mother, but I also believed that being a mother would give me freedom—freedom from my mother's drinking and the hurt she caused me. I believed I would need less from her and be freer to have compassion for her while personally remaining safe. My energy could be redirected.

For some reason, after all the disappointments regarding her drinking and my being let down, I held on to the belief that if I had a baby, it would heal and right everything. There was no connection except in the expectation I placed on these possibilities with all my heart. When I lost this baby, I was heartbroken. I felt as if I had finally been defeated and I was not slated for conventional happiness.

I became convinced that I was not allowed to be normal and that I would not be allowed to have babies. I got very dark.

My first call the next day was to my mother. She was very sad but quickly added that as long as I was OK, that was what mattered. We would have another. And that was it. She had no other words of empathy.

I could not believe the pauses on the other end of the phone.

"Mom, are you sure there is not anything you want to tell me?"

"Nope."

"Well, OK. I love you, Mama."

"I love you, too, sweetheart."

I hung up and finally got really angry.

Wasn't this the moment when the mother was supposed to say to her grieving child some words of empathy or compassion from her own experience? We'd hardly talked about the mysterious Baby John since my outburst all those years ago, but I knew Mom, too, had experienced some kind of a loss and she might be able to identify with me or offer support.

And even if Mom had no connection to such a personal loss, wasn't she supposed to come up with something like "Oh, honey, it is much more common than you think. It's your body's way of telling you the baby was not strong enough." Or even, "There is another angel in heaven, my darling."

I just couldn't believe that she could not finally come clean about the baby boy she had supposedly lost after delivery. I was in pain and sad and I had nowhere to turn.

I dialed her house once again. "Mom, are you sure there is *nothing* you want to share with me at this moment in my life?"

"Nope, not that I can think of."

"OK, well, can I ask you a question?

"Sure."

"Was there ever a baby . . ."

Pause.

"Was there . . . like, a boy . . ."

"Ah, why would you want to talk about such things?"

"Well is there a . . . grave?"

"Maybe."

OK, then, if this is so painful for her that she can't even help her only daughter not feel so alone, at a devastating time like this, then . . . I got nothin'.

I let her off the hook and never brought it up to her again. I would never know any more while my mother was still alive and physically able to communicate.

We would go through six IVF attempts after the first successful transfer. The difference was that because of the violence of the miscarriage, the scar tissue on my cervix had been stretched enough for me to get pregnant vaginally. The first successful attempt at implantation had been completed via my belly button. This would be the possible spiritual "reason" for the loss. By the time we got to the sixth try, we were exasperated. I had had some frozen embryos and some were fresh (six in all), and I could barely take it anymore.

I told the doctor I did not care if I had triplets; I wanted all six to be implanted in me and we would see. Lucky seven it was, and we finally returned home from a routine visit with a positive pregnancy test. And miraculously only one took. And unbelievably, the one embryo strong enough to make it had been a member of the original bunch. She had been frozen for two whole years.

This time we kept it a secret until we heard the heartbeat.

We called our parents during the sonogram and put the phone up to the machine to hear the heart. My mom recognized the sound immediately and began to cry. "Oh, my darling, I'm so happy for you." (Probably just for me—she didn't mention "that man" [Mom's favorite moniker for Chris] to whom I was married.) My dad thought it was a dog panting. We shared the good news with a slightly tempered excitement simply because of the long journey we had been on to get here. We did all the tests, including the amniocentesis, and we were relieved every time we got good news. When I got the formal call that the amnio had been normal, I burst into tears. Chris's parents were in town and we were having pizza at John's, uptown. I nervously picked up the call, and when I hung up, I was going to be a mother.

I don't remember telling my mom about the amnio. I also don't remember ever letting my mother feel my belly when the baby was moving. It seemed too physically intimate.

Chris and I bought a loft in SoHo with great light. The plan had been to stay in LA as long as possible because Chris had a job there and then come to New York City later in my third trimester. I wanted our baby to be born in New York City and Chris was on board. Plus, I was considered a high-risk pregnancy because of my compromised cervix, and the doctor did not want me doing too much traveling. I always loved that term: *compromised cervix*. As if my cervix had been involved in a lengthy legal negotiation and had been forced to reach some settlement. Well. It was better than the word *incompetent*, so I took it.

This high-risk state also meant that I could not visit my sick father. I needed a specialist in these types of deliveries and nobody wanted to put me or the baby in jeopardy.

Three weeks before leaving for New York City to deliver my baby, I was at the LA dog park saying bye to some friends when my cell phone rang. It was my stepsister.

"Say what you want to your dad, and say it now."

She put the phone up to his ear and I said: "I love you, Dad. And I've always been proud you were my father. Please don't be scared."

According to Cristiana, Dad moved his toes.

That was the last time I would ever talk to him. He passed away that afternoon shortly after we were on the phone. We had already chosen a first name for the baby, Rowan, and I decided Dad's first name would be her middle name. She was to be Rowan Francis Henchy.

I phoned my mother to tell her that Dad had died, and she began to cry, repeating, "Oh, Brookie, oh, Brookie."

We had not really discussed my dad's illness. Through her lonely tears she asked me if he had said anything about her to me.

"*What?!*"

"Did he mention me?"

"*No, Mom,* he did not mention you. How could you ask me that right at this moment? No, he did not talk about *you!*"

I knew that was being cruel but I said it anyway.

I sobbed the entire plane ride to New York City.

I went to term.

Chapter Sixteen

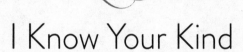

I Know Your Kind

was eight months pregnant and a good friend of ours from California was throwing me a coed baby shower in our newly acquired SoHo loft. All my life I'd lived on the Upper East Side, but moving downtown was the best decision we ever made. It felt like a fresh start. It was a bit grittier than the Upper East Side but more forgiving and varied. We decided not to cancel the shower because of my father's death but to instead try to celebrate his life as well as the one growing inside of me. I was incredibly sad that my dad would never meet my children, but I tried to forget the reality of the loss.

I had not seen my mom in a while and I was very nervous because I was pretty emotional and didn't want her to cause any trouble. But when she arrived she was surprisingly happy and not even sneaking alcohol. It was a beautiful and intimate shower, even if it was slightly bittersweet. I was shocked, amazed, and unbelievably relieved that Mom did not drink, and probably would have lost my mind if she had. Maybe somewhere in her subconscious she sensed that, but I doubt it. I just got lucky.

Three weeks later, in mid-May, my water broke. It was 5:00 A.M., at

the crack of dawn, and I had gotten up to use the bathroom. It was a few days before her due date and two days before my father's birthday. I had hoped she would be born on my dad's birthday. But Rowan was breech and chose to turn the night before my water broke. I'm sure she did it on purpose just to make sure I knew she was her own person.

When my water broke I did not go right to the hospital or call anybody. I called out to Chris, who had been up all night celebrating at the upfronts, which is when networks present their new shows to advertisers and affiliates. I yelled to him from the bathroom and asked him to check the *What to Expect When You're Expecting* book to see what to do when your water breaks. He waited a few moments and then said that the book said to go back to bed. I brought a towel to bed, went back to sleep, and had an amazing two-hour nap. I had a blowout scheduled for 9:00 A.M. so I figured I could go to the hospital with smooth hair. I hoped I would not go into labor until after the blowout was done.

I awoke and called my stepsister, Diana. I casually mentioned that my water had broken and she screamed at me, "Why are you not at the hospital?"

"Because I'm not having contractions and they'd probably just send me home."

"Oh my God, no, that is not right. Go to the hospital now. You can get an infection if your water breaks and you don't tend to it."

I lunged at Chris and asked him to tell me, again, what the book had said.

"What book?"

"Oh my God, you didn't even look at the book when I asked you! The baby may get an infection or I might because my water broke and I did nothing. Get me to the hospital *now*!"

Once safely at the hospital, we began phoning relatives and some close friends. I did not get an infection and I ended up needing to be induced. However, after being on Pitocin for twenty-four hours with practically no dilation, I needed an emergency C-section.

Mom and Chris's parents had all arrived at the hospital. As I was being wheeled into the OR, I saw Mom from my lying-down position on the gurney and I had such a strange feeling inside. I knew she was going to kiss me either on the lips or the forehead and I was instantly sick to my stomach at the thought that she might have cold, slightly clammy lips. I was sure she was nervous because only Chris was allowed to be in the OR with me.

I also resisted yelling out to her to tell me I was going to be OK. I suddenly felt like I could never ask her that question ever again. I knew for the first real time that she could not possibly know the answer to this question that I had been asking her since she was able to make it rain. I sometimes weaken and ask Chris this question. Sometimes you just want to hear someone say, "Yes, it's all going to be fine," even if you know that they couldn't possibly know the truth.

The delivery was horrendous. I was conscious and had had an

epidural but I was very aware that things were not going smoothly. First of all, I heard the doctor yell, "Cord wrapped, cord wrapped!"

Evidently, when Rowan turned the night before, she had wrapped the umbilical cord around her body and neck in three places. Thank God I did not push.

My uterus had herniated and I had lost a tremendous amount of blood. Another doctor was called in to assist. The baby was fine, fortunately, but the doctor had to concentrate on trying to keep me alive. The nurses took her away and I told Chris to go with them.

"Go with the baby, go with her."

I had heard that babies got switched sometimes and I was paranoid.

Once I was alone with the team of doctors and nurses, the terror set in. I was terrified of dying. I suddenly did want my mommy to tell me I was going to be OK after all. I had just had a baby, but I felt more like a baby than I have ever felt in my life. "Mommy, where are you?" was ringing in my ears. The doctor was able to assure me that the worst that would happen was a blood transfusion and a hysterectomy. I couldn't have cared less about losing my uterus. I wanted to live.

I also instantly got jealous of Chris for being alive and with our baby and hated my mother for being so careless with her own life by abusing her health with alcohol. And here I was split down the middle and fanned out like an opened minibox of cereal! It all came out as feelings of abandonment. I was sad and miserable—I couldn't believe how cold the OR suddenly felt. I got stitched back together and was allowed to own my uterus for another twenty-four hours. Ooh, goody! They were going to watch me, and if the bleeding stopped, I would not need the hysterectomy. I had always been fascinated by the fact that the word *hysterectomy* was born out of the word *hysteria* and was designed to fix women who were acting crazy during menstruation. It made sense to me now.

Once I was back in my room, they brought Rowan to me to

breast-feed. My mother had never breast-fed me and, while watching the nurse hold my newborn baby up to my chest, had the strangest look on her face. Mom kept herself tucked in between the side table and the side of my bed and draped her left arm over the back head-board of the hospital bed. I felt crowded but also strangely glad she was quiet, while making her best attempt to be near me without try-ing to control something she knew nothing about. She was shock-ingly still sober. Maybe she was deeply afraid something was going to happen to me.

I was exhausted and beginning to really struggle. I was beginning to feel stranger and sadder than I had ever felt in my life. I felt like I didn't recognize anyone around me. I knew who they were, but I felt they were all on a shore celebrating while I was underwater trying not to drown. I have pictures of the nurse holding Rowan up to my breast and I have fear all over my face. My mother was quiet and non-communicative. She looked like she was in shock.

Chris's family and some friends were milling around and all fo-cusing on the baby. Chris held her practically the entire time. I don't remember ever asking to hold Rowan myself. I had seen so many photos of friends and relatives from their hospital beds holding their newborns and looking at them with utter devotion and loving awe. I am sitting bare breasted and hooked up to machines, looking at al-most everybody else except Rowan. I had this overriding feeling that she already did not like me.

This was obviously the beginning of severe postpartum depres-sion. None of us knew what it was yet, but it would last much longer and cause damage to all of us in different ways. Thank God Rowan would remain unscathed. I eventually wrote a book about this ex-perience, *Down Came the Rain*, but at the moment I had to concen-trate on avoiding both a blood transfusion and a hysterectomy. My twenty-four hours of being watched were not yet over. I was not out of the woods yet and I could not seem to focus on anything other than my health and my own life.

People who wanted to see the happy mother and child came and went, and I kept a close eye on my mom. She seemed so out of sorts and slightly sad. I kind of felt like shaking her, but I didn't know what I would say. She seemed to want to be needed but she was so uncomfortable. It was as if she felt like she did not belong. She was as much related to this baby as Chris's parents, and yet she seemed to be receding into the background. In a surreal way, we both were but for different reasons. We were both out of sorts, equally at risk of not surviving. Mom dealt by being eerily quiet and I, too, chose reticence as a way to stay afloat.

It was time for Rowan and me to rest. Mom and Lila went to P. J. Clarke's to eat and I slept. Rowan was in a crib next to my bed and was attached to a light to help build up her bilirubin. She was a bit jaundiced and needed the vitamin D. She looked like a little alien on a mini wooden stretcher. I can't remember when Mom and Lila returned but I recall them coming back separately. Lila came in first and was mumbling something about how Mom had not wanted to leave the restaurant.

Chris had set up chairs in a kind of circle in the middle of my room and inclined toward my bed. He knew many people would be coming and going and want to hold the baby. Mom arrived after Lila and she walked into the room totally hammered and ready to fight. A male nurse, with whom she was overtly flirting, was guiding her into the room. We got the feeling that Mom had been in the building for a little while and had inappropriately made her presence known. She may or may not have pinched or slapped him on the butt but he ushered her into the room and then made a quick exit. I had an inkling that because she was my mom they were stretching their tolerance.

Mom came in the room as the family members were passing Rowan around to be held. They all took turns, and when it was Mom's turn, she reached out to hold the swaddled newborn, only to almost drop her in the process. Rowan only weighed seven and a half pounds, but Mom fumbled her and the baby almost fell to the floor. I could tell she was drunk, but I could not even speak. I was mute and exhausted and felt like I was out of my body and hovering unnoticed. I watched in stilled horror and felt as if I had just been forced to ride a terrifying Ferris wheel for a second time. As if the operator would not let me get off.

Chris leapt up, grabbed the baby from her hands, and got right up in my mother's face. He told her that she was not allowed to hold Rowan in her condition. He took a strong stance and told her she was drunk and could do whatever the hell she wanted to herself, but was not allowed to jeopardize our baby. His face was red with anger, and he said, in fact, he would like her to leave this room right now.

Nobody else said a word. I don't even remember Rowan uttering a peep. Chris followed my mother to the doorway to make sure she didn't do anything sudden. She turned face-to-face with him in the doorway, pointing at him and tapping her forefinger on his chest in a threatening way.

"Oh, I know your kind," she said.

She pushed back and staggered off and out into the night.

Chris came over to me immediately and apologized and said he was so sorry, but he had to draw the line at our baby. I was relieved she was gone but profoundly sad that it had to be that way. I thanked Chris for defending us, even though I knew he was just defending his daughter. That was the man I knew he was and the father I wanted for my children. But overall, I was just fatigued by everything.

My in-laws were trying to act normal and were successfully

avoiding discussing anything but this perfect baby. I could tell Lila was angry and sad and hurt and frustrated by having to deal with Mom again and again. Nobody had any authority over my mother. Even in this supposedly blessed and happy moment, she could not be happy or healthy.

My heart was breaking for a few reasons and it would soon become evident that I had reached an emotional limit. The cumulative and recent pain and sorrow had caught up to me and I was breaking apart. My heart ached for everybody I loved and was now breaking for myself. I fell asleep that night looking at this little stranger under her orange light and I envied her. This baby was allowed to be helpless. I had never been permitted to be so.

The next day the doctor came and told us Rowan's hips had not fully formed and she would need to wear a strong Velcro brace for a few months. I sat there on my hospital bed and could not grasp anything. I hated breast-feeding, I had lost a lot of blood and was weak, my baby was yellow and needed a paddle attached to her with intense light, and now her hip sockets had not formed and she needed to wear a brace that made her look like a marionette whose knees were stuck bent up. I did not have the strength to feel happy or available to the present potential of joy. Rowan was in a brace, but I felt like I was in a straightjacket.

I was able to keep my uterus and my life and I was soon released.

At home, it seemed that nobody could help me. I continued to struggle with breast-feeding, I could not stop crying, and I had horrible visions of Rowan getting hurt. I would get dizzy at the powder smell of the diapers. I'd huddle in the shower with hot water pounding down on me and not move for extended periods of time. Food had no taste or appeal. I actually still haven't eaten lasagna since my mother-in-law made a pan of it that first week. I had taken one bite and could not even swallow. I had such trouble producing milk for my baby because I was not nourishing my own body.

On one incredibly low day, Chris went out to get a changing table because we were totally unprepared for the arrival. For some reason I had not been proactive about setting up a nursery. I knew the due date but had not bought the necessary furniture and had only set up the nursery by getting a rocker that had actually been a gift.

Chris came back from a store (ironically called buybuy Baby), empty-handed. He sat down on the edge of the bed and began to cry. He said he had seen happy mothers holding their newborns, and pregnant mothers smiling and shopping.

"What is wrong with you? You don't sing to her or kiss her."

I felt my world end. I could only answer that I did not know and that I was so sorry. I left him in our room and hobbled out to see my mom, who was sitting on our leather tufted coffee table in the living room. I slumped in the chair in front of her and began to cry. She asked me what was the matter, and I looked at her and with dismay said, "I made Chris cry."

"I made him cry?" she asked.

"What?! Oh my God, Mom, *no*, not *you*. *I made Chris cry! You* are not the important one here. Get out of this house right now or I am going to jump out of the fucking window. Get out—I mean it!"

She just sat there motionless and trying to be invisible. I cried and escaped back to the bedroom, disgusted. I knew her hearing was deteriorating but I could not believe that she heard something about her—and not about Chris or me—in what I was crying about. Just like when Dad died and she asked me if he had asked about her, my husband was crying and she thought she had caused his tears. It was all about her in her mind, not out of narcissism but out of fear and insecurity. Mom had just stared at me and had become helplessly still. Her eyes looked like those of a scared little kid witnessing something horrible.

I realized the problem did not actually concern her. There was something terrible wrong in my life and it affected all those around me. I did not know where to turn.

I would soon get a baby nurse to help out for a week, which turned into a year. I got help from a doctor who referred me to a pharmapsychologist who prescribed me the proper combination of medication. I also began to eat better and began to exercise again by taking Rowan on long hikes around the neighborhood in New York and LA.

Things settled down and I stopped hating my mother for not knowing what I needed. How could I expect her to talk about her experiences from a place of wisdom and understanding when she had never spent any time on self-reflection? I realize today that she was scared most of the time and lonely all of the time. I was eventually even able not to punish my mother for continuing to call Rowan "Brookie." We invited her out to California because, no matter what, I wanted her to know my baby and I wanted Rowan to know this grandmother as well.

I didn't realize, though, that this was the beginning of a new phase in our relationship and my mother's health. Mom started being more and more helpless. The next few years would be a challenge in an all new way.

In the months after Rowan was born, there were a few times that Mom visited us in LA and seemed to be in a quieter place. I was going back and forth between New York and New Jersey and LA, but for the beginning of Rowan's life we were primarily living in Santa Monica. Chris was working on a new TV show and we were living in a house on the west side of town. Rowan was only a few months old but was getting so big so fast, and I really wanted Mom to see that I was

doing a good job taking care of my baby. She enjoyed playing with Rowan and putting pink sponge rollers on her few bits of baby hair. Mom would spend the first few days seemingly not drinking, but by day three it was always clear she did not want to be under my watchful eye.

Not watching my mother was never something I could do. I always fell right into a codependent routine of scrutinizing her every move and trying to anticipate those I had yet to see. I wanted my mother around because that way I knew she was alive. But she made me crazy in ways I could not believe. She would say things under her breath or I'd see an expression of judgment in her eyes and I would have to address or fight it. Even if I left the room and counted to ten or practiced deep breathing, I would have the urge to wrap my hands around her throat and squeeze. Even when I'd try to be sweet, it felt forced because she made me nervous. Oh, how my mom could unsettle me and undo all the work I had done on myself to live a healthy and self-actualized life. And why did I still seek her approval?

I still would rather have her be around than alone and in an echoing house in New Jersey. It was a relief to have her arrive safely off the plane and a relief to see her leave. She was OK with Rowan but was never left alone with her in those early days.

I wanted to have her go on these walks with me while I pushed Rowan in a stroller around the neighborhood. I had had such good deep conversations with Gemma, our baby nurse, on these walks, and I would have loved the Hallmark moment with my mom as well. Sadly, Mom's knees were bad and her arthritis was making it very hard for her to do any walking. She was perfectly comfortable to sit and watch movies for hours. It seemed it was the only activity we occasionally still enjoyed together. For some reason it bothered me when she sat doing nothing all day, just watching movies. And for some reason I didn't trust that she was not also trying to snoop around my office or even pocket little things just because she felt entitled to do so. It was very strange but Mom wanted any form of control she could find, even if it meant stealing back a little ashtray or coaster we had gotten in Europe on one of our earlier trips.

Her health did seem to be declining and it was beginning to be apparent that alcohol consumption was not her only issue. It would be years before the problem would be diagnosed, but she was somehow increasingly different and booze was surprisingly no longer the only problem.

When I once went back to Haworth when Rowan was about six months old, it became even clearer to me that drinking or not, Mom was not completely coherent. She would get confused or not be able to follow a story. This particular night in Haworth, Rowan was sick and I really did not feel secure with my mom helping. She began drinking, only in the evening, but I realized that I was totally alone in caring for my sick infant. I had no car because I had been dropped off at my mother's for the night and her car was in the shop. She had had her license taken away from her anyway, so she wouldn't be needing a car. I was going to help her sort through some closets that needed cleaning out that evening, but Rowan had gotten a fever and instead I had to keep a close eye on her.

Chris told me to call a car and leave immediately. Leaving abruptly was proving problematic, but I figured since I was near a police station and hospital I had a potential escape plan. I called the doctor and he said just to keep an eye on her fever. If it got past 103, then I should worry. I tried to cool her face off with cool compresses.

It was a real traumatic night for me because I felt so alone and so afraid for my daughter. I had my own child to care for and it really hit home for me that I could not rely on my mother to help. All my life I felt secure knowing I could handle my mom and take care of myself. I also always believed she actually did take care of me growing up. I had survived, hadn't I? This feeling with my own baby girl felt very different and deeply unsettling. Suddenly all bets were off and I hated my mother and her incompetence.

I consciously separated myself from my mom and her issues, and survival kicked in. But this time it was not for myself but for my infant. Something deep within me shifted and I made Rowan my only emotional and physical focus. My daughter became my only priority. I realized, completely, that I could not count on my mother to help my daughter or me. And most likely not even herself.

All throughout my life I had held out hope that my mother would one day ultimately show up for me and give me the freedom not to worry about her or put her needs ahead of mine. In these moments of fear for my daughter's health, I realized that it was up to me to reclaim that freedom on my own. She would never be able to bestow on me such peace and autonomy. Rowan slept and I stayed awake to watch her breathing. As I lay awake listening to Rowan's labored breathing and praying for her fever to break, I hated my mom and I redefined my loyalty. By dawn Rowan's fever had broken. I was exhausted but buoyed by the fact that the worst was over. I returned to New York City and never discussed any of it with my mom. There was no point.

Two years later, living in New York again, I was planning to appear in the musical *Chicago* for the second time as Roxie Hart, this time trading London's West End for Broadway. I had called my IVF doctor to say that I wanted to start the process of getting pregnant during my run in the show. I would need a few months of medication, and being in a show was the best time to do it, because I am always my healthiest when performing. After some routine blood tests the doctor called back to tell me that the process would not be necessary because I was already pregnant. I was stunned and elated but now suddenly afraid of doing eight shows a week while pregnant. The doctor said not to do any extra exercise and I would be fine.

Mom came to my opening night on Broadway and seemed happy to be included, but very distant. She seemed uncomfortable and unable to articulate herself. I had been getting more short and curt with her recently because she couldn't even seem to order the food she wanted at a restaurant. She whispered instead of speaking loud enough to be heard, and I would often impatiently hurry her on and speak to her in a condescending tone. I could not seem to stop myself from lashing out. I would get frustrated and oddly embarrassed.

I would get impatient and raise my voice, saying, "Mom, *what* do you want to *eat*?"

I would then just pick for her and apologize to the server out of embarrassment for my mother's lack of focus. I felt mortified that she was acting like a little kid and I was ashamed of my own impatience. Later, Rowan would stick up for Toots and tell me not to be mean to her, scolding me.

Other strange things happened as well. Chris came into the kitchen one afternoon and saw my mother place a ceramic bowl of soup onto an open flame on the stove. He stopped her and said, "Teri, that should be in a metal pot."

"I know but it's faster this way. Take out the middleman."

Luckily, he managed to avert disaster by offering to help and, in fact, serve her. This soup incident sent up our first warning sign. This was beyond my mother's normal eccentric nature.

Soon after that, I decided to get rid of my entire set of Fiestaware dishes and cups that Mom and I had collected over the years at various flea markets. I now wanted clean, uniform-looking china. I went to Sur La Table and bought simple white bowls and plates and mugs. As I was taking the stickers off the bottoms of the mugs it occurred to me that this task might be something my mother could help me with. She was thrilled that I asked for her help. She stood at the kitchen island and began peeling off the tiny SKU labels from the bottom of the pieces.

I watched her out of the corner of my eye and was sadly fascinated by the precision with which she picked away at the edges with the tip of the painted red nail of her index finger. She moved slowly and with focused concentration, and added each little sticker to a mounting pile stuck to the marble top of the counter. She reminded me of the autistic children I had studied temporarily after I graduated from college as research for a part in a shitty movie I did. She was at first quiet and seemingly content, but she could not seem to finish the job. I kept watching her while pretending to do other things. She skipped some stickers and labored over others, and then would get distracted and forget she was working on a task at all. A task that should have taken fifteen minutes took over two hours and was completely disorganized.

Watching her inability to complete any seemingly simple task spurred deep curiosity in me. Was she brain damaged from a ministroke she had suffered a few years back? Was the hematoma that I had seen and touched at St. Vincent's when I received the dead turtle more damaging than I thought, or was excessive alcohol all to blame?

I tried another kitchen task. I asked Mom to set the dining room table with the new flatware I had also just ordered. I gave her enough for twelve settings. Now, it had been my mother who had taught me the proper way to set a formal dinner table. She was from Newark but she made sure she was skilled in proper etiquette. I learned from a young age which utensil went where and why. Mom disappeared into the dining area to set the table. We were not having a dinner, but I did not tell her that. She was gone for about two hours. When I checked in on her, nothing she'd done made sense. She could not seem to finish the job. I can't say I handled it well. I would like to be able to write that I calmly helped her and encouraged her like I would a child. I did not. I got disgusted and impatient and used the moment to chastise her and shame her. I was striking back and felt ugly and ashamed but I could not stop this lashing out.

"Seriously, Mom, you can't even set a table. Really?"

She got that terrible wide-eyed—scared, cornered, and broken—look in her expression and she went still again. Instead of lashing back or cursing at me as I had seen so many times, she looked like a little kid being shamed by her mommy. I was not proud of my behavior but felt so pouty and bratty. I wanted to stamp my feet and cry, "It's not fair!"

It was as if I had reverted to that little brat from Mom's return from St. Mary's.

It is a very unsettling feeling to see your parents really helpless and vulnerable. I was so frustrated that I had taken care of her my whole life, and that now, when the big dramas seemed to have subsided, it felt even worse. I was getting angry that when I had thought she might have finally settled down a bit and had finally become a sweet or calmer grandma, she now seemed impaired and even more helpless. The promised land I believed in had never materialized and now we were in a different kind of hell. What had it all been for?

Something was not right in her head. Was her brain pickled by booze? Or was it something else?

Part Five

I will always be your daughter and you my mother even if the manifestation of that is not what either of us dream of.

—*Card to Teri from Brooke*

Chapter Seventeen

Tag Sale

Life around my mother began to be even more unsettled and intense, but for entirely new reasons. I was beginning to get worried and sad because alcohol was seriously beginning to be the least of my worries. For forty years my focus had been on her drinking. Now I almost wished that the booze was the problem. My chest would tighten every time I saw the look of fear on her face when she was asked a question. She looked like a little kid in a foreign land having been separated from her mommy.

Chicago went well and I finished my run just as my belly was beginning to look like I was hiding half a soccer ball in it. I told my mother I was pregnant and called her again when I heard my daughter's heartbeat. Mom cried this time, too.

It was about this time that I really began to feel distant from my mom. When I had Rowan I was still so enmeshed with my mother, but with this baby I felt a new level of freedom. I am not sure what to attribute this liberation to, but I really just started to feel like I was finally growing up. Time had passed since my dad's death. I didn't care, honestly, if my mom drank or not. And I was about to have two children under the age of three. Life was shifting.

Sadly, the realization dawned on me that I was becoming a mother at the same time I was beginning to lose my own. I am reminded of the fact that in every Disney movie from *Bambi* to *Frozen* the mothers all are dead or die within the first few minutes. Is that what it takes to start your own story? One's narrative morphs with one's current perspective of the truth. But must one's mother die for a person to fully individuate?

I started getting the heavy feeling that it was too late for my mom to ever really be happy and for me to make up for the time I had lost whenever she was drunk.

Maybe when I blurted out "If you die, I'll die" all those years ago I was onto something. Maybe a part of me would have to die to continue. I used to honestly feel that if Mom died I would actually stop living. Now I had my own children to live for and I had my own life to fully live.

It started getting very sad to me when I realized I was actually, slowly, losing my mother and there was little to be done about it. I felt like I had lost her my entire life. I had fought for her and had fought against her for so many years and was not sure what I had to show for it. She was fading just as I was beginning to come into focus.

Mom was mostly living in her new condominium in New Jersey. It was becoming evident that this would probably not last long. It was getting harder and harder for her to take care of herself. She was starting to show real signs of forgetfulness and she began speaking less and even more quietly. She was hardly drinking and when she did it wasn't to excess. I had actually given up trying to get her to quit drinking. In fact, I began to pour her wine like I would for anybody else at the table. Why not? I had contacted lawyers and begun the legal process of being designated her health and legal proxy. It was evident Mom was on a path toward being declared incompetent with regard to her personal care. She had a couple of friends who'd drive her places and I'd arrange any other necessary travel. I was no longer worried she could drive, and I just had to make sure she didn't hurt herself by accident in some way while unattended.

I visited her when I could. In my spare time I continued to go through her storage units to take inventory and sell some more items to help her pay her bills. Over the course of our lifetime together Mom and I had owned six homes. There was a period where we owned them all at the same time! Once I convinced my mother to start unloading some real estate so as to maintain some financial liquidity, we suddenly had more furniture than we could ever use. That did not stop her from buying more. Mom often bought furnished houses, but every time she sold a house, she kept its contents. My mom could never part with a thing. After the collection expanded out of several storage units, my mother ended up renting a warehouse in Paterson, New Jersey, that was literally the size of an airplane hangar. She filled it top to bottom and had been paying rent on it for years.

The big problem, however, was the actual manner in which Mom stored her treasures. There was no rhyme or reason to any of it and hardly anything was marked. The boxes were stacked on top of each other, reaching up as high as the ceiling. She had clothes, linens, silverware, fabric, jewelry, more clothes, books, art, film reels, bikes, toys, tools, stereo equipment, countless rugs, built-in cabinets she had ripped out from places, machinery of sorts, Hollywood memorabilia, and furniture galore. Most of it was real quality. But who needed four rolltop desks or the built-in cabinetry from our town house on Sixty-Second and Lexington Avenue? My assistant Dan started helping me sort through everything. We never knew what we would find, but you knew there would be a story attached.

For example, she had two wardrobe-size cardboard boxes chockfull of Beanie Babies. She had become one of those people who collected them with the plan of cashing in one day. She never traded or sold them, though, but simply kept buying hoards of the little ridiculous stuffed animals. The whole thing creeped me out. But I had learned to pick my battles. Either they would sell or I would find a place to donate them.

I thought I would donate the boxes to a children's hospital but was told they could not take stuffed animals because of the germs. I then found out that my aunt Lila knew somebody who would fill a suitcase and bring it to children in developing countries. She could only take one suitcase, however, and would not be making another trip for months. I decided to rummage through the boxes before separating them to be sold. My assistant thought it was a waste of my time. They were obviously just boxes full solely of Beanie Babies.

I explained to him that he did not really know my mother. Something told me I needed to go through all of them. Well, at the bottom of one of the wardrobe boxes was a little piece of crumpled-up tissue. Inside said tissue was a 14-karat gold, diamond-encrusted Harry Winston watch. Mom had always hidden things places and then forgot where they were. I found lose semiprecious stones in dental-floss containers and a 24-karat gold purse inside another flea market clutch. There were real Louis Vuitton and Chanel bags mixed in with knockoffs, and I had to beg Dan to go into their stores and ask for help telling the difference between them. I don't think it was about fear of theft as much as she was just eccentric and loved being in control. Mom would go to all lengths for a laugh or just to have something over on somebody.

In April 2006 our second daughter, Grier Hammond Henchy, was born. Now I had two daughters under the age of three. Even though Grier was born in LA, we had decided that when she started school we would move the girls back to New York and get their education in Manhattan. I had always wanted to have my girls have a New York

City upbringing. Mom had been making reckless decisions—like letting a guy who worked at the gas station move into her living room. She was found wandering barefoot and confused around a school parking lot.

We decided it was time to move her to an assisted-living facility.

Mom went willingly, but when she arrived she hated it because she was not like "these people." It was just like it was back in rehab all those years ago. The way she saw it, she was never as bad as the other people in these places. The tough part for me was that Mom really didn't look as old as the other residents. They all actually did seem older and more out of it than she did. She didn't mumble as much as they did and had not begun to shuffle with her socked feet wedged into bedroom slippers.

As soon as she was checked in she started asking me when she could leave. I have to admit that although it was a relief to have her accounted for, I felt terrible that she needed such a place. I felt guilty for "putting her away." She used to love to paint the picture to people of her being eventually locked up and me sliding a tray of food to her under the door. "Peter and the tray," she called it, reminding me of the Peter-like betrayal she'd always expected.

I justified it all by saying to myself that it was temporary. I secretly felt she was somehow superior to the others. I thought she would snap out of it. She had to. It couldn't end like this.

Having her in a facility gave me the freedom to handle the sale of her homes and have tag sales for the excess crap. I discovered that she had been shopping on QVC and HSN for copious amounts of jewelry. She had burned through money I had allotted her over the years and had even siphoned from a retirement fund. There were hundreds and hundreds of little boxes and bags filled with birthstone rings and earrings. I had never seen so many cubic-zirconia items in one area. She bought in bulk and had intended to give it all away to friends and employees and one of each to her granddaughters. It was insane. In addition she had various collections of everything from taxidermy, vintage record players, quilts, tiles, antique doors, or orange crates filled with door fittings. She had milk-glass table settings, Depression-glass collections, rugs, sterling-silver settings for twelve, over a thousand vintage tablecloths, assortments of paint-by-number art mixed in with period oil portraits, bolts of fabric, multiple pieces of antique furniture, and unfinished crafts from the seventies.

I had to sort through it all and decide what to do with it. I basically kept the good stuff and put the rest up for sale. We had three massive two-day tag sales to rid ourselves of the clutter. We made a good chunk of money on these sales and the money went directly to her living costs.

One day I called to speak to my mother and they said she had gone out with a male friend. My mother had two friends at this point and I was one of them. The other was an accountant's assistant who had been helping Mom pay bills. She was a woman.

I asked with whom she had gone out and to where, and why had they not called me?

They said that a man came to visit her and that Mom seemed to know him, so she left with him. The jailbreak had been a success. He was not on the accepted list of visitors and these idiots had no idea that they were allowing my mother to be checked out by a *National Enquirer* reporter. My head exploded with rage.

This bozo snuck Mom directly to the bank, at her request, and she had tried to take out money. I actually guessed she would go back to Haworth, because she maintained her account there and was always talking about money and being stolen from. She wanted to flee and this was her ticket to escape. I hung up on the numbnut attendant at the facility and immediately called the bank and asked if my mom was there. They informed me that yes, she was. A man in fact had accompanied her. She was trying to withdraw money from her account at that moment.

I explained in an agitated tone that this man was not a friend and had basically kidnapped her. I begged them to please not release any funds, saying that she had been under psychiatric observation and was currently living in an assisted-living facility. I had no legal right, technically, to stop anything, because the account was in her name. I made a dramatic, agitated, yet crystal-clear case and explained that my mom was not of sound mind and would do something damaging with any money. They agreed to deny her access this time but would need more documentation on the legal restrictions, which were already being prepared.

I thanked them profusely and said I would get the paperwork ASAP. I had by then known these bank clerks, policemen, and mailmen for over twenty-five years.

Mom got very angry that she was denied access to her account and stormed off. The bank had said it was some paperwork mix-up and told her to ask her daughter to help. The slimeball reporter next took Mom to a diner, where she proceeded to blab all about her horrible daughter over a cheeseburger. She told the dramatic details of how I "divorced" my own mother and stole everything from her. She went on a tirade about evil Perry and how he had brainwashed me. She loved saying I had basically joined the Agassi cult. Mom painted herself as a true victim and me as the ultimate betrayer. "Hiya, Peter!"

He took copious notes and had the story of a lifetime. America's Sweetheart was actually a Daughter Dearest! He had gotten everything he wanted, and Mom loved being able to vent and be heard. She felt wronged in every way and was letting the world know the "truth." He dropped her back at the facility with the same ease with which he had had her removed.

I moved her out of the facility the next day and sued the *Enquirer*. I won the case and gave the money to Alzheimer's research. The story was blocked and I was ultimately protected.

Because of the wandering situation and the trust in strangers, as well as her mounting paranoia, I had Mom analyzed and consequently declared incompetent. My request to become legally affirmed her health proxy and guardian was thus immediately facilitated. Once again I was taking care of her, but this time it was out of necessity, not obsession. I tried to be up-front about it with her but was worried she would feel like I was trying to find more ways to betray her and steal from her. She seemed not to grasp anything that I tried to explain. Having more control made it much easier with regards to real estate sales and other legal decisions. I found another facility in New York City that specialized in patients with Alzheimer's and the many other forms of dementia. It was located on the Upper East Side at Eightieth and York. It only took two trains to get to and was close to Mom's and my old neighborhood.

Plus, I could sleep at night knowing she was closer to me in New York City, and with any luck I would not be getting any more phone calls from the police. In addition I could have my children still spend visits with her, which made her smile.

As a part of the entrance protocol, Mom had to be taken to a psychiatrist to be analyzed. I took her to a small office on the ground level of a big brick building. The doctor asked Mom simple questions about the weather, the day, and who our president was. It happened to be Presidents' Day so the question regarding our president was clearly appropriate.

But when asked the question, Mom couldn't remember the president's name. It was a cloudy day, and when asked about the weather, Mom smiled and said it was a great day outside because her daughter was with her. She recalled her birthday and other details about herself with no problem, but it was clear there was some sort of impairment.

The next part of the test involved her answering some comparison questions. There was clearly one best answer to each comparison. This showed me something so extraordinary and sweet and heart-breaking.

"How are a boat and a vehicle the same?"

"They both have motors."

"How are a baby and a bud the same?"

"They both smell really good."

She failed.

This last question killed me, because it was so clear as to the way she thought. She thought with an innocence of a child. Some boats did have motors, and buds and babies did smell pretty delicious. She would not get cognitive credit for being anything but literal. Varied interpretation was not the desired goal. I tried to argue that they were not entirely wrong answers. Yet again I felt the need to stick up for my mother in front of a total stranger. The doctor later explained to me that based on all the tests and the brain scan, Mom was showing signs of developing dementia. All my frustrations, fear, and worry and what little anger I really and rarely possessed melted in abject, gut-wrenching, and profound sadness.

Of all the things I thought my mother would be dying of, dementia was not one of them. Her brain had so long remained seemingly sharp. Because of her wit and ability to notice details in human be-havior, I thought her mind would be the last to go. I was sure it would be her liver that went. She was also from hearty German and Irish stock, and because her mother had lived past ninety, I was sure my mom would outlast all of us, or at least her wretched mother.

I took her back to the new facility. It still didn't feel as if Mom really belonged in a place like this. She didn't seem like the other people, at least from my perch on self-denial hill. She still had the capacity to communicate with the staff in a way that did distinguish her from the others. She still had her wry, sarcastic approach to some things, and the staff got a kick out of her. Mom started going to Saturday Shabbat ceremony with a rabbi who loved to sing. She told him she liked the singing and the music.

As time went on, she seemed to settle in a bit more and I made my kids visit more often, even if it was only to do their homework or take her for coffee. I went as often as I could but I really hated going. The moment I would see her I would get a sick and sad feeling in the pit of my heart. She reeked of sadness. She cried every time I started to walk to the elevator to leave. I always promised to come back, but she looked like a puppy in the ASPCA commercials or a starving UNICEF orphan with tears in her eyes.

This might have been the time to talk to her and get some type of closure, but all I could ever do was tell her I loved her and run away. It was too much for me to see. But hearing "I love you" seemed to light up her eyes for a moment and I took it.

But I needed and wanted more. *Please come back, Mom*, I thought. *Let's try this again. You can do this.*

Mom was already too far gone to have any real conversation at all and nevermind the dual apology I had imagined.

But back at home, my family was thriving. We had fully moved into the new town house downtown. Both girls asked to have their beds moved to be against the wall. I smiled inside, remembering that first night Mom and I spent in our new apartment on Seventy-Third Street. I thought about the mattress being on the floor and against the wall and wondered if genetics were playing a part. There is something very cozy and seemingly womblike about having a wall to push up against.

I resisted moving their beds for them for as long as I could because the rooms were not set up that way and moving the beds would mean blocking a window in each room. The thought of the head of a bed right under a window made me nervous, but we don't live in LA, so earthquakes are not a concern. All my fabulous decorating down the drain. My girls were not concerned with the fact that the house had been featured on the cover and inside *Architectural Digest*. They wanted beds moved and crap hung up and taped everywhere!

"OK, fine, I'll help you move your beds."

"You're the best, Mom!"

"Yeah, yeah."

I have never told my girls about the apartment on East Seventy-Third, but they both wanted to shove their beds against the wall and stack the multitude of stuffed animals all along the side. They wedge their warm little sleepy selves with their backs to the wall and now sleep through the night. My younger daughter comes in my room in the mornings and she asks to cuddle and spoon. I now pull my own little girl into my body and I am the outside spoon this time. I am constantly reminded of the glorious nights' sleep in the bare apartment and being spooned by my mommy, but my daughter and I differ when I ask her whether my arm is too heavy. She often says, "Yes, a little, Mama." I would have never told my mother her arm was heavy even if I could not breathe. God forbid she lift it off me. I guess I should feel proud my girls feel secure enough to express their feelings to me.

I look at my girls when they are asleep and I marvel at how stunning they are. Their smooth, pure faces and tiny features seem to glow. Granted, it is also because they are asleep and not fighting or talking back, but I do understand how every mother's child is divinely perfect.

I always thought I would be a great mom. I could handle babies and take care of them and was never scared to have them entrusted to me. I could soothe them and make them smile. I could always make them fall asleep in my arms and I could get lost in their skin and delicious smell. I was never disgusted by their diapers or bored with having to attend to them constantly.

But I *never* intended for them to grow up!

I never thought past the baby stage. I assumed I'd be a good mom because I could handle infants, never once considering their being eleven.

Now, after many years, I realize that my girls could not be further apart in personality from one another. Rowan keeps her emotions deep inside whereas Grier is a walking, ticking emotional time bomb. They eat differently, dress differently, think differently, and react differently. As I write this, Rowan is eleven going on twenty-two and Grier is eight and wants to be back in my womb. In addition, they could not be more starkly different from me, and how they relate to me is nothing like how I related to my own mom.

It took me a while to realize that just giving birth to them did not mean I knew who they were. It also was a shock for me to find out they weren't me, either. I assumed that because they were babies that I understood who they were inside.

I have to ask my girls who they are. They are not me. I am not them. It is easy to want to mold them. There is a difference between teaching and crafting. It is our duty to protect and love and impart what we think are life's truths, but we really need to support our children in ways that nurture their individual selves. And I remind myself that I'm still the parent anyway.

For instance, Rowan is very clear about how her friends treat her and what her needs are. Grier once told her that her best friend was not treating her well, but she kept wanting to spend time with her. Rowan said, "Well, she is obviously not your best friend, then, because best friends don't treat each other that way!" Later I found out the reason why Rowan said what she did was that I told Rowan the same thing when her best friend was treating her a certain way. She took what I said, remembered it, and applied it to Grier's situation. But back when I was a kid and my mother's daughter, I, like Grier, would have taken the bad treatment just to have people like me. Wow, did I actually teach her that?

I admire Rowan so much because of how sure she is of herself. When she was a baby, I would watch her at the playground trying to get kids to play with her. She would sometimes get rejected over and over and she remained unfazed. I'd hear her say, "No? . . . No? . . . No? . . . OK," and she would then simply start to dance and play on her own. She was completely content, and sure enough, in a short amount of time the same little kids would start to gravitate toward her. Before you knew it, she was like the Pied Piper.

Rowan has always been very straightforward and black-and-white. When she was two years old, she was in her car seat in the back of my SUV and I was pulling out of our driveway in LA. I had just gotten really mad at my mother for something. I can't remember why I was crying but I was upset and quietly crying in the front seat. I was trying not to be obvious, but sure enough Rowan didn't miss a beat. She quickly asked, "Mama crying?"

I had a decision to make. Do I lie and say no, I just had something in my eye? That would send the message that it was shameful to cry in front of others and that her instincts were not correct. I had to quickly think of what my little girl needed. She needed to hear the truth but also needed to know that her world was right and her mom was OK enough to be able to keep her safe.

"Yes, bug, Mama's a bit sad, but I'm going to be fine and I love you."

"Mmn, Mama's crying."

And with that she put her thumb in her mouth and looked out the window completely satisfied. As she stared at the passing trees I thought, *What! That's all I get? I'm upset here! Come on! Nothing?*

This thought made me chuckle. How different I was from my own mother and what a different childhood Rowan was experiencing. I never was able to stop being concerned about my mother and her emotions. I could understand how she wanted my continual doting. I felt a bit lonely as I sat in the car but ultimately proud that I had not made my problems Rowan's. I don't think I ever fully believed my mom was OK or safe herself. I grew to believe it was my responsibility to keep both of us safe. Anxiety became a constant in my life beginning at a very early age, but how I handled it changed over time.

Rowan actually scared me at times growing up because she seemed so independent that I felt she didn't need me. All my mom wanted was to be needed and wanted. As Rowan grows older, she fights me on so much that our relationship often causes me confusion, frustration, fear, and pause. But every now and then she surprises me with unsolicited affection or nuanced humor. My mother and I bonded the most through our humor. It was our go-to remedy when we were having problems. I believe that comedy is one of the only ways one can truly live in the moment. I have always used humor as my biggest defense mechanism. I believe I homed in on this part of my personality early on and used it as a way to cope with life. It helped me escape Mom's alcohol. Mom and I shared a bond in comedy, and if we were laughing, we were temporarily OK. It became my vocation on and off camera.

Humor has become a point of connection between Rowan and me as well. Instead of it diffusing angst, it is just another way for us to be honest as well as vulnerable. I'll never forget the first time Rowan launched into a full-on impression of an old lady from the Bronx. She was incredible at it. For a moment I saw my younger self in her and felt emotional and strangely proud. We were with my half sisters over Thanksgiving when Rowan suddenly began asking me questions as if we were two old ladies sitting and gossiping on a stoop in the "old neighborhood." She shocked me and I jumped into the impromptu improvisation and felt so close to her. We all laughed hysterically. It was oxygen in my veins like it had been with Mom. I flashed back to skits my mom and I used to do just for one another and was very moved by all of it.

Grier and I have a very different relationship. She rarely challenges me and is incredibly affectionate with me. She had the most fun with Toots because Mom was regressing by the time she was born and could play with blocks and toys with Grier for long stretches at a time. Grier is also a mini-hoarder in training. Like my mom, who was the queen of collecting, she loved all the little dust-collecting tchotchkes my mom would give to her. Grier loves to put a coin in her "maybe need pocket" of her jeans, and it's the same kind of mini-pocket in her own jeans that Mom had pulled a nickel from when she was in the holding cell in New Orleans.

Grier is extremely emotional and once said, "You are everything that's wrong with my life!" She was mad at me for putting her sister in a time-out and crying and hated me for it. Not long after this outburst she added, "You know, Mom, the minute I say something mean to you, I wish I did not say it, but I can't stop it before it comes out of my lips." I love when my girls express such raw emotions so honestly. It hurts my feelings at times but I have to admit I am relieved that they can be so honest with their emotions and possess the freedom to express everything they feel. I think I was always way too concerned with my mom's feelings to even notice my own. The same drama that Grier embodies when she is mad is the same she shows when she is happy.

"Wow, I can't believe you love me, Mom! I don't know why I just said that!" she'd say. Or "I just love you so much it *horts*." Or "Mama, you are my heaven!"

As beautifully layered as my relationship is with my daughters, I do believe it is a much healthier one than mine was with my mom. Mine was deep and wonderful at times but extreme. It was not founded on security but on a sometimes irrational love mixed with intense codependence.

There was never any lack of love, but that's what made it hard. There was also a good deal of fear from both sides. She always feared I would leave her. I always feared something would happen to my mother or that I was not good enough for her. I never doubted her love for me but I was perpetually worried about her well-being and self-esteem—the things mothers usually worry about for their children.

My girls don't doubt my love for them, either, but they are also quite secure being away from me. They rarely feel they need to check on my state of mind or my whereabouts. I had to work on not being threatened by their autonomy because I grew up thinking that real love had to be based on codependence. Independence equaled abandonment.

In late 2011 my mother began to fade further. She was very settled into the Eightieth Street residence and I had settled into a new routine with my life and her care. I was doing *The Addams Family* on Broadway. One night after the show I was walking into one of my favorite little pubs that sold my favorite Belgian beer, Duvel. As I sat and ordered, Carmine, my bodyguard and driver on all Broadway shows, got a phone call from the facility.

Mom had complained of shortness of breath and heart palpitations. She was being taken to the emergency room. I had not yet taken off my Morticia makeup but was just going to have a quick beer before going home. I had to come straight away because she was asking for me. I chugged my beer, and Carmine and I ran out.

When I arrived at the hospital I went in to visit Mom, and an aide from the residence was feeding her bits of a ham sandwich like you would to a baby. She seemed very content being hand-fed. But Mom took one look at me, bolted up, and started to move to get dressed.

"I'm ready to go home now. I am ready to go."

She thought I had come to take her away, like Calgon, and I am sure some place deep in her consciousness, she knew if she had any emergency I would show up. I settled her a bit and told her I needed to talk to the doctor to get some information.

I stepped outside to speak to the doctor on rounds. He explained that she was checking out fine but that he was a bit concerned about her blood pressure and how disoriented and scared she seemed. He said he could not say she *had* to stay overnight, but he did suggest that it wouldn't hurt. It was late and maybe she should sleep.

That was music to my ears. I wanted her watched and accounted for through the night. And I needed to sleep. At one point in this discussion, I glanced through the small window into Mom's room and she saw me and started to sit up again, except this time she began ripping the IV and tubes out of her veins. I burst into the room and there was blood spurting around like spin art. Here I was, with my white Morticia face and bloodstained red lips and dark kohl-lined eyes, trying to control Mom and the whipping-around tubes. It looked like a scene from *Tales from the Crypt*.

"Mom, Mom, Mom, please calm down and relax. You need those IVs to stay in for a bit."

"But I want to go home. With you."

She had not yet ripped her heart-rate monitor off and I could clearly hear the beeps of the machine. It became like a cartoon, because every time she heard something she wanted to hear, the beeps slowed and became steady, but every time I told her something she did not like or want to hear, it sped up.

"Mom, calm down, I am here." . . . Beep . . . Beep . . . Beep.

"You can't come home with me right now." . . . Beepbeepbeepbeepbeepbeepbeep.

"I will come back in the morning, which is only in a few hours, to get you." . . . Beep . . . Beep . . . Beep.

"But, Mom, you have to stay here tonight to rest and have the doctors make sure you are OK." . . . Beepbeepbeepbeepbeepbeepbeep.

"But I'll be back." . . . Beep . . . Beep . . . Beep.

I finally settled her and they gave her something to help her relax. Carmine and I belly-laughed hysterically about the heart-monitor symphony the whole ride home. You could not make this stuff up.

Chapter Eighteen

They Die Feetfirst

The building that housed the facility we'd moved Mom into stood alone and was dedicated solely to those various forms and stages of dementia. It would prove a great fit for Mom. The staff was attentive and loving and there were many activities. There was a salon and outings and crafts and musical events. A rabbi came to offer services and a priest came every Sunday.

Each floor had only eight residents and was well staffed. The higher floors were designated for those patients further along in their decline. Mom began on a lower floor and could often be found sitting at the small reception area fully dressed and perpetually ready to leave, lipstick and all. As the first year progressed she stayed on a lower floor, but as she entered her second year the director suggested that Mom be moved to a higher floor. She was beginning to show signs of incontinence and was taking her Depends off and hiding them behind her armoire in her room. She then would have accidents and . . . evidently it was not pretty. I did not want to hear the details, but to them it was just another day at the office. The first time the situation was described to me, I got instantly sick. I had just gotten past the diaper stage with my daughters a few years prior. This was an utterly different thing. My God. I was not prepared to deal with adult diapers.

In the summer of 2012, Mom was moved to a higher floor and I visited as often as I could. I remember a woman I had seen often at the facility around that time, whose husband had also been suffering from dementia, asking to come in to say a word. I always thought this lady was incredibly put together. She was beautiful and effortlessly chic. I would be in my sweatpants and sweater, feeling like I was somehow being disrespectful by not dressing up more. I would see her thin frame in a woolen herringbone suit with an A-line skirt, telling her husband she loved him over and over in a cheery tone or feeding him pastina. It made me well up with tears. She came in and said she wanted to thank my mom. She wanted me to know that my mom had made the place "real" for her.

She explained that in her early months at the residence she would see my mom dressed up and with her lipstick on downstairs sitting with the receptionist for hours at a time. Mom wanted the company and to be the welcoming committee. This woman said that Mom had always been so nice and thoughtful to her, complimenting her on her outfit or jewelry whenever she'd arrive to visit her husband.

The truth was I'd been watching the woman for months. I'd see her dancing with him during holiday get-togethers when there was live music. I'd think about them dancing at their wedding, and then consider how tragic it must be to have your husband not recognize you. I guess I was projecting to avoid the sadness that engulfed me the day my mom could not recall my name. In the summer of 2012, I asked her what my name was and she just stared and appeared to be searching for some clue. She lit up every time she saw me and could point to my pictures in magazines but could not access my name. I was familiar to her but she could never retrieve my name again. I even joked to her once that I was an "icon," and surely she was able to recall the eighties? Nothing.

Even though I retained my humor, it all kept chipping away at my soul.

I began spending even more time with Mom and would sometimes just go sit with her and read a book. But one night, when I was away, I got an alarming call. She must have fallen in the bathroom, and was complaining about pain and acting agitated. The facility decided to send her to the ER. I was called and went to go see what was happening. There were so many doctors coming and going and asking me questions that I couldn't answer. I was supposed to be the closest person in her life, but I could hardly answer one question regarding her wishes or her medical history. In the end, they discovered that she'd broken her arm, but things quickly got worse.

I called Lila in Arizona and told her Mom was in the hospital and also hadn't been eating. She had gotten a feeding tube and evidently had gotten pneumonia because she was not swallowing and her lungs had had some fluid in them. The main doctor handed me a form and asked what my mother's wishes were regarding DNR. I had actually never heard of a DNR (which means a "do not resuscitate" order, but to me at that moment I could only think "do not run").

I stood out in the hospital corridor on an iPhone whose reception went in and out because of all the machines and signals, and I told Lila my mother might need surgery and asked her if my mother had ever given her any inkling as to her wishes should she die on the table during an operation. Her reply was the last thing I expected.

"All I can think about is that little boy."

"Excuse me?"

"All I can think of is that little boy."

"What does any of this have to do with what I just asked you? Does she want to be resuscitated or not?"

"Oh, your mother never planned on dying."

Holy fuck! I thought. I was going insane. The doctors were all waiting inside the tiny room for me to check a box and they gave me the impression that time was of the essence, and I was just now actually learning a hugely powerful piece of information. I settled my reeling mind and regained my composure.

"Are you intimating that there is a grave some place and I need to start to find it so Mom can be buried next to a brother I never met? And does that mean she wants DNR or not?"

"Well, I remember a medallion that the priest gave your mother and me. I had it for years but it fell down the drain and when I found it, it was all black. He gave them to us after doing a small Mass for the baby. I think he was buried but can't remember where."

"You know what, I'll call you back! Thank you, and I'll keep you posted as soon as I get more info."

I checked the box for "Do Not Resuscitate." I reasoned that if she went, she would not be able to withstand the defibrillator paddles anyway. She was Catholic so I assumed she would let God make up his own mind. And even if Mom had wanted to be kept alive at all costs forever, I didn't want that. I was sure I couldn't handle it.

I signed the sheet, and as I was bent over the clipboard atop the tray table, my mom's favorite necklace, which I'd recently begun wearing, swung out over the page. It was a big gold medal of the Virgin Mary that some guy had given her along with a little aluminum disk, exactly like the one that Lila had just described to me. I had seen this medal my entire life and never knew why she wore it. I went home in slight shock at the day's events.

I was informed that the doctor had chosen not to operate on her arm for fear that the surgery might be too stressful. Mom was actually recovering and would probably be able to leave the hospital in a day or two, once the pneumonia cleared. DNR was no longer on the table, but the medal still was.

It was time to deal with the other matter. I got a glass of wine and called Lila back.

Now, finally, I heard the true story about Baby John, a secret Mom had kept almost her whole life. Mom had gotten pregnant with a man named Philip Brady. She gave birth to a boy and named him John after her dad and brother.

She had met the father at the Peppermint Lounge in Manhattan. He was married. He knew she was pregnant. Mom promised not to get him in trouble for having an affair. She must have said she wouldn't say a thing to anybody or ask for money, but wanted to have the baby. This was obviously Mom's modus operandi, a modern and sadly sweet one at that.

As far as I can tell, Mom had also been with Murray (the same boyfriend she'd surprised by removing her fur coat), who was eighteen years her senior. Somehow they were dating when Mom went into labor and he was at the hospital for the delivery. He was convinced the kid was his, and his name was put on the birth certificate. She had the baby, but Lila told me that he died in the hospital within twenty-four hours. The baby maintains Murray's last name and supposedly is buried somewhere in New York. At the burial, a priest evidently performed a service and then returned to give that saint's charm to both my mom and Lila, her best friend and my future godmother. I assume Lila had been meant to be named godmother to Baby John as well.

It all made more sense now. Her terror when she had me so early. The fear, the squeaky door, the poop, the worry about the crib turned to the wall indicating a kid would be adopted. The strap attached around the chest. She panicked because she'd had a loss before. She was gripping on to a life—hers, mine, and Baby John's.

The memory must have been too devastating for her to drudge up, and my own miscarriage must have derailed her and thrust her back to that horrible memory of her own loss. No wonder she couldn't help me.

I remember sitting on the floor with my friend Stephanie years earlier, after my failed attempts at conception and my eventual miscarriage, thinking, *Why am I not allowed to be normal and have a baby like anybody else? I don't work properly. I am a failure.* Mom always wanted me to be special, and I worried that this failure to become a mother was a by-product of being so "unique." Of course I wasn't normal. I was Brooke Shields. I wasn't perfect, though, obviously, was I?

No matter what it all meant, I had finally learned the whole story, or as much as was available.

Once Mom was back at the residence, it seemed that she was exhausted and began spending most of her time in her own room instead of in the floor's common area with the TV. She had totally stopped her reception-area visits. Her sister-in-law and nephew and nieces came to visit, as did Lisa, Bob, Lila, Stephanie, and Lyda and a couple other close friends of mine who knew my mom in her later years. Her full-blood sister never bothered. It was tough on Diana and she explained she did not want to see Mom the way she was. She was satisfied remembering the laughter and the fun all of us had had together.

I was with Mom the whole time at the end. It was so hard to watch her all bent and rigid as if rigor mortis had already begun to take hold. Except for the liquids that gave her pneumonia in the hospital, Mom had not eaten in almost a month. We called in hospice to start to visit once or twice a week. When I told them how long she had gone without food, they said they had never seen anything like it before. Of course not. This was Teri Terrific. She defied the odds. This was about a few weeks until the end.

Her face was becoming pale and twisted and she'd bite anything that got near her mouth, including Lisa's neck once as she was trying to tuck in a sheet. Either her lips were tightly pursed or her mouth gaped open. Her skin was remarkably smooth, soft, and unwrinkled.

The only sounds she emitted were dry mumbles, where her chin would flap like a ventriloquist dummy and her lips would dryly flutter. Cries of resistance could be heard every time someone tried to move her at all. Her fractured arm must have been excruciatingly painful. Her hospice aides flipped her over like a dead body in order to wash her and change her diaper and powder her. The bizarrely green-brown contents of her body were just the same color as an infant's.

Her fists were clenched, and whenever I tried to open her fingers to clean her palms, she would try to bite my hands and scream through clenched teeth. She once bit the lose skin that covered my knuckle. She clenched down and simply would not let go and just bit and bit. As at the elbow, there are no nerve endings, so I just let her bite as much as she wanted. She wasn't strong enough to break the skin. She was never able to relax, not once during that time. To get disengaged from her clenches, I pried her jaw open like I do with my dogs when they pick up something from the ground and won't give it back to me. Biting never seemed to give her any relief, either. I guess she simply did not want to go. The feeling of fear radiated from her and all throughout the room.

At times Mom had fits of emotion, widening her eyes and looking terrified. At others, she would gaze up with a deeply worried expression and stare at a spot on the ceiling, scared and with seeming anticipation toward something. Lila told me she was looking at the angels, but she looked too frightened to me. She looked like she was seeing the Grim Reaper. I thought anything divine was supposed to elicit beautiful and relaxed emotions. Mom's eyes pooled with fear and panic.

The end finally arrived in late October 2012. As the fates would dictate, it happened that this period of time was devastating not just for me but for the entire East Coast as well. Hurricane Sandy had ravaged New York City as well as the entire coastline.

It was the deadliest and most destructive of the year and the second costliest in US history. Unofficially known as Superstorm Sandy, it hit New York and New Jersey on October 29 and created havoc. In the city alone we were experiencing a widespread power outage and a halt to life as we knew it. I was getting the feeling that Mom was getting close to dying because she was so unresponsive.

I did not have the awareness or the perspective to see the personal symbolism in all of it. New York City had no electricity, no water, no public transportation, and the National Guard was patrolling the streets. And those of us in Manhattan were considered the lucky ones. Other parts of the city looked like war-torn areas in need of real relief.

There was no gas to be bought, so when our car made its last trip uptown for me to get to Mom I had no way of getting back. So I stayed there. There was a declaration of a statewide state of emergency and Governor Cuomo had requested a pre-disaster declaration on October 26. I joked to my mom that if only I had gone to her years ago and requested a pre-disaster declaration, maybe things would have turned out differently.

I came to refer to all of it as Hurricane Teri. Close friends would nod in agreement when I said it was all by design. My mom would never allow herself to be overshadowed by anything, especially not a hurricane with a name like Sandy. It was as if Mom were spiritually declaring, "Fuck you, Sandy! I'm Teri and ya ain't seen nothin' yet!"

I'd joke that she had orchestrated the whole thing so I would have to stay by her side. I was by no means minimizing the pain and loss and devastation that Sandy created and that countless were still enduring—I was trying to stay present and intact, and humor was once again my only resource.

On October 30, the night before she died, I was sitting in a chair next to her bed and three women from the staff, who had ended their workday, popped their heads in and asked if they could say good-bye. I was surprised. I'd been coming there for weeks—how did they know now was the time to say good-bye?

They handed me a three-quarters-full bottle of Poland Spring water. Since we were smack in the middle of Sandy's wrath and were rationing everything, I made no mention of the cracked seal on the cap. (It didn't cross my mind that this residence had generators and hoards of supplies should disaster strike. Everything was available that people needed.)

I took the plastic bottle and held it in my hand and thanked them. The more maternal one of the three kept saying, "We are worried about you. You have not eaten or had anything to drink in a while and we are worried you are not staying hydrated."

I said I was fine. A friend of mine had brought me soup earlier, and to be honest, I was (shh . . .) planning on having a snuck-in Duvel in a bit. They stood for a while and then suddenly, strangely, all plopped down on the floor in Mom's tiny room. Well, I figured they were planning on staying for a while so I joined them. Mom was propped up as usual on multiple pillows and showed no signs of awareness that anybody was in the room.

The same staff member reiterated that they were concerned that I was not staying hydrated. I needed to drink! *OK*, I thought. *Wow, stop bugging me. . . . I will show you that I will drink.*

I took a huge swig of what I thought would be water from my little plastic bottle, only to discover that my throat was on fire with pure, marshmallow-flavored vodka! Not wanting to seem unappreciative or square at all, I sputtered, "Wow . . . thanks. . . . I needed that!"

Smiling and nodding, one of the ladies proudly announced it was very new and was called Fluffed vodka. Wasn't it delicious? Huh? I felt like gagging. I hate any flavored anything. I drink my vodka straight and with a twist. No chocolate, cake, eggnog, or cotton-candy-flavored vodka for me, ever. But, I guess, it was time to make an exception. Down the hatch with another smaller gulp.

Then one by one each of these beautiful, hardworking, warm relative strangers began pouring shots from their own vodka in plastic bottles, into tiny pill cups, like I'd seen in the movie *One Flew Over the Cuckoo's Nest*, and raising them to my mom. The toasts began. We raised our mini "glasses" as each person told her version of how my mom had affected her life.

One woman still in her hairnet began by saying, "I call her 'My T.'" Another said she liked to call her "Teri Town." Others preferred "Mamma T" or "T" or simply "T-town."

Mom lay catatonic in her bed, mouth open, seemingly oblivious to what was happening. The bottom half of her body looked like it had melded into the mattress. Only her head and shoulders, propped up on the pillows, seemed to be in the room.

One story involved Mom going up to a woman and saying what a beautiful smile she had—the first time she had ever received such a compliment in her life. Another told a story about a daytime attendant who always asked incredibly obvious questions. Mom's new friend was wheeling in the lunch tray, like she did every day at the same time, and this person asked if it was lunchtime. The attendant rolled her eyes, and Mom, seeing the exchange, made a face accompanied by a rude gesture, signifying that she, too, thought the question was dumb. Mom made people feel noticed.

Another toast included how Mom knew when one of the ladies was having a bad day and was trying not to show it to the residents. Mom went over to her and said that no matter what was going on in her life, it would all end up OK in the long run.

She touched these women in varying ways and they kept repeating how much the staff as a whole had adored her. One of the women said that she always knew that Mom "had a little Dominican in her." As did I, evidently, from the way I "gulped down that vodka!" This comment incited a mini-debate over whether Mom was more Dominican, Puerto Rican, or Cuban and what the merits of all were.

This woman had once been asked by her supervisor to get a bottle of wine that was hidden under my mom's bed. She was to tell Mom that she could have the bottle but just not keep it under her bed. The bottle would be safe in the main office downstairs and Mom could have it whenever she wished (I had no idea Mom was getting access to wine from the inside, but it didn't surprise me). She entered her room and asked Mom for the bottle, and Mom complied readily by proceeding to pull out from under her bed an entire *case* of red wine as if it was the most normal thing in the world. Why have just one bottle at hand when you can get a whole case? Makes sense. Take out the middleman.

I shared a story about how Mom once used a turkey baster to infuse the breakfast melons with vodka while we were on a river-rafting trip down the Salmon River. The ladies loved that one.

These stories continued until the staff had felt like they had gotten a chance to tell me what Mom had meant to them and how funny and sensitive she had been. I was not at all surprised by any of this, because it had always been my mother's way. She always immediately connected with the staff at places to make sure that they never felt like she was better than they were. She always said that the working people were her people. Mom had a talent of making strangers feel special. She put me on a pedestal while placing herself, pinned, under it.

To end the good-bye, the first staff member held up a plastic pill cup filled with Fluff vodka and motioned to me that she wanted to put a bit on Mom's lips as a toast.

I said, "Sure, it's not like it's gonna kill her. Go on, give it to her." Now, Mom's mouth had been open for days by this point. The cup was pressed to her lips, and in the same reaction that caused Mom to bite my finger and Lisa's neck, Mom's teeth clamped onto that cup like the Jaws of Life. Even though she basically did that to anything that got near her mouth, it was pretty funny. I didn't ruin the "funny" part with an explanation. The women all squealed with laughter and a declaration of Mom's love of booze. All at once there was a ceremonious raising of the last cup to God, and Mom, and life, and those we love. It was one of the most surreal moments I have ever experienced. It was tragic and sweet and real and odd and funny and profoundly heartbreaking.

Finally, it was time for them to leave. I thanked them for what was now my empty bottle and I was then alone again with my near-death mother.

The Fluff vodka had made me tired, thankfully. I had no way to get home because of the continued mass-transit strike and lack of gas. I had no place to be. My kids were fine, bunking with evacuated friends at my home, where we had a wood-burning fireplace and candles. The city was shut down entirely and I had had Fluff vodka for dinner. I decided I would get into the bed with Mom and get some rest.

I slept in the bed with Mom the whole night, not waking up once.

I raised the side rails so I would not tumble off during the wee hours and set off some alarms or sensors. I slept hard. I have no memory of my dreams.

That next day the daytime hospice nurse arrived at 9:00 A.M. and changed Mom's diaper and bedding and washed her hair. Mom loved animal prints. In her tiny freestanding blond-wood closet she had two leopard-print blouses. One was made of slightly stiff cotton with neon accents. The other was silk with a smaller print and no accompanying obnoxious color. I started to give the aide the silk one and then selfishly and morbidly changed my mind. I wanted the silk one for myself, and with dark humor joked to myself that it would be a shame to burn the more expensive silk one. I knew that if it had been anybody else in that bed and Mom and I had been making the same decision, we would have made the same joke.

Mom was now dressed from the waist up with her hair combed. I tried to pry her fingers open to put in some talc. Her fingers were so clenched, and as had become the ritual, she screamed through a once again clenched jaw and tried to pull herself up to bite me with the front of her teeth. I gave up and just calmly said, "OK, Mama, it's OK, no powder."

The attendant tucked in the sheets and was changing Mom's socks. I rolled my eyes and shook my head when I saw that both pairs of socks were actually the gray unisex kind with no elastic that the airlines sometimes give away. The no-elastic part was fine, but it still struck me as funny, typical, and gut-stabbingly tragic that they were the same socks the airlines provided. They are usually offered only in business class, though, so maybe Mom thought them special and herself fancy. Mom just loved anything free, including the menus on airplanes or the tiny dishes for butter. Back in the day, Mom would take everything from everywhere. She wiped clean anything travel-size she could get her hands on at hotels and on planes and from cleaning carts. She even pilfered the linens from Japan Airlines' table setting from first class.

The worst was one year on Halloween when she decided that instead of candy, she would make little care bags of mini toiletries to hand out. I begged her not to and suggested we instead donate the stash to a women's shelter. Disaster and humiliation diverted as mini Butterfingers and Hershey's Kisses replaced the shampoos and conditioners.

Well, this day was Halloween and the recollection gave me pause. This pause would turn out to include the last smile I would feel on my face while she was alive.

I was shocked out of the moment by the insensitive aide, who grabbed Mom's airline-sock-covered feet and announced, "Oh, so cold. Yup, in my country we say they die feetfirst. Yup, that's what they say. . . . Feetfirst!"

I did not know or care to which country this woman was referring. I did, however, wish she was currently in it. I could not believe the lack of compassion she was exhibiting. However, I did go feel my mom's feet, and they were indeed colder than the rest of her and colder than usual. But it was almost November so I overlooked the callous comment. I could never really bring myself to say she was dying.

I put the blanket over Mom's gray socks and pulled my chair around to the side of the bed. I sat in it facing her. I put a classical music station on my iPhone and held it up to her left ear. I saw no flicker of acknowledgment of the music but tried to believe the people who told me that the hearing was the last thing to go.

I sat trying to read a book and kept glancing up at her eyes to see if there was any movement under the lids. I periodically held the back of my hand to her open mouth to feel air, just like the mirror Mom held to my mouth to check for steam. I'd also stare at the sheet over her chest to make sure it was still rising and falling with her breath. All of a sudden my iPhone chirped and it was Lisa calling. The phone call interrupted the music. There was still almost no movement from Mom. But every so often a slight, almost imperceptibly faint rise in the white cotton sheet would occur. I breathed then, too. Mom's body seemed so heavy and flat, as if it had melted into the bed like Silly Putty in the sun.

I picked up the phone and with the other hand touched Mom's left arm. I had long since stopped trying to hold her hand because she would clench her fist tighter if I even tried to shove my fingers in between hers. I was giving Lisa the update when Mom suddenly and violently clamped closed her mouth with a smacking sound, teeth crashing, and then equally as quickly and forcefully sucked in a wide-mouthed breath. She then brought her lips back together. I blurted out to Lisa that something was happening and I had to hang up. I dropped the phone and stared at Mom's chest. It was still slightly rising up and down like the pulse of the light on an at-sleep computer.

I worriedly shot a glance over at the aide, who was sitting in the comfy chair at the window, oblivious and fully engaged in her Sudoku puzzle. As much as I hated this woman and her cold-footed country, I still thought it better to have her around in case I was missing some kind of sign. This was a ridiculous idea, because she was not paying attention and, in the end, I had resented her being in the room.

Then it happened again. Another gasp of breath followed by a tight clap together of her lips. My adrenaline started pumping and I began to panic. I counted beats in between these gasps: one, two, three, four, gasp, shut . . . one, two, three, four, gasp, shut.

I just stared and was startled off my seat with each lurch of her breathing and accompanying gaped mouth. The time in between them varied as did the seconds in the open position. There would be nothing and I'd think maybe she died and then, bam, another gasp. There was no rattle like I had anticipated. Finally I said, "Ah, Mom? What are you doin' to me!?"

I was on the edge of my chair in a surreal and seemingly suspended state, focused and watching and waiting, but unclear as to what for! I was holding my breath in sync with hers, and it was like she died a hundred times! I took another quick peek to see if the aide was watching, which she was not, and returned to Mom. When her mouth was clamped shut I kept uttering "Ahhh?" in an attempt to ask the oblivious aide if *this* was *it*? But then Mom would pop her mouth open again and grab a mouth of air.

Mom continued to do this for what felt like an hour but what was, in actuality, only about thirty seconds. I stared, waiting for each gasp. And then, as suddenly and as without warning as it had all began, it just stopped. I waited for it to occur again. Nothing. It was the opposite of what I thought would happen. I always thought it would be an exhale—a slightly pushed-out pop of air coming from the back of someone's throat—that signaled the end. That was what the movies showed, often. Instead, my mother's mouth simply stopped opening. Nothing else happened.

It all just stopped happening. *She* stopped happening.

I exclaimed, "Ah, is that it? Is this It? Did it just happen? Ah, excuse me, whatever your name is, is she . . . ah . . . done?" I checked my phone for the time. It was 11:37. I couldn't help but release a quiet crying chuckle and say, "Oh, Mom, of course it's a thirty-seven."

Thirty-seven had always been my mom's favorite number. I never remembered why and always forgot to ask her, but I did remember that we always bet on horses or picked numbers that had a thirty-seven in them. I had been desperate for signs of any kind during the entire dying ordeal and instantly prayed that this thirty-seven was one of them. Of what, though, I could not tell you.

The aide got up in slow fucking motion and came over to feel for a pulse. Now it was my mouth that was open. She just nodded at me and muttered that she had called it. . . . "Yup, they always go feetfirst." Oh, I wanted to punch her and stick a plane ticket in her mouth. This woman then suddenly acted sweet. She gently placed my mom's hands back on her stomach, slightly overlapping each other like you see on dead people in open coffins. She then whispered some quick words that felt like a "Go with God or peace" or some sort of a sentiment, but I did not comprehend any of it. I could no longer decipher sounds. I felt like I was in a sound booth with the volume for the outer room turned off. Only the sound of my own heart pounding in my head kept me from passing out.

Oh my God. . . . Wait, no, wait a minute, can we go back?! Just for a minute. I have to grab something. I just need to get it.

I had this overriding urge to believe that I just needed to go re-trieve something and therefore Mom could not die just yet because I needed to get my stuff. She had to wait to leave. She had to say some-thing to me. Please, God, bring her back just so we can say good-bye with words and sounds and with closure. She needed to tell me some-thing, anything and that she knew that I had always loved her deeply and that I was sorry if she ever felt hurt.

Wait—if I stare long enough at her, she will wake up for sure.

I took a deep inhale to calm down, cleared my eyes, and stood up over Mom to look at her face. I hoped she could somehow pop up and comfort me. I still wanted my mommy to tell me she loved me and it would be OK.

It was not that her face looked "peaceful," but it was true that she was no longer grimacing. What struck me, however, was that she no longer looked like my mother. She was not in there. Her skin was still so beautiful and almost iridescent. It was like silk velvet and her fore-head was still warm. I desperately wanted to kiss it before she got cold so I could still feel the warmth of the living. I kissed her and told her I loved her and then added that she could come back . . . *now.*

But I was talking to a stranger and an it. I wanted to shake this being and tell it to give me back my mother. Then I realized I was not talking to a dead person but was addressing something else entirely. Something that looked nothing like Teri, or even human really. The woman I had shared life with was no longer in there. This thing lying in the bed was an inanimate object—an emptied package. I had heard all sorts of versions of the body being only a vessel, but they had never really struck me until this moment.

Maybe it is the soul or the spirit—or a myriad of different labels— but all I can say is my mom was no longer in the room. Her essence seemed to have instantly disappeared. I said out loud but to myself, "She's not in there anymore. Who is this body?" The room got very foggy and it felt alien.

I felt the panic starting to mount yet again and my eyes darted all around trying to find something I could recognize. Where had my mom gone? Where was I? Flashbacks of when I was a little kid and did not know my mother's whereabouts coursed through my body. On a floral chintz-covered armchair (oh, how my mom loved her floral and especially her chintz fabrics) sat a huge stuffed doll I had made when I was nine. It had a completely disproportionate body made out of heavy white linen. The chest and lower half formed a square and the arms and legs were tiny and stuck out like a brontosaurus. She had glued rows of thick yellow yarn on top of and around her head. I had given her a blue-jean-overall skirt. That was the best I could do and had to rely on my mom to sew in the blue eyes, small nose, and little lips that looked like a perfect bow. It had been one of the first things I had ever really sewn and Mom made me feel like it had been worthy of awards. I recognized this doll as the only real thing left in the room.

My mom was no longer occupying the space, and I did not know where she had gone. All I knew was that I had to *leave*. I had to get out of that room.

I grabbed the doll, a tiny stamp-size photo of me as a baby in a sterling-silver heart frame that was by the bed, and my purse and opened the emergency door. The buzzer always buzzed while the door was open and I had gotten used to it. Today, however, it seemed suddenly extra loud and long. I ran into one of the downstairs offices, half-thinking she'd be right behind me and I was busting her free from a cell. I brought with me a charger I had borrowed. If only I had thought to bring the charger down a little earlier, Mom would have waited longer to die. I was sure of it. That was the thing I needed to do to keep Mom alive. I tried to explain to the staff that I just had to return their charger. I just had to. I was never coming back there again to do it. "Here is your charger. Thank you." I knew when I turned to leave that I would not be back. I ran out to Eightieth Street and turned west toward First Avenue.

I got to the corner and stopped, not sure what to do next. I needed to get back to some place. I remember feeling like this on 9/11. I ran out of my apartment on Fiftieth Street and just started speed-walking up First Avenue. That day, like today, I had no idea where I was headed. Some taxis had begun to run again but I was suddenly afraid to get into one. Chris was in LA and not picking up his phone. I left him a message about my mom and just began pacing in a small radius on the southeast corner of Eightieth Street and First Avenue.

As I was looking up and down the avenue, a beautiful foreign girl was crossing the street in front of me. She may have been from Brazil or Spain—I couldn't tell—but she was very pretty, except for the cigarette that was hanging from her red-lipped mouth. As she passed, she recognized me and started excitedly to try to talk to me about "*Laguna Blu*." I began to feel like I'd black out right there. I think I said thank you and that she had pretty hair and then I tried to look away.

She was staring at me with a kind, questioning look. She asked if I was OK. I blurted out to her that I was not OK and that my mom had just died. Could I have one of her cigarettes? I do not smoke. I have never been a smoker. The times I have been drinking and have tried to join in, I felt incredibly and uselessly sick. But in this moment I wanted to feel that sick sensation even just to know that I was in fact still alive. I wanted to fill my body with disgusting smoke and nicotine and get that head rush and feel the sweating that precedes vomiting. She gave me one and went on her way after trying to say something sweet in broken English. I took two drags on the cancer stick and threw it out. I was alone on the street again and had no idea where to turn.

I did not look for a cab but instead went inside a kosher meat market on that block. Standing by the refrigerated items, I called my friend Stephanie and asked if she'd come meet me here because I needed to go home and cook steaks. I was crying and saying how horrible it was to see what I had just seen and that I was afraid to be alone.

She said she'd meet me ASAP and told me to hold it together. An old couple was buying some meat nearby and had obviously heard me on the phone. I had not tried to be discreet. In fact, I believe I had purposely talked loud enough to not be alone. I knew they, too, had recognized me, and I secretly hoped that if they knew I was sad, they would say something wise to offer me comfort. It is amazing to me the comfort of strangers in moments of dire straits.

I was beginning to have the feeling I used to get as a teenager when I felt like I was disappearing. It usually happened in large crowds and I believed that if I screamed, nobody would hear me. I caught their eyes and tried to smile. Maybe they would understand my fear and pain. The old man nodded and said, "We know who you are." The woman then chimed in with some type of "circle of life" comment and I instantly hated them. I was so jealous of their old age and their seeming happiness and of the fact that they had one another. How could they know what my mom felt or how I was doing? How dare they try to help me? Who did they think they were? Fuck them!

I nodded, bought my meat, and went to wait on the street. I started to beat myself up for talking loudly on the phone and for looking to strangers for recognition of my pain. It was an affliction of mine of which I thought I had been cured and felt angry to have seen it rear its ugly head once again. Thankfully, Steph got to me and we drove downtown together. By the time we arrived at the house, Lisa was already there. She knew something was going to happen and cleared her day. I must have called her to tell her but did not remember much from the previous hour. Chris got me on my cell and I told him I couldn't talk because the girls were with me and if I stayed on the phone all I would be able to do was cry, hearing his voice. My mom loved Lisa and Stephanie like her own daughters and they knew her better than any of my friends. It made perfect sense to have us all together.

Another friend from our school arrived as well. I must have called her, too. I don't remember calling anybody but Stephanie. All I remember from the rest of the day and night was a big fire in the living room, steaks on the grill, and lots of wine. We managed some morbid humor so as to keep me from careening off a cliff.

Overall, I was numb. I was not tired but I knew I could not handle being awake much longer. Being awake was simply too dangerous. I was offered a sleeping pill but was terrified that I would have some kind of hallucination and not make it through the night. Some more wine seemed to do the trick, and I promised my friends it was safe for them to leave. My girls came home from a friend's house and let me sleep. Chris must have told the girls about their Toots. In the morning I opened my door to find a note from Grier that read, "Dear Mom I am sorry about your mom but she will be OK. It's OK to be sad. . . . I love you. . . ." She had erased something under the "I love you." "You will see her soon. . . ." I cried at how sweet the note was and then burst into hysterics at the part she erased.

It was October 31. The day that Hurricane Sandy dissipated, Mom dissipated, too.

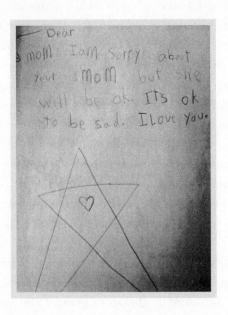

Chapter Nineteen

Cremation/Look, Ma, No Pants!

The funeral home came and took Mom's body. I had gone there a few weeks prior to make all the arrangements. The funeral director had told me to also contact the church ahead of time, which I did. Afterward I even stopped at Finnegans Wake for a cold beer after speaking to the priest. It was a mini-tribute. One of Mom's old haunts when we lived on Seventy-Third Street. It was easiest to find her there because it was often the first stop and was just at the end of our block. I didn't even have to cross the street.

My assistant Mike had flown in from LA to help me prepare for the memorial. In the two days that he had been in New York City I suddenly decided to have him go through all my closets with me. We did a massive frenzy of a purge. I needed to stay busy because I was afraid to feel. I could not stop myself from whipping around my house and cleaning it all out. I combined my stuff with my mother's from the residence and we lugged four grossly heavy black garbage bags into our car. Mike had finally found gas, from a Hasidic Jewish man who had a minipump under a bridge in Brooklyn. It was surreal but

Mike followed up on a tip from a buddy and we had wheels to get to the Upper East Side funeral home. Mom had a favorite thrift store that had been around for decades. It was the same one in which she bought her Puccis and my infamous gauchos.

Parking was hard and we could only find a spot five blocks away. Sweating and running, we lugged the bags across middles of streets and finally reached the store. I deposited the mother lode, and the little ladies behind the counter were thrilled. They recognized me but, when they heard my mother had died, did not ask for a picture. I explained it was my mother's stuff as well as mine and she had died two days prior. I needed to keep saying it to believe it was actually real. I joked to Mike that I should have said "the mother loaded," because Mom would have thought it funny and a bit outrageous. We rushed home because we still had no power and the house was empty and without an alarm.

The funeral director called and explained to me that they were going to use a different facility for cremation because their regular one had lost power due to the storm. I told him Mom would prefer the one without the power! I think he got the joke but was afraid to laugh. Funeral homes make me laugh nervously. Otherwise it is all just too horrible.

They had taken Mom's body to be embalmed so I could view her and say good-bye. Two days later I was called and told she was ready for me to see. I was first shown the vessels to choose from for after cremation but was unhappy with the choices so I said I would buy my own.

I was then sent up to the ice-cold viewing room. It was huge and empty except for Mom's basic wooden coffin at the far end. They said they have to keep the room cold because if not the bodies thaw. A detail I did not need to know. He closed the door and I stood for a moment before moving. I then walked across the huge empty room and it felt like an hour-long trip. There she was in her shitty stiff cotton leopard-and-neon-printed shirt and nothing on the bottom. I looked.

Under the cover was just a plastic tarp and I did not see her big grandma panties, either. I did not inspect too closely for obvious reasons but I had to know about the stuff they don't show you. It did strike me as morbidly funny and knew that Mom would get a chuckle out of it all as well.

"Look, Ma, no pants!" I said. "Oh, Mom . . . here we go. Haven't you taken this far enough? You are not getting up, are you? I love you, you know that, right? God damn it, Mom. Really? We could have had more laughs. My babies are really funny, too. I am sorry."

And with that, I put the weird square-bodied doll in the box with her and placed my picture in the little heart frame, which by the way was one of the party favors from my sweet-sixteen birthday. Mom had over two hundred made with a picture of me as a baby inside. We would always find the extras hidden in surprising places. I tried to put the small frame in her now freezing hands but once again could not open her fingers because this time she was actually dead and stiff. I attempted to wedge it under the clasped part but it felt too Sopranos-like. I settled on placing it on her sunken chest and pictured it rolling off during her transfer to the crematorium facility in Long Island City.

I had to kiss her forehead, which was indeed freezing and such a contrast to the moments right after her death. I am glad I did it, but wish I had not. My lips will forever remember the cold, smooth skin. She still didn't jump up or tell me it was all OK. And it wasn't OK. None of it had been but here we were. This was indeed it. The moment I had been afraid of my whole life.

"I love you, Mama. Bye."

I walked out, looking back once more and wanting to rush in and shake her. I was so truly alone. And she was so not ready to go.

I was quiet in the car as we drove away.

Three days later I got another call from the funeral director. He was hemming and hawing and I could tell something was wrong.

"Yeah . . . hi. . . . Well, you know how I said that we were using a different facility to do your mother's cremation?"

"Yes?"

"Well . . . yeah. . . . OK, well . . . we um, we started the process. . . ."

"Yeah?"

"And then, um, well, that facility lost power as well. So we had to then have your mom sent to a different one."

"OK . . . So was she . . . ah, lumpy . . . or just done from the waist down, or . . . You know what, *don't* tell me. I don't need to know. . . . I am good. . . . Thank you."

I went shopping at antique stores for a sterling-silver container of some kind. I even toyed with the idea of its being a martini shaker as an inside joke. I could not find one big enough. Neither did my mother, obviously!

Anyway, I ended up buying a sterling-silver round jar with a lid that probably had been used for biscuits or cookies. It must have been some kind of retirement gift because it had engraving in a foreign language and a date around the lip of the lid and was very heavy. My plan was to put her on my bar and nestle her among the array of glass bottles and sterling knickknacks and stirrers. I figured this way she could remain forever close to the two most important things in her life: me and booze.

I know the joke would not be lost on her and that she would actually appreciate it. It is not against Catholicism to cremate, but a burial and a headstone is more often the norm. But "dust to dust" sounds more like cremation than decomposition if you ask me. There is not even a skeleton left after the oven. Catholics love funerals and a place to visit their dead, so I will eventually find her a spot in a mausoleum in the city if I can. But cremating her was what I wanted, and I did what I wanted to do. I did not like the idea of her in a box under the ground because it did not feel finished to me. She was never a woman to be contained. She was the kind who would rather go down in a blaze of glory than be in a box. It seemed fitting. I wanted her with me as well as near or in her favorite places.

This would end up being easier to do than expected because she, of course, did not entirely fit in the cookie jar. When the funeral director handed me the jar, he also handed me a canvas bag with the name of the funeral home printed on the side. It was shockingly heavy. I felt like I had just visited a gift shop in a theme park that had happened to be death themed. The director sheepishly said that she didn't fit in the jar, "So the rest of her is in this plastic sealed bag and blond wooden box. Sorry about that." At this point that was the least of my worries. I was just glad they finished all of her.

The wooden box sits next to our beloved dog Darla in a cabinet. I have yet to decide what to do with either of them. The sterling biscuit container indeed sits on my antique marble bar table amid the beautiful bottles and antique decanters and items we collected from all over the world. I can't wait to feel her watching me.

While Mom was dying I tried to keep giving myself the benefit of every doubt. I was there and loving. Toward the end, I consciously made myself breathe and stay present in every moment. If I drifted in attempt to escape the situation, I would snap back and touch her arm and tell her I loved her. I said what I thought I wanted to say. I said what I thought she would want to hear. I said words but it never felt cathartic or sufficient. And I will never know if she heard me or not.

I would have to remind myself that every time I visited her I did hug her and tell her I loved her. It had to have an impact. But it never seemed enough for either one of us.

It never felt satisfying and I never exhaled. I didn't think I started early enough, while she was able to respond. I kept beating myself up for not doing something differently. I kept having that gnawing feeling that I waited too long to start really spending time with her. But then I remember how impossibly hard it had been to be around her. I had created a distance so as to form my own life. I had to leave so I could return.

And yet I look back, and I realize I really tried. I did my honest best. I never fully abandoned her all those years. While in the facility I always went back in for another hug or to say I love you again. She would sometimes smile and mumble it back or she'd start to cry as I was walking away. Had my lifetime of devotion registered with her at all? It really was not supposed to end this way. Or maybe it simply was?

In the end I wanted her to forgive me for the "divorce" and for stripping the entire office and for putting her in a facility. I admit I do carry some residual guilt. But I did get a bit of a reprieve when Lisa told me that Mom said to her, "I can't believe Brookie did that to me with the office," then with a pursed-lip smirk added, "That took *balls*." Lisa said it was as if she was proud and had taught me well.

I got nothing like that from her during her dying days. Before she left this earth I never had that moment with her alone where she gave me peace of mind and heart. I never did with Dad, either. But the problem is they are the ones doing the dying. They can't make it about us, the living. But if she had been peaceful I might have been able to exhale. I don't know if my mother had ever been at peace.

Now that she's gone, I'm not sure what I miss. I miss the earlier years and who I believed she was. I missed our unabashed laughter. But most of all what I think I miss is potential. I was always waiting for the drama to be over. I believed one day it would all be fine. She would be normal and sober and happy and we could relax and enjoy all we had experienced in life. Her alcoholism permeated our lives and it was on a rampage to steamroll our dreams. Mom was not strong enough to fight it. But honestly the alcoholism didn't kill me. What did me in was the *hope*. I was never ever released from the hope. There was never any freedom from it.

I miss my mommy, but do I miss the idea of her more? I wanted to feel more relieved for her when she passed, but I don't feel that way. Mostly I just feel sad. It seems like such a shame and such a waste actually. And yet maybe if she had been healthier, my life would not have turned out as extraordinary. I can't regret any of my life but I do regret for her. I am OK. I was always going to be OK. She was not and that is simply sad to me. All I ever really wanted was for Mom to be happy and healthy minded. I wanted this mostly for her but it would have been an amazing gift for so many.

I also wanted my mom to accept me entirely and support my decisions. But like I have said about my own children, we are not the same people. I wanted her to agree with me and it could not happen. I often had to force myself to go against her. I wanted her to be independent, and at the same time I wanted her to help me be independent. Two things that threatened her to the core. Independence equaled loneliness for her. She claimed she was independent, but it scared her to death.

There's an Erich Fromm quote I love: "The mother-child relationship is paradoxical and, in a sense, tragic. It requires the most intense love on the mother's side, yet this very love must help the child grow away from the mother, and to become fully independent." I did become my own person, but am not sure I was or will ever be completely independent of her. I was born from her.

Once we stopped living together full-time I didn't want Mom to be alone. I wanted her to maximize her many creative talents. She used to help cast male cowboys for Bruce Weber. Why not go into casting? She collected linens. Maybe open a linen shop? I wanted her to streamline her life and not become a slave to her possessions like she warned me against becoming. I wanted her to not be lonely. Admittedly, I would have been jealous—and even squeamish—if she had a relationship. But I'd get over it, because I'm a big girl. Plus, if she'd had one, it could have freed me considerably. At times I wished I had a sibling from her to carry the burden. I envisioned her traveling or having a fabulous shop in New York and fun colorful friends. I wanted us to have great holidays and family gatherings. Nothing is ever like it is in the movies.

I guess I harbored such romantic visions about who she could have been because I really believed they were options. I saw it all. Why couldn't she? I wanted her to never drink a drop of alcohol ever again and be released from her crippling addiction. I wanted her to know how fabulous I thought she was and how much more I thought she could enjoy. I wanted her to feel loved and to have truly loved herself. But that last key desire of mine never happened. Instead, she was sad inside and alienated everybody around her. Her loneliness was epic and I felt like I was watching a life squandered.

And, because she was not communicating at all at the end, her dying was even more frustrating and I felt increasingly helpless. I could not snap my fingers and change any of it. It is a crazy, gut-churning feeling to be alive while somebody is actually dying. We should not have been done yet but maybe you never are. Maybe it never is enough. Maybe that's the point. Maybe life just needs to be lived, period. Mom was leaving this world and I could not stop it from happening. My mother did not want to die but she spent a lifetime killing herself.

I will never feel like I said good-bye to either of my parents. But honestly, nothing would have been enough. I prayed she would hold my hand once more, make eye contact, or say I love you. They say that the hearing is one of the last senses to go and that she could hear me telling her I loved her, but I will never know. I will never know what she was or was not feeling. She seemed horribly scared to me and not at all peaceful. Maybe people just make that stuff up to help the living, grieving people? I have played and replayed those last few days and her last moments. I've done it drunk; I've done it sober. I've done it in therapy and out loud to myself when I'm alone. And I still can't fucking grasp it. I wanted to be there, and I was, but the horrific image will be etched on my retinas for the rest of my life. I would have beaten myself up if I weren't there, but I will forever regret seeing what I saw. I cannot believe my mother no longer exists. She is no longer present in this world. I simply can't believe it.

I understand nothing more about death than I ever have before. In fact, because I can no longer just imagine what it would look like, I no longer have the luxury of painting it the way I want to see it. I did *see* it and I did not like one bit of it. I saw it and I still don't get it. I have no clue as to what really happened or happens.

For me it helps to believe that there is a God of some kind because it means that maybe Mom is not alone.

I hope and pray that our loved ones find peace and are only dead to the material world. I wanted nothing more than to know Mom ended happy in her heart. Maybe that's why she looked so unfamiliar the second she died. Maybe the body is just a temporary house. There has to be more than this. There has to be something else. I know this world can't possibly be all there is. I have to believe she went somewhere, because otherwise it's just that she no longer is. I simply hate to bear that thought. I wanted some sort of proof she still occupied somewhere. I wanted a sign or to feel a "presence." But that is not the way it worked for me, evidently. I now know why people seek mediums or psychics. They want to believe and will take any proof.

Now Mom is just ashes. If I think about it too much, I can work myself up into a frenzy. I can get claustrophobic and sweaty at the thought that I can't touch her or go back to the way it was earlier and in good times. Now she is not anywhere I can get to or even get away from. She has been reduced to dust divided into two containers. Not sure what to do with that reality. My religion only tempers me to a certain extent. I love it in theory but when somebody you love goes away forever, it just feels so final. I know love never dies, but if given a choice I really would prefer David and my dad and my dog and my mother to all be alive. I would only want my mother to be alive if she was sober and happy, though! Otherwise, keep her until she's prepared to be so.

My kids dealt differently with Mom's death. Grier cried when she was sleepy and brought up angels and heaven a lot. Rowan was stoic and only worried that it meant I would die soon, too. I always hated when people said how we are all constantly dying so I did not respond to Rowan with that. I reassured my daughters that I was fine and would be around a lot longer. I believe all kids deeply want to hear that.

Just because I no longer had a mother it did not mean I was no longer a mother. It actually hit me as very strange not to gauge any of my actions toward my children based on my mother's reactions or opinions. Even though Mom did not spend a great deal of time around my girls and me together, I always had her in the back of my mind. And she only had me in the front of hers. It was as if I alone existed in and for her life. I can still hear her opinions in my head today, but because she is now not actually alive, I don't feel the need to defend myself or yield to her way of doing things. The noise of her is turning down its volume in my thoughts. This is a bit of a relief because I no longer have to feel not good enough for her. She is dead and can't affect the course of my days anymore. That I welcome.

One night in bed Grier made two half ovals with both her hands as if she were about to bite into a burger. She said that this was us. We were together. I saw it as we were separate but also whole because of the other half. We started pretending we were eating big burgers and saying "*Yum.*"

She then made one half oval move a bit up and the other slightly down so they were no longer parallel. "This is Rowan and me," she said. My heart cracked. I prayed her relationship with her sister would improve but right then it was all about fighting.

I explained that it would not always feel like that between her and her sister. I promised that Rowan loved her younger sister and said I believed that they would one day be closer.

She then made half a heart with her left hand and fingers and then did the same with her right hand. She first held them apart and then slowly closed the two sides to form the heart. She then said, "Mom, it's like this *heart* is our home."

Often it's at bedtime that I am moved to tears.

The other night I was lying down with Grier as I always try to do before she goes to sleep. Rowan stopped asking me to stay with her a while ago so I am savoring the one who still wants me. Grier asks to cuddle and I have to fight not falling asleep and waking up at 4:00. Sometimes I ask what she is thinking. Lately she has been saying she often thinks about Toots and Pop-Pop. I can tell she knows this will touch me and she wants to let me know she cares. I asked her what she was thinking about them. She never met my dad but hears stories all the time about him. She said she was thinking of what she would be doing with them if they were here now. I asked her what that would be. "Well, I think I would be reading my journal to Pop-Pop and I'd for sure be showing Toots my gymnastics."

I asked her if she was sad or missed Toots. Mom scared Rowan as time went on, but she played with Grier like a kid and had deteriorated mentally by the time Grier was old enough to know her. They played like buddies together and adored little trinkets. Of course Mom had bought the expired Happy Meal toys from a tag sale and kept giving them to Grier. I kept throwing them out because I hate the clutter my mother always represented.

Grier said she did miss my mother but was not sad because every time she felt like she missed her she would just realize that she could talk to her and that she would always be in her heart. Grier tapped both her hands on her chest and mentioned that even in school if she thought of Toots she could think of her as being inside her own heart.

"Right here. And I don't feel sad. I can talk to her from here." This blew my mind and I promised to try to do the same thing. Mom once told me that she was trying a new therapy that when she wanted a drink she would tap on her chest bone with her fingers to remind her not to take the drink. She said it was supposed to trigger some kind of sense memory and help with addiction. Of course, she probably was just doing it at a bar and the bartender thought she was signaling that he serve her another drink. Anyway, I told Grier that that was beautiful and I would do the same from then on.

I know I have said that we keep those we love forever in our hearts, but hearing her repeat it with her little hands over her heart and in her tiny voice made me weep. I hope I can find that same comfort in my own heart that I seem to have taught her to have. Or maybe I didn't teach that? Maybe she taught it to me?

Grier provided one sort of comfort to me. Rowan did, too, but in a very different way. Rowan convinced me to let her get her ears pierced at the age of ten. It was six months after Mom died. I recalled that I was twelve when my mom took me to get both our ears pierced. She had never had hers done and wanted to do it with me. I went first!

I actually had always intended to only let Rowan get her ears done when she was twelve, but walked into my own trap. She had asked me at age nine and I said no, not until you are double digits! Forgetting completely that ten and eleven were indeed double digits prior to twelve, I had to follow through. I did go to college, I swear.

She and her cousin wanted to get them done together and it was to be a special birthday event for Rowan. Her cousin graciously waited until Rowan's actual birthday to get hers done at the same time.

My oldest half sister, Marina, lives uptown and suggested we go to her dermatologist. I had thought Claire's would have been the better bet and cheaper, too. Not that I try to ever skimp on my daughters where their physical well-being is concerned, but I had gotten my ears pierced at a mall in New Jersey when I was twelve and my ears didn't get infected and fall off. The mall kiosks did countless lobes a day and had it down from my point of view. I did not yet realize that the venue would turn out to be the least of my worries. But Rowan wanted to go uptown to be with her cousin, and my sister made an appointment.

Rowan and I were rushing late as usual and her cousin had already gone in. By the time we arrived, the cousin was smiling with two wonderfully pierced ears. Rowan sat down next and the doctor came in. She drew the dots on the lobes and asked me what I thought.

Remember, when I was young my mother was never, ever wrong in my eyes. She always had a question or a suggestion when we were at the doctor's as well as every other area in which she was completely untrained. She possessed impressive instincts in a variety of situations and I always trusted her above all. She often questioned the professionals and they often complimented her on her observations. She was also always bluffing her way through. I, however, thought she was God. Mom, therefore, could have had the lower right side of my chin and the outer left side of my eyebrow each pierced and tell me they were even and I would have looked in the mirror and seen perfect symmetry.

Unlike my mother, I usually ask Rowan her opinions before voicing my own. But in this case I spoke up first. I looked at each lobe and said that I had to be honest—I wasn't sure the dots looked centered. I wanted them each centered in the middle of the lobe. The doctor exclaimed that that was exactly why she asked the mothers. She wanted moms to give the stamp of approval. She did not say if she agreed or not. I felt so good at the moment—Rowan must have thought that her mother was even smarter than the doctor.

What I had not taken into consideration was that first of all, I was *not* a doctor, and second, my daughter's lobes (like the rest of the population's) were different in size from one another. The board-certified surgeon was, in fact, taking this into consideration. The dots were redrawn and the deed was done. I took one look at the final product and, getting instantly sick to my stomach, realized that I had inadvertently caused the holes to actually be uneven. Yes, thanks to my expertise, each lobe was pierced in its center, but when looked at head-on, one gold ball was, in fact, a bit higher than the other. I did not say a word, partially because I could not breathe, but mostly because I was terrified of my daughter's reaction.

I paid the ridiculously large bill, we all made a big fuss at how big our girls were, and we separated. I took Rowan back downtown and envisioned my sister and the family all celebrating my niece's perfect lobes. I was resigned to try to suppress all the feelings that were creeping into my consciousness. "This too shall pass" had become a useful mantra for me over the years, and I was reminding myself of it once again for comfort.

I continually tried to forget about it but with little success. However, Rowan didn't seem to comment so I thought maybe the bullet had been dodged. It gnawed at me, as things tend to do, and try as I might I could not suppress my self-hatred for having marred our firstborn.

A few months passed and Fourth of July weekend was upon us. After being asked the same question every week leading up to this holiday, I finally told Rowan she could indeed put on new earrings for the first time. I took her to get some fun earrings and the choice was a monumental one. After about an hour, I was numb. She chose a small cardboard square full of multicolored little Gummy Bears. We went home and the ceremonious changing of the earrings began.

Because I could not find music associated with the changing of the guard at Buckingham Palace, I found Bob Dylan's '78 single with that exact same title and gave it a shot. As we were swabbing each lobe with alcohol and talking about how exciting it would be for her to show off her ears to the families who were soon coming over for the Fourth of July BBQ, Rowan breezily said, "Mom, I think when you switched the dots on my ears, you actually made them uneven."

I almost instantaneously threw up. I no longer heard any music and had the feeling that I was falling into an abyss. My world suddenly narrowed. Mustering a voice that wouldn't betray my true emotions, I calmly retorted, "Really? I don't know, I think they look great."

We completed the switch and I sent her to put on her bathing suit. I quietly snuck into the next room and asked Chris if I could have a word. He'd definitely have a solution. I began deep breathing and when he arrived, I said I had something I needed to tell him and that I really needed his support and his help. I begged him first to tell me that we could fix it and it would all be OK. He had such compassion in his eyes and in the past has repeatedly met such frightening moments like these (for me) with true calm and honest but practical advice.

But his face changed with the news and he just turned and left the room to look at our daughter. Suddenly he burst back into the room and blurted out, "One Gummy Bear's feet are sitting fine and the other Gummy Bear's feet are dangling off her lobe. She looks ridiculous. You are not a doctor. Why did you interfere? I can't believe you."

I was stunned and in shock. He had never reacted to me like this. He was defending her and was so angry and disappointed in me. I myself could not believe it. I was also instantly jealous of Rowan. And after I emotionally prefaced the entire situation by saying I felt terrible and needed help to fix it. This was fixing nothing.

Seething, I silently put on a bathing suit and a long caftan cover-up. I got a fresh bottle of sauvignon blanc from a local vineyard from the fridge and brought the whole thing out to the pool, just as I had seen my mom do countless times, except with red. I had every intention of finishing the bottle by myself, but to maintain a modicum of dignity and a semblance of being a lady, I was sure to bring a glass. Never let it be said I'm not a lady! I calmly went out to a chaise lounge by the pool and settled in for the long haul through my rambling and conflicting thoughts. Looking like the mother in *August: Osage County* before needing a binge, I hunkered down.

I stayed on that lounge chair growling inside and steadily drinking that entire bottle of wine. Maybe I was more similar to my mother than I thought. Friends began showing up for the BBQ but I did not move one limb, nor did I speak. I just lay their stewing, bottle in hand, and nodding like an old silent-film star to friends as they arrived. Everybody made himself or herself at home. They knew me enough to just let me go through whatever it was that I was going through.

I let Chris be host and invisibly watched the scene unfold. I was so hurt and mad at my husband and so enraged with myself for interfering. I was angry with my mother for always seeming to be right, in my eyes. I was mad that I could not become the same sort of maternal superhero I thought she was. I was mad at Rowan for questioning me. As the backyard began to fill with noises of screaming kids and mingling adults, my wine-calmed mind drifted to an old video. In it I was about nine years old and Mom and I were on vacation visiting with Lila in Phoenix, Arizona. She was working at the Biltmore Hotel and they had a huge pool and great pizza and frozen yogurt. Lila must have been videotaping me in the pool.

In the video, Mom is teaching me to dive from a diving board and swim the length of a pool. It was in the early afternoon and already blistering hot, but there she was, sitting on the edge of a metal and plastic slatted lounge chair in blue jeans and a button-down blouse. Just like a coach training his Olympian hopeful, Mom was calling out instructions to me with the utmost confidence.

Mom kept declaring, "Brookie, think out, not down, when you dive. Think out, always think out and to the other end of the pool." I can see her left arm swinging up and out, indicating a forward fluid motion all the way to the far end of the huge pool. I repeatedly dived off the board and resurfaced with the same gasp, spitting out the important question "How'd I do, Mom? How was that?"

It was seemingly very sound advice and made a great deal of sense. I guess it is important to always aim in the direction of where you want to end up while diving or doing anything else in life. However, I am not quite positive that her directions were founded on any true knowledge of how to dive. And she was so sure of her own advice, I took it as absolute truth. I just breathlessly continued on in my pursuit of the out-and-far dive, trying not to throw up from the inevitable belly flop.

It wasn't until years later, while watching this video, I remembered that my mother never learned how to swim! Mom avoided water—her uncle had drowned and I'm sure her mother never taught her—but I never knew any of that until I was an adult. I always just thought Mom didn't like being in water. She would wade in the shallow end at times or I would hang off her legs as she sat on the edge. On a cruise ship once, when I was about five, I went swimming and the water started sloshing around. I began to flounder. Mom didn't jump in but grabbed a server and he pulled me out to safety. Looking back, I never had any real evidence that she could swim. I had pictures of her frolicking in the ocean, but I don't remember her ever actually swimming, let alone doing a dive.

What struck me was how convinced I was that my mom knew of what she was instructing. I never doubted my mother's ability in anything she did. Why would it ever cross my mind that she could not have been able to save me were I to have begun drowning?

Back on my chaise I was wakened from my daydream by a loud cannonball in the actual pool in front of me.

I looked at Rowan frolicking around and thought, *How come you question me so much? Why am I not your queen?* Suddenly, after years of professing that I wanted and planned on nurturing my daughter's independence and raising her as a healthy, secure, and unique young girl, I now wanted to take it all back and instill in her the same blind faith I held for Mom. I had always professed that I wanted to nurture my girls' independence and help thwart inevitable insecurities. Yet as soon as I became threatened, I changed my tune and wanted her to be as dependent on me and reverential toward me as I had been on and toward my mom. I wanted my daughter to look up to me with that vintage, unconditional love I had always had in my heart and mind for my mama. I did want her to believe I was always right. Of course I hoped she was self-confident, but I sure as hell didn't want her to challenge me or think me fallible.

I realized I envied her independence. I was threatened by the fact that even at such an early age, she had begun to individuate. I ached from loving her and all the feelings that brought up.

In that doctor's office I had just wanted to be right. I wanted Rowan to think me smarter than everybody, including the trained professional. In recounting the earring story to her friends, I wanted her to say, "My mommy is the best; she knows even more than the doctors do."

After yet another cannonball the dog started barking. It was a signal to shift my focus back to the present. No more time to wallow in my self-pity and anger. I was beginning to get self-conscious alone on the lounge chair, and I shifted my thoughts. I had the reality of the uneven holes with which to contend but could not immediately do anything about them. In my defense, the corrected dots were clearly centered in the middle of each of her lobes. However, one had to look at only one lobe at a time to see that. Look at my daughter head-on and it was another story.

Fortified by the haze of the sauvignon blanc and renewed by the desire to fix what I had broken by myself, I settled the dog and resolved to contact the doctor the next day to review the options. Just as I experienced a hint of relief and renewed focus, a game of chicken was loudly being assembled in the pool.

It was Rowan on her dad's shoulders against another schoolmate on her dad's. Right before the match began, Rowan called out to the crowd. "People, I have an announcement to make. People . . . I . . . have . . . pierced . . ."

Oh my God, I thought, *here it comes—she's going to throw me under the bus!* I braced myself.

"Ears! Yes, that's right people, I, Rowan Francis Henchy, have . . . perfectly symmetrically pierced ears! *Bam!*"

She did some hip-hop gesture with both her hands to punctuate this declaration.

Stunned, I just stared at her. Emotionally inverted by a joy I had not expected, my eyes welled once again. Rowan had obviously intuited the whole picture so clearly and wanted to take care of me. I slammed up against feelings of relief and joy as well as guilt and embarrassment at how much I, too, needed her approval. This dynamic was so complex and layered.

I felt so proud of my little girl's heart and her innate spirit, yet shrunk with shame that I had created a situation in which she felt the need to care for me. I silently vowed not to make my shortcoming her responsibility ever again. I should have remembered how I acted when she asked about my crying in the car all those years back. Rowan was being her grounded self, wanting everything to be OK. Standing chest-deep in the water with Rowan on his shoulders, Chris just shook his head and half smiled. His expression suggested pique, defeat, and pride.

We all celebrated the day of independence, and the irony was not overlooked on my part. I, too, shook my head.

That night Chris and I did not discuss the events of the day but instead quietly readied ourselves for bed. He broke the silence with the acknowledgment that a bigger conversation was necessary but sleep was calling.

The next day, after reaching the doctor and explaining my dilemma, I had a plan to offer. Taking Rowan aside, I admitted to having made a mistake and explained that we could take one earring out, let the hole close, and get it repierced. I emotionally added that I loved her so much and I had just wanted it to be perfect and for her to think her Mom was cool. I thanked her for what she did in the pool and said I really appreciated it. She asked me if I thought her ears looked OK. I said I honestly did. Rowan looked at herself in the mirror and then turned back to me and said, "Mom, you didn't do it on purpose and besides nobody is going to ever notice. Can I go play now?"

I exhaled and was awed by how self-confident and forthright my ten-year-old was. Had I had anything to do with that?

I realized once again I still had a lot to learn. I forgave my husband completely. I would have been mad at me, too. I admitted to my own mistakes and where my own insecurities reared their ugly heads. I brought up the necessity of our being a united front at all times in front of the girls and we could always hash out our own differences in private.

It is not about not becoming my mother as a mom. Nor is it about being her. It is about being as much of myself as possible and defining my individual relationship with my girls with respect for how they feel as well as how I feel. Using those lessons I have learned that I value and leaving the ones I don't behind. Rowan and I were both free enough to be ourselves and together managed to find an honest and healthy way out of a decent-size problem. I don't know all the answers but together we can learn.

I have to come clean and say that this was not the end of the Gummy Bear saga. A year later Rowan out of the blue asked if she could repierce her one ear. I said sure and we went to Claire's that afternoon. A new hole was pierced and it was not dangerously close to the old one. She even convinced me to get a third in my left ear. How could I say no? It was a little bonding moment and funny that this time, too, she went first, just as I had when my mom and I got our ears pierced together when I was young.

Who knew that little, uneven, plastic Gummy Bears could penetrate so many layers. Literally!

Chapter Twenty

Returning Home

I n January 2013, Chris and I began looking for a house out at the beach. I hadn't spent time in the Hamptons in years. My dad's family had moved to Palm Beach and soon those beaches replaced the sand of my youth. However, Chris and I and the girls soon began getting invited to visit with various families from school who had Hamptons houses. Driving back into the city on Sunday night we'd talk about how much fun we all had and how relaxing it had all been. I began to reestablish a bond with the area, visiting the playground on which I had skinned my knee and crawling under the trellis under which I used to find tiny frogs. I'd run into people of all ages that I knew from my childhood. Invariably after I'd introduce them to my husband and daughters, these old friends would begin to reminisce about my father and tell me how missed he was. I even got to show Chris and the girls pictures of my grandfather that hung on the walls at the Meadow Club.

It was all very familiar and somehow comforting. It felt different, though, and as if this time my entry into this community had been generated by me. It was via my husband and girls that I had come to want to celebrate my roots. After a while, it became clear that Chris and I wanted our own place somewhere at the beach.

One random day, after years of wishing for and working toward the possible purchase of a second home, Chris just said, "What are we waiting for? We work to live, so why don't we invest in a house and enjoy it? It doesn't have to be in Southampton, either." We began the hunt and after a fun and exhausting search during the dead of winter, just three months after Mom's death, we found the perfect place—a modest, yet roomy house in the town of Southampton, about a mile from the water. It was fully renovated, would fit many guests comfortably, and had a big backyard and a freshwater pool. Our dream house was finally a reality.

We had cast a wide net and had looked everywhere from South-ampton to Montauk. How funny it was that we should end up right back where it had all begun! Suddenly, I was with a Realtor, driving past the place in which I learned how to swim and do the box step.

How serendipitous it had been to have been accepted at the perfect school and then become friends with people who all lived near one another in the town I actually loved. And how strange and amazing that it was my daughters who had brought me back to the place my mother had loved and to a life she had coveted. And how strangely sad it was that Mom would never see it.

The sale went through and I set out immediately to decorate. Given my mother's inability to ever finish decorating any of her homes, I was even more intent on quickly assembling furniture in every room. My goal was for each room to be livable and uncluttered. I promised Chris that I would not spend any money, but could easily furnish the place with what I currently had in storage. Dan and I had spent al-most five years going through my mother's storage spaces—Beanie Babies, Louis Vuitton purses, and all the rest—and it happened that we were just about to finish and leave the space for good.

The day we emptied the unit completely and had trekked to Paterson for the last time it seemed almost too good to be true. Mom had been moved to the new facility in Manhattan and had declined in mental health so that she had given up trying to fight me on the warehouse. She just knew I had sold some stuff and had money for her. I assured her I kept the jewelry and most of the art and special furniture, but maybe we did not need twelve Erté sculptures. Two would suffice. She seemed to be mollified by the amounts of cash we made at the three huge tag sales and the tax deductions from donations. As we drove away from the now cavernous unit, I looked out the window and saw the bronze monument of Lou Costello and a little park dedicated to him. He had been from Paterson. Abbot and Costello had always been a favorite for both my mom and me. We'd rush back from church Sunday afternoons to watch it together on Seventy-Third Street. Amid the seediness of this area stood this plump little man with a smile on his face. It looked as if he were waving me good-bye.

Now it was time to start decorating the beach house. Chris was away the weekend the movers came to Southampton for the big move, so I had free reign. I called in my personal troops and was determined to use as much preexisting stuff as I could.

For three full days, three of us worked nonstop, getting all of my mother's furniture and art scattered and perfectly placed. We staged it as if it were a movie set. We put down rugs and hung art. We made up the beds with various antique linens. In every room we found mismatched but functioning end tables, lamps, chests, and more. We moved a huge oak table by ourselves down a flight of stairs and into a basement to be used as a wrapping, craft, and work table. I wanted it to look cozy and eclectic and like we had lived there for years. We were able to fill the small pool house with towels and couches and a few coffee tables. An enormous collection of earthenware green vases that Mom and I had collected from various antique markets lined an old oak baker's rack. The Van Briggles, Roseville, and USA pieces added color to the room. We'd only take one break a day to eat dinner.

By the time Chris arrived I was shattered physically and mentally. I was an emotional wreck, having engaged with my mom's belongings so intensely over the past few days. Many memories were attached to all the pieces, and it felt like each one was imbued with her spirit. My mother's stuff was finally being put to use after decades of being paid for and transported all over the United States. This was the first time some of the pieces had ever even been put to use. She would collect just to collect. She amassed for future homes she wouldn't even buy. Seeing it all finally staged perfectly in a home Mom would never see gave me pause. Mom never arrived at a place to actually use and enjoy her things.

Chris gave me a huge hug and was obviously blown away by how much work we had done. He marveled that it looked like a "completely decorated home." But I couldn't help but think his comment was like what you say when you see an ugly baby for the first time and don't want to insult the parents. He must have caught a glimpse of an expression on my assistant's face as he hugged me that suggested he tread lightly. He smiled and said, "It's great, babe. I'm starving; let me shower and take you all to a great meal."

At dinner Chris, sensing my fragile and fatigued state, lifted a glass and made a toast to us and to all the hard work we had accomplished. Cheers to our new amazing home! He then added a special toast to me, calling me "Mom" and saying he knew how much I was doing and that it was all truly appreciated. I felt so relieved he was there and let out a sigh that represented a mixture of weariness and relief. I drank my martini straight up with a twist and didn't realize the poignancy of the order until later. That had ultimately been my mom's drink of choice. We all counted our blessings and talked about all the things we wanted to do in our new home.

Later that night, I lay in bed, wide-eyed and staring up at the ceiling. Chris asked, "Babe, what is it? Are you OK?" In a trancelike voice I responded, "I hate everything, I'm getting rid of it *all*."

Suddenly, I hated everything. It was eclectic all right, but seemingly done by a color-blind crazy hoarder person. I hated the old-fashioned style, I hated the smell, I hated the fact that Mom saved it all and that we had paid for the storage all these years. I hated her hoarding it, and us waiting and waiting for a dream house and a place in which we would be happy and at peace with one another. I hated that I gave so much of my own time to the navigation of it all.

What was meant to have been a fresh start for us all had developed into an experiment in clutter, in being stuck in the past, and in how *not* to decorate a beach house. I had hoped and believed the pieces would work and that this eclectic amassing of furniture and things would make for a charming beach home. But the truth was, I had outgrown the stuff. Assembled all together, after all this time, it just seemed dated. None of it felt like my taste anymore. I was no longer that person. I had changed and was no longer "shabby chic meets uptown Manhattan meets tramp art meets Connecticut housewife."

I felt sad, stupid, and slightly frustrated by the years that had gone into these past three days. I lay still and felt an unsettling sense of rage and sadness inside. I was surrounded by the things my mom savored, in a house she would have loved, yet she was not there to see any of it. And I didn't even like it in the end. It felt it had all been for nothing.

I knew not whether to scream or cry, but I was clear about one thing: I had to rid myself of almost everything. I realized it could possibly be considered excessive, but I knew it was necessary. Suddenly, I didn't care about spending money on new pieces. I had some cash left from the tag sales and I wasn't going to go on a crazy buying spree. I just needed this home to reflect the *me* I was today and the family I had created. Some might say I was ascribing way too much to inanimate objects, but this was my entire past and my upbringing and the life I had only shared with my mother. These things represented our unfulfilled dreams. Now I saw it all as only holding an obsolete promise. I had attached so much to these *things*. I saw in them a feeble chance to go back and make right the "almosts" in our life. I saw it all laid out and knew I could never go back. Mom and I never finished a home and enjoyed it together. We just kept chasing the stuff and the destinations and never inhabited them. It felt like a real end to a huge period of longing.

The next day I started peeling away the things that gave me the most anxiety. I found an antiques dealer in the next town over and engaged him to help me sell most of it. He was hesitant at first because he said people often came to him with pieces left to them by family. They usually held only emotional value to the individual but usually little else.

Undeterred, I sent him photos and measurements and we were in business. I have to say that the pieces were all exquisite. They had real value and were in pristine shape. This guy said that in all his years of being in this business, he had never seen such a cohesive, quality, beautiful collection. He could easily move this stuff and give me half the proceeds. I then could buy items we all really loved and wanted to live among. It made sense, and I did just that.

I soon realized that this had actually been an important part of my particular mourning process. I had needed to go through the entire process—cleaning out the storage space, seeing everything that was there, placing it all in our new home, paying tribute to what my mom and I had collected and the path it had taken, and then being *done* with it.

I kept a few special items with which I could not part and decided to work just enough of them in to feel good and connected to my mom. With the money I received I bought and decorated the place to reflect my husband and me and us as a family. It was a liberating process and a telling one.

Six months later it was our first Christmas in this house, and to quote my girls, it promised to be "the best one ever!"

For the first time since I can remember, I was also not alone in the holiday decorating. As a kid I decorated our tree every year all by myself. I'd take a minimum of four hours to place the multicolored mini-lights on practically every needle. I would then deck out the tree with so many ornaments you could barely see the branches. I loved the ritual of it all. I would stay up all night if I had to use everything. I was methodical and maniacal and felt such commitment and peace doing it all by myself. Mom never liked doing the tree.

I would start after dinner and then we would go to midnight Mass. I always resumed after Mass and would sometimes stay up to 4:00 A.M. I never turned on the lights until the whole tree was done. My favorite part was when I'd finally take the ridiculously long assembly of plugs that had been stacked and attached and put the last one in the socket. The tree would glow and it was so bright you could read a book under it.

I'd switch it on and enjoy the light and the intense quiet. Mom would be getting ready for bed and I'd do the reveal for her—"Ta-da, Mama!"—and then go into my room and go to bed, incredibly excited for Santa to come. I'd leave the tree without presents and in the morning there would be so many wrapped packages surrounding the base that one would not believe we were a household of two. Most of the gifts would be spilling out of a Christmas stocking the size of a young child. Mom had found the enormous stocking at some store and thought I deserved it.

Christmas morning was always amazing and we would usually go to Bob's family's house for an Armenian-style family Christmas. The day after Christmas I'd go to my dad's house and have the holiday with my family there. Mom's relatives were never a part of our lives in these later years.

Now it was my turn to create traditions in my own home. And I was taking it incredibly seriously. I roll-called my platoon and we put together a plan. Everyone happily got to work. I dreaded the day my girls stopped believing in Santa (and vowed to never pass out like my mom had done so many years ago and reveal the truth). Santa would come during the night when they were all asleep for as long as possible.

This year one daughter did the outside lights with Chris's mom, another child did the fireplaces and powder room, I completed the dining room table, and we all did the tree together. For the record, I did not redo the placement of any of the lights or the ornaments when my girls were not looking! The house was stunning. Because it was to be the first family dinner at my new special table, I wanted it to be just right. I had recently convinced my husband to let me get a large oval zinc-top table that had two massive debarked tree trunks as its base. Even though Chris started out being unsure, thankfully, its dominating presence grew on him and we kept the table. Since the table was my domain, I went about the decorating in a way that would make Colin Cowie proud.

First, I placed two fresh garlands from a local farm along the length of the table crossing in and out of the other through the center. I next wrapped tiny battery-operated mini-lights on thin wire, which I had splurged on from Restoration Hardware, around white balls made of seashells. I made two pyramids of three balls each and encased them under glass domes and located them toward the center of the table amid the green garland. Two sterling candelabras that my mom bought at an antique place ages ago bracketed my center masterpiece. To finish it off, I scattered a few huge pinecones and nestled a few silver birds and mini-conches into the green. I thought I'd add a bit of beach into Christmas. I lit the candles, stood back, and as the holiday music wafted through the otherwise quiet house, I thought it was the best-smelling room and most beautiful table I had ever set.

Chris made a feast and we all sat down and toasted to it all. As I sipped my glass I slowly looked around the table at the smiling faces. Everyone was eating, talking, and enjoying the meal and the setting. I suddenly thought, *Who are these people and why are they in my house?* I started to feel like I was receding into the atmosphere. What were they all doing in my home and at my table? Where was my mom? I looked at all their faces and finally settled on my girls' backlit silhouettes. They seemed to have left me. They looked so happy and in their own skin. They were playing some joke on their "Opah," which is what they call Chris's dad, and it occurred to me that they, my daughters, were actually related to these people. They were blood, and I, somehow, was the outsider.

This thought seemed to suggest to me that all the people at this table were related to each other except me. I saw Chris and his sister, Michele (who the girls call Aunt Mimi), both their parents, and the sole Henchy grandchildren. All of them, including Mimi's husband for some reason, were all one big happy family rejoicing in Christmas. Where had my family and my life gone?

Sitting there, as the noises became more indiscernible, it slowly dawned on me that I no longer had any parent with whom to share this day. I felt orphaned.

I started to feel as if I could sneak away from the table while they all laughed and celebrated and walk out of the house and just keep going. My kids would be fine. Look at the great family they had! They might miss me, but not for long, and they would grow up just fine. Look at all those Disney princesses—their moms had been vanished from their lives way earlier than this and their futures turned out to be more glorious than they could have imagined. Maybe it was even better for my kids if I, too, vanished.

Chris startled me by repeating some question even louder and I regained consciousness and tried to shake off my mood. I got a huge lump in my throat and tried to smile it down. I lingered with the feeling for another second, though, and recognized it as similar to a sensation I encountered years back and at the beginning of my bout with PPD. I resisted the urge to panic.

I finished my glass and slowly refilled it with champagne, watching every bubble trying to stay afloat and feeling slightly like one of those helpless bubbles. Nobody seemed to have noticed my "absence" and I attempted successfully to reengage in the table chatter.

After dinner, as I was clearing the table, my husband said, "I see that look in your eyes. You are leaving again, aren't you? You are retreating and I want to go on record and say that I am a witness to your starting to disappear." I looked at him with tears starting to well up my eyes and said, "I have no parents." He held me tight and said he understood.

Do you? I thought. *Does anybody really know what it feels like to lose a mom, until it happens?* No matter what the quality or situation of one's life, the end of a living mother is profound.

I was happy for Chris's sake that he didn't know from experience what I was feeling, of course. And I also knew that he was really just saying that I had him and the girls, and that he was aware I was struggling. I didn't feel like Christmas-crying anymore. So I took a deep breath and told him I loved him and the girls, so much it "horts."

Later that night I went over it in my head. How could it be that I had everything in place, but there remained a huge void?

I found the wonderful husband and grounded relationship, my kids were healthy, we had the full and vibrant home with the tree and the decorations and the music, and even the *snow*, for Christ's sake. I had everything I had always wanted, but now I had no mom. She used to be my barometer for joy. If she was happy, I was happy. I wanted to show her how well it had all turned out. Sure, life had kicked us in the ass for various reasons but no one's exempt from that and there had been and currently was a tremendous amount of good. The blessings were continuing. I wanted to show off my beautiful table and how I had utilized the special possessions she herself had taught me about and collected. I knew she'd love it when she saw it.

Denial can be so very shrewd. The first year after Mom died didn't seem to be so bad. Because Mom had been failing for a while, there had been a few recent celebrations during which we were not together. That first year I just tricked myself into thinking Mom was not with me because she was still at the assisted-living facility. But this Christmas was a shock. It had been about a year and two months and I still had not had any dreams about Mom or any emotional outbursts. I suppose it was crafty denial, but I was beginning to realize that my mourning had only just begun.

I now needed to do what Mom was never capable of doing—let go, even just a little bit. Because I wish she knew she didn't ever have to let me go. All she needed to do was stretch her arms out farther and relax her fingers.

Epilogue

Dear Mom,

My first feeling is that I miss you very much. It is hardest on your birthday and on my birthday, because those were the days that we celebrated each other. I never thought I could live without you. To see you dying in that bed with its rails and thin sheets, in a curled-up and scared position, devastated me. Watching you actually die was one of the hardest, more unreal things I have ever experienced, and it was the day I had dreaded most my whole life.

I never felt as though I told you enough how much I loved and appreciated you. I wish we had had a heart-to-heart while you were still of sound mind. You always said, "Let's talk," but it never happened. I think we wanted to avoid disrupting the good times. Or, when we did try, we'd just fight or not know what to say. It was as if the intimacy was too scary and embarrassing.

I still feel as though I knew and understood you better than anyone else in your life, and that was hard to do because you so rarely told anybody how you were feeling. And yet I feel as though I never got the full story. I think I hated your drinking so much because the you I knew existed and loved was stolen away from me.

I was always free enough to sob to you, but it did not bring us closer. I think that was because I was your baby in those moments and you felt needed. But as I grew up and tried to make changes, these moments were fewer and farther between. It was as if we no longer knew who we were together.

I also have to believe that because you never really lived in sobriety, even your dry days were colored by your addiction. You were ambitious and street smart, and although also intensely loving, and often well intended, you were also an addict. It was as if you were not only addicted to alcohol but also addicted to me. You never did the work to fully embrace sobriety, and you robbed yourself. I became the meaning in your life when it would have served you to find the meaning from within.

I see now how much pain and sadness you carried. I believe your heart was such a fully feeling heart that you were not strong enough to heal each time it was broken. I have read some of your old journals and was deeply affected by how you regarded yourself. You always proclaimed how tough you were and how strong you were, but you never seemed to feel good enough. It is hard to love ourselves, but I have learned to love who I am inside. I can always strive to be better, but I am enough. I don't know if you ever really did love who you were. I don't believe your mom ever helped you to believe in your own self-worth as you did for me.

I know I fought you, but it never meant I did not love you or did not need you. Your approval meant the world to me, as did your happiness. That was the hard part, because I wanted your approval for my growing up independently of you, yet I feared my independence was the root of your unhappiness. But if I had not fought to differentiate myself from you and from our tight bond, I would not have been able to survive. I'm sorry for the way I handled our "divorce," but I did not have the strength to break away from the life we were living without taking drastic measures.

I loved you so much, Mama, that for so long I put you before me. I blindly defended you because you were my mom. It was often just that simple. As a mom, I admit I sometimes wish my daughters looked up to me with the same undaunted devotion as I did you because I imagine it felt good. But I also don't want them

*to have to carry that burden. I carried you because I loved you
and needed you, but I needed to learn to care for myself, too. I
remained conflicted because I felt like you never really let me in,
yet you absorbed me so far in that I could hardly find my way out.*

*I appreciated you and all you gave me in my life. It was very
hard to get past the alcohol and yet, when you were not drinking,
we were so unique and glorious together. The laughter healed
everything.*

*I am just so sad that you were so sad and that you could not
get your life straightened out or fully actualized. And yet, it was
your life, and you chose to do with it what you wanted.*

*I remember when we were being interviewed by Barbara
Walters when I was sixteen. When Barbara asked you what
message you wanted to leave with the public, you simply and
resolutely said, "I'm not going to change." And you didn't. But in
life I believe change is healthy and necessary for growth. You saw
it as defeat, and I believe that was unfortunate. I knew you meant
that you were never going to take criticism lying down or cave to
others' wills, but it also carried into your life.*

*I realized that up until the end I was fighting the same fight. I
was navigating your demons. I was trying to do for you what only
you could do for yourself. I was never going to "fix" you. I see, too,
that much of your unhappiness was independent of anything I did
or was, but as a child, one carries that responsibility. I did not
have faith that you would be OK, so I kept trying to be the source
of your happiness and self-worth.*

*I wrote this book as a way to shed light on your complicated
yet vibrant and, at times, tragic personality. I wanted you to live
longer. I wanted you to be a more integral part of our lives, but the
booze killed everything. You died too early. You had more to enjoy
and do. We had more to laugh about.*

But we did share an extraordinary life together, and you taught me so many wonderful things. I learned about humor, survival, and perseverance. I learned the power of observation and the necessity of generosity and good manners. I learned how to always work hard and try my best. I even learned how to have better posture. "Stand up straight, Brookie. . . . And keep your head held up high."

I learned how to "never take no for an answer" and how to fight for what I want. I learned how to pick myself up when I fall and never allow defeat to define me. You taught me to cast off any negative comments often hurled at me and not to "sweat the small stuff."

You taught me to look for the good in people and to admit that life could always be worse. You taught me how to adapt to my surroundings and to jump into life with both feet. You taught me how to find treasures at flea markets, to love both NECCO and Choward's Violet candies, sneak into a second movie, and be silly for a laugh. I learned to dab perfume in various, and even precarious, places because "ya never know where you might be kissed." And most important, you taught me to "never say fuck in front of the B-A-B-Y!"

Throughout the good and the bad, I would not have traded you for any other mother. I would have exchanged some of your behaviors, sure, but I can say that about practically everyone I know, including myself. You did the best you could, and so did I.

It is sad, though, and that was the overriding emotion that permeated my life throughout writing this book. Sadness. I wish I had written this letter while you were still aware.

Neither writing the book nor this letter felt at all cathartic. People speculated it would, but in actuality it all just gave me a heavy heart. But soon I will only remember the good.

I am choosing now to concentrate on and revel in only the wonderful memories. They are as much a part of me and us as are the bad ones. I have always loved you, and I am thankful for all you were. That will be your legacy.

From now on, when it rains, I will know it's just you up there being bossy. And from now on when I throw my kisses at the moon, I will hurl some your way.

I love you, Mama,
XX, Your baby girl

Acknowledgments

I wish to say thank you to my literary agent, Stephen Barr, for his layered insight and basically just for the way his brain works; to my focused and incredibly organized and attentive editor, Jill Schwartzman, for filing every tiny random memory I sent to her at all hours of the night; to her assistant, Stephanie, who didn't let a little thing like pregnancy derail her when it came to getting my changes transcribed and in on a deadline; to my godmother, Lila, for her years of support and for helping me reconstruct history; to my great friend Lyda for being attached to the past in the same way I am and for helping me remember all the details; to my friend and archivist Mike for knowing more about my life than I do and for caring and for tirelessly keeping track of every bit of the past forty-nine years; to my babysitters Kelly and Lauren for keeping my kids busy and alive while I slogged away at writing this book and for listening to me read out loud and for typing faster than I will ever be able to. To my assistant Dan, for caring for me and for becoming a part of our family. To Lisa, for remaining my "sassy." To my husband, Chris, just because he asked me to marry him; and to my smart and stunning daughters, who inspire me to be a better person and who take my breath away because I love them so deeply. And finally to my mom, for loving me.

A Conversation between
Brooke Shields and David Gilbert

1. **You've been interviewed a thousand times. Do you ever find yourself tripping into the set response in your daily life and you have to say,** *Wait a minute, I'm not being real, I'm being the persona,* **or** *I'm giving them the answer that they want and that I can give easily?*

My real friends never ask me the typical tabloid or PR types of questions, but sometimes I will retell a story I may have told on TV to a friend and I lapse into a bit of a showman. In storytelling, there will be times when I'll be talking to someone and I know how it works. I know where the funny is, so I will jump into that, but I'm very cognizant of it. The argument can then be that I'm never real, but it is actually the opposite. I am not being fake at all. I am embracing the theatrical part of myself. I just know which parts of the story will be enjoyable to people. And they're all real parts of me, you know?

2. **Do you like talking about your celebrity or your career with friends? When we met, you were probably ten years old and I was nine. We were talking about our summer, and I said I was at camp. You said you were on** *Mike Douglas.* **And I thought,** *Okay, that's a*

different kind of summer activity. But you've always had a really great group of real friends and you're a real person, which, when I think of how long you've been famous for, it's shocking that there's anything real about you. Honestly, people want these stories. When someone—maybe another mother at school—says to you, "Tell me about *Blue Lagoon,*" is your thought something like, *Okay, I have to perform this a little bit,* or is it, *Yeah, this is fun to talk about*?

It's really fun for me to talk to people who I know I'm safe with. If these conversations started at kindergarten at my children's school, I would be thinking, *Oooh, people don't know what to talk about.* It's fair—I'm the elephant in the room. Okay, let me be the elephant and I'll be the first one to [makes elephant trumpet sound].

So now when anyone asks about my career or my work, there's absolutely no threat. I'm not worried that they're going to look at me differently. There will always be people who can't help themselves, and I know who they are and I don't fault them. People are human, and who knows how they experienced me before they met me.

3. Obviously you were very well protected by your mother. You were also normalized by Dwight-Englewood and by Princeton.

That was my mom's doing, and she and I both fought for it. She did everything she could to keep my life as normal as possible and make sure I had companions around me to make me feel like a regular kid. At her memorial, one of the lawyers who had known us forever came up and said, "It was unprecedented. Your mother would ask for three airline tickets. You couldn't get one ticket, but she was like, 'Well, I'm taking her and she needs a friend.'" So I'm taking my stepsister, Diana, taking her all over, to Japan and Manila and all these places, and I think my mom knew that was really important to me.

I always had this can't-let-them-beat-me attitude. Whether it was my mom's mottos, "Never let 'em see you sweat," or "Fuck 'em if they can't handle it," or just my own stubbornness. Whatever it was, if I was pushed against, I just went further. And that attitude helped me stay grounded, strangely enough.

However, having my first daughter obliterated me. It took away all my power. All of a sudden I was experiencing something so foreign, which I had no response for. I had no resources to rely on. It was not simply about being the good girl, or being polite, or doing my job. A little human being was involved. It was not just me and my mom. It was me and a stranger and no mother for me. The rug was pulled out. And with the level of depression I experienced, I was just waiting to figure out how to slip away. It was so acute. Becoming a mother didn't ground me at all. At least in the beginning. I had felt so much more grounded on my own than with my baby.

4. Because you had this strong, particular kind of mother, it must have been really intimidating to suddenly have to take on the role of mother yourself.

I resented it. I truly resented it. It had nothing, strangely, to do with my baby. Because I'd been spending my whole life taking care of my mother, and now my mom was not capable of helping, and there I was having to do all the mothering again. And yet, having babies was the only thing I always knew I wanted. I have always wanted a baby and I have always wanted to be a mother. And then all of a sudden I was looking at her like, *What can I do for you?* I needed to be mothered. I felt incapable of all of it. It was very shocking, very literal to me. But once I got help and the right medication, I became more balanced. Then it was such an escape for me to have kids because I could say no. I had an excuse. Because I'm never someone who says no—God forbid I won't be liked—but suddenly I realized, they were the priority. I didn't have to show up for anybody but my children, and that in turn helped me be selfish and look to my own needs for the first time in my life.

5. I found that having kids opened up my social world a lot, and it seems like for you growing up it was just you and your mother. You'd have your father's family who would come in, but in specific little chunks, so it wasn't like you had a normalized suburban backyard existence or even an urban let's-go-to-the-playground life. Has that been an eye-opening thing?

First it was like a shiny penny, because this real-life stuff is fun. Playdates and mommy-and-me groups and the park, and then you see the inertia of it, and the conversation becomes so vapid. You're just talking about pacifiers and suddenly you think, *Oh God, I don't want to do that. I don't fit into that.* So then I considered that maybe I'm more of the carry-the-kid-to-every-art-opening mom, and that worked for a while because I loved having Rowan in tow. But then that gets to be too much at times and the older they get, the more they need routine. I did the same thing with the school. I think you jump in and it's all-consuming with the families and the kids and the volunteering at school events. I went in thinking I had to be über-mom—that I could have a career and be a full-time mom. You want to prove to yourself and the community that you can do it all. Eventually, over time, you realize you can't be everything all the time, but you can try to be your most. Socially it levels out as well. You go from thinking you have to be friends and liked by all the moms and then you realize you don't. You settle a bit. I've got a solid but varied group of families as friends and I genuinely like the parents, and the kids genuinely are friends, and we all play well together—I don't need too much more. I used to love that feeling of chewing up something in my mouth and giving it to my kid, like that mama bird. It was like a badge of honor, you know? And it was like I am better than everybody because I'm cool and nurturing. Then the reality of being a parent kind of kicks in when they're not babies anymore, and then you realize, *Oh God, these are humans whose worlds I am shaping. I better not fuck up.*

6. Your mother had so much chutzpah, yet she was always battling being an outsider. How much of that do you think was a role she was playing to mask how insecure she felt? A lot of people have that kind of tough exterior. Did you see that crack clearly, or did the drinking disguise that?

I think, to a certain extent, Mom felt she always had to play a role because I don't think she ever felt she fully belonged anywhere. She came from Newark but felt she needed to get out. She learned the rules and played the Upper East Side rich lady for a while but then fought the protocol involved and tried to brashly resist it. Then, as a team, we became recognizable in the fashion/entertainment world, which thrust us into another realm of people altogether. Mom wanted to feel important and necessary in all the worlds we frequented. I used to think it was cool that we could go anywhere, but as I grew older I began to question my real roots and where our home really was. I think she was just always opting to play a part because she never believed she was really enough anywhere. This is why I believe she welcomed the escape of alcohol. I maintain that a big part of why Mom never felt worthy was because of the way her mother regarded and treated her. A mother plays an irreplaceable part in building a child's self-esteem. My mom never got the validation from her mother that she needed.

7. I also got a sense in this book that your mother seemed like a really lonely person. You never really quite say it, but between the lines there was a real depth of loneliness to her that was kind of heartbreaking.

I don't think I really knew it—or maybe I always knew it but I wasn't able to admit it. I was in the position to fill that loneliness. It would have devastated me to think that her loneliness was not something I could fix.

I think loneliness was at the root of her insecurity. I watched how she answered the phone. She would be alone in this big house in New Jersey. The phone would ring, she'd be right there, and she'd let it ring a second or a third time, and then she'd pick it up quickly, as if she had been running to get it, and she'd say something like, "Put that right there, just one second, I've got to go take this— Hello?" And there wasn't even a cleaning lady around. I'd say, "Mom, I know you're alone, there's nobody in the house." She couldn't say, "I know, isn't it funny!" or anything like that. She'd say, "You don't know that." But I did know that! And yet, she had to keep up the facade.

It also makes me so unbelievably sad for her. She was loved and admired. But something deep inside kept her from believing it to be true. Recently Bruce Weber was marveling at how talented and creative Mom was. She'd find people everywhere for him to photograph. If he needed a certain type of guy, she'd say, "Hmm, I'm going to church so I'll see what I can find." She would return with one or two perfect people. He wanted her to go into casting because she had such an eye. People needed her, they loved her, they celebrated her. But I think because she really was so insecure and sad, it made her unable to absorb it. At her core she felt lonely to me and I will never not cry for that. So when she'd say, "It's us against the world," I think she really meant her. She never allowed herself to be loved and yet wanted it all the time, cried for it, begged for it. And drank to forget it.

8. It comes through in the book that you could never really love her enough because it was impossible for her to accept it.

Right. And it's not like I could have done more. It was that she believed so deeply in being abandoned. She believed that I abandoned her the moment I was born. Instantly all bets were off. There I was, the next thing that was going to leave her, *inevitably* going to leave her. Can you imagine? Just as a mother, it crushes your heart. It's like a vice. I can't even imagine how sad that was. She probably had some postpartum depression and she was probably sleep-deprived and exhausted and thinking, *Where am I?* and *It hurts to love this much.* She was alone on Fifty-Second Street in an apartment with a five-and-a-half-pound, premature baby, who in her mind will probably die—because her other baby died. A prominent politician had just lost a kid to SIDS, so it seemed like danger was everywhere, and Mom knew my dad was too young to really handle it. . . . Then you add the alcoholic piece that I spent my life trying to fix for her. For a long time I kept trying to find ways to prove to her that I loved her. She needed to believe she was lovable, and that was the one thing I could not do.

9. How did your dad fit into all this?

I didn't find out most of this until after my mom died. Mom had gotten pregnant, and Dad wanted to do the right thing. So he insisted they marry quickly, which they did, but my dad had to go to London soon after I was born so Mom was left alone. In one letter, he says how he promises to give her a church wedding one day soon. It's interesting, in reading all the letters now, I really see how he was struggling: wanting to be a good man and trying to reconcile his young life and how it had not gone the way he had thought it would. I think my mom just sort of knew, so she cut bait, but she did it without him knowing. She must have been afraid of how it would work out, and as she always did, she ran before she was left. She probably rationalized, *He's going to come back and it's not going to work out and I'm not going to be good enough for him so, ah, you can't fire me, I quit. I'm gonna go do it for all of us. All I need is this baby.*

10. What's also interesting to me is that you've always been a worker, and in some ways that's how you filled your self-worth, with work, work, work. How do you balance that with being a mom today?

I'm still working on that, trust me. For me, if I want to be a good mom, I often have to step away from my first love. I was in love with my work way before I met Chris, way before I had babies. I have a primary love, you know what I mean? It is a balance that I don't think you ever really strike but you must continue trying to find. I need both sides of my life. They each inform the other. But the work thing is really hard. I say in the press, "Oh, I'm a better mom because I allow myself my creative outlet and I want my girls to see it's important as a woman to work." Those are all the pat answers. I have to keep believing it and trying to be my best in every area. That's all I can do.

11. That's what I think people forget, or they don't take into consideration. You love acting. There are so many moments in the book where you say, "God, I wish I took it more seriously." But I think that also saved you in a way, made you more grounded in your love of acting and your love of being a mom.

Acting is like my oxygen and it's been emotional trying to balance it with my life as a mother. I don't feel like I am ever really doing enough, but this doesn't stem from my relationship with my mother, believe it or not. It's because I wanted to have it all and I have a very full life. I do always feel a bit lacking in all areas. Then I just have to stop judging myself and enjoy everything I do have and embrace it all.

What shocked me is how sometimes I look at Rowan as if she is the symbol of my mother. I let her get to me the way my mother did. I want Rowan's approval so much and I have to be very careful. It's the same feeling that I had with my mother, they both had/have a certain power over me.

Rowan recently said, "Oh my God, Mom, it's going to be so funny when we bring up the earring story and I tell *my* friends about the day my mom messed up my ears." And instantly I got all twisted up and felt horrible and mad at the same time. And to think that I was envious of Rowan's independence and her ability to criticize me. It felt unfair that my daughter did not revere me with the same blind devotion that I did my mom. It's been interesting. I had to really work on that in therapy because I had to not make any of my issues Rowan's problem.

My mom always used to criticize what I was wearing or my butt size. The other day, Rowan put on this outfit and it was exactly something I would wear. She said, "It's my mom outfit. Cool, right?" It was all I could do not to weep and thank her. I felt validated; I felt like Sally Field! I told her I loved her and said, "Yeah, it's great! But you make it look cooler." It's the little things. I just have to take it all a bit more in stride.

12. Do you think—and this is an impossible question to answer but I'm going to throw it out there—if you were not *here*, do you think your mother was destined to turn you into something? If it wasn't going to be model/actress, would it have been a Nobel Prize–winning scientist? Or do you think it just all happened in a weird kind of way and being your mother was a role that she took on?

I don't think she had a plan for anything, except that she would see a shiny object and go, "Oh, that looks fun." Or: "Hey, let's try this." She never had a premeditated plan. She flew by the seat of her pants. One day there was this baby who she thought was the most beautiful baby who ever existed. I became her sense of pride. She thinks, *Out of all the children, I have the Baby.* She thought she was blessed, that God gave her the blessing of this child. She was going to pour all the love she never got into me and my career. She had strong street smarts about her, a ferocious wit, and a protective nature.

13. She could have been a great agent/manager for *everyone*.

She would have been an amazing casting director but she couldn't love anybody more than she loved me! She'd say, "I can't fight for another person because that means I'm not fighting for you." I was it! I was her, I was her soul. Her beauty was really important. She was a model, sort of. She was surrounded by photographers. "Take pictures of *my* baby!" And the baby is beautiful and well-behaved and has a demeanor that somehow works, and then people want what she has. To which she would say, "Really? You want this? You have to go through me to get to it."

14. Did she allow you, as you got older, to take credit for your success, or was it like you were blessed, destined for this success?

When I started performing, in that *Friends* episode, *Suddenly Susan*, and then *Wonderful Town*, she always gave me credit. She thought I was better, smarter, funnier, prettier than everybody. *Suddenly Susan* was the first thing I did totally without her as a manager, but she didn't resent it. In general, she always gave me the credit, but she would say, "You know you got your good looks from your father, but you got your brains and sense of humor from me." So she was always going to give herself a *little* credit. She was always fighting to show her value. I don't know if she ever believed it, but then she sees it in me, and she thought she was right about me all along. You kind of want every mother to feel that way.

15. Her instinct to protect you is so amazing. That's why this book is also important for you to have written. Was that the persona of her being a stage mother?

I don't know how she really felt about being called a stage mother. She'd always laugh and scoff at the idea. We both believed that this was not the case because she was never the Mama Rose type who wanted the spotlight for herself. She didn't have the self-confidence. She'd say, "Let them think that. And if it is true, then I rival the best." But the day I fired her as a manager she called it a divorce. It broke her because I said I didn't need her. And if *I* didn't need her as a manager then where was her importance? I said I wanted her to be with me as a mom. I think that threatened her, and somehow taking away the business piece of our relationship terrified her. I was abandoning her. It was finally happening. It wasn't martyrdom but the belief that she was leaveable. She wasn't enough to hold on to anything. What a way to live. No wonder she was an alcoholic. It was all too much for her. . . .